ST. MARY'S COLLEGE OF MARYLAND
ST. MARY'S CITY, MARYLAND

THE TRAVELER'S BOOK OF VERSE

TEMPLE OF VESTA, THE SO-CALLED TEMPLE OF THE SIBYL, TIVOLI

38188

THE TRAVELER'S BOOK OF VERSE

EDITOR
FREDERICK E. EMMONS

ASSOCIATE EDITOR
T. W. HUNTINGTON, JR.

Granger Index Reprint Series

 BOOKS FOR LIBRARIES PRESS
FREEPORT, NEW YORK

Copyright 1928, 1956
by
Holt, Rinehart and Winston, Inc.
Reprinted 1970 by arrangement

STANDARD BOOK NUMBER:
8369-6110-2

LIBRARY OF CONGRESS CATALOG CARD NUMBER:
77-108582

COPYRIGHT NOTICE

For permission to use the copyright material included in this volume, the editors are indebted to the following publishers, whose courtesy is here gratefully acknowledged:

The George Matthew Adams Service: "On Traveling," copyright 1927 by Edgar A. Guest.
Edward Arnold & Co.: "At Fano," by Sir Rennell Rodd.
The Atlantic Monthly Company: "Santa Maria del Fiore," by George Herbert Clarke; "The Chain of Princes Street," by Elizabeth S. Fleming.
B. J. Brimmer Company; "Charlemagne" from *The Wagon and the Star*, by Mary Sinton Leitch.
Burns, Oates and Washburne, Ltd.: The poems by Aubrey De Vere.
The Century Co.: "Near Amsterdam" from the *Complete Poems of S. Weir Mitchell*.
Dodd, Mead and Company: "The Rolling English Road" from *The Flying Inn*, by G. K. Chesterton.
Doubleday, Doran and Company, Inc.: "Trees" from *Trees and Other Poems*, by Joyce Kilmer, copyright 1914 by George H. Doran Company; "Castilian" from *Black Armour*, by Elinor Wylie, copyright 1923 by George H. Doran Company; "Night at Sea" from *Little Houses*, by Amelia Josephine Burr, copyright 1922 Georgett. Doran Company.
E. P. Dutton and Company: "Evening: Spain" from *The Dark Wind*, by W. J. Turner.
E. P. Dutton and Company and John Murray: "The Spires of Oxford" from *The Spires of Oxford and Other Poems*, by W. M. Letts.
John I. Fisher Publishing Company: "In Old Rouen," by Antoinette De Coursey Patterson.
Harper & Brothers: "In Florence" from *Lyrics*, by Cora Fabbri.
Hodder & Stoughton: "The Little Bells of Sevilla" from *Madge Linsey, and Other Poems*, by Dora Sigerson Shorter.
Henry Holt and Company, and James B. Pinker & Sons: "England" from *Collected Poems*, by Walter de la Mare.

Copyright Notice

By permission of and by arrangement with:

Houghton Mifflin Company: The poems by Thomas Bailey Aldrich, Hortense Flexner, Oliver Wendell Holmes, Henry Wadsworth Longfellow and James Russell Lowell.

Aldred A. Knopf, Inc.: "Bagpipe Player: Nuremberg Fountain," by Leonora Speyer.

J. B. Lippincott Company: "Venice," by Thomas Buchanan Read.

Longmans, Green & Co.: "San Terenzo" from *Rhymes à la Mode*, by Andrew Lang.

The Macmillan Company: "Umbria" from *Selected Poems*, by Laurence Binyon; "The Book-Stalls on the Seine" and "In the Galleries of the Louvre" from *Spirit of France*, by Charles Lewis Slattery; "Heather" from *The Great Dream*, by Marguerite Wilkinson; "London Town" and "Sea-Fever," by John Masefield.

Macmillan & Co., Ltd. and Alfred Knopf, Inc.: "The Venus of Milo" from *Poems*, by Wilfrid Scawen Blunt.

Methuen & Co., Ltd. "By the Arno," "The Grave of Keats" and "Rome Unvisited" from *Poems*, by Oscar Wilde; "Skies Italian" from *Skies Italian*, by Ruth Shepard Phelps.

John Murray: "A Passer-by" from *Poetical Works of Robert Bridges*.

Oxford University Press: "Versailles" from *Fireside, Countryside and Other Poems*, by Godfrey Fox Bradby.

L. C. Page & Company: "The Enchanted Traveller" and "The Wingèd Victory" from *Later Poems*, by Bliss Carman.

G. P. Putnam's Sons: "Gargoyles: Strasbourg Cathedral" from *A Florentine Cycle and Other Poems*, by Gertrude Huntington McGiffert.

G. P. Putnam's Sons and The Ryerson Press: "In Flanders Fields" from *In Flanders Fields and Other Poems*, by John McCrae.

Charles Scribner's Sons: "Albert Dürer's Studio" from *The Complete Poetical Writings of Dr. Josiah G. Holland;* "Pictures of the Rhine" from *Poetical Works*, by George Meredith; "America for Me," by Henry Van Dyke; "Dawn on Mid-Ocean" from *Dust and Light*, by John Hall Wheelock; "Ode: The Mediterranean" from *Poems of George Santayana;* "Nightfall in Dordrecht" from *Poems of Eugene Field*.

Frederick A. Stokes Company: "Edinburgh" from *Collected Poems*, by Alfred Noyes, vol. ii, copyright 1910 by Frederick A. Stokes Company.

Copyright Notice

Yale University Press: "Browning at Asolo" and "The Name Writ in Water," by Robert Underwood Johnson.

A. P. Watt & Son: "The Rolling English Road" from *Wine, Water and Song*, by G. K. Chesterton.

Personal acknowledgment is also made to the following poets and individual owners of copyrights:

Laurence Binyon, for "Umbria."
Godfry Fox Bradby, for "Versailles."
George Herbert Clarke, for "Santa Maria del Fiore."
G. K. Chesterton, for "The Rolling English Road."
Robert Underwood Johnson, for "Browning At Asolo" and "The Name Writ in Water."
Mrs. Mary Sinton Leitch, for "Charlemagne."
John Masefield, for "London Town" and "Sea-Fever."
Gertrude Huntington McGiffert, for "Gargoyles: Strasbourg Cathedral."
Dr. Houston Mifflin, for "Dawn in Arqua," by Lloyd Mifflin.
Ruth Shepard Phelps, for "Skies Italian," (published as "Foreword: to A. U." in *Skies Italian*, copyright 1908 by Ruth Shepard Phelps).
Bishop Charles Lewis Slattery, for "The Book-Stalls on the Seine" and "In the Galleries of the Louvre."
Mrs. John E. D. Trask, for "The Angelus," by Florence Earle Coates.
George E. Woodberry, for "Shelley's House."

"As the Spanish proverb says, 'He who would bring home the wealth of the Indies must carry the wealth of the Indies with him.' So it is in travelling: a man must carry knowledge with him if he would bring home knowledge."
                                    Boswell, *Life of Johnson.*

CONTENTS

GENERAL
		PAGE
Bridges, Robert	A Passer-by	3
Burr, Amelia Josephine	Night at Sea	4
Byron, Lord	To the Ocean	5
Gould, Gerald	Wanderlust	8
Harper, John Warren	He Never Took a Vacation	9
Masefield, John	Sea-Fever	10
Wheelock, John Hall	Dawn on Mid-Ocean	11

ENGLAND
Beaumont, Francis	On the Tombs in Westminster Abbey	15
Browning, Robert	Home Thoughts from Abroad	16
Chesterton, G. K.	The Rolling English Road	17
de la Mare, Walter	England	19
Gray, Thomas	Elegy Written in a Country Churchyard	20
Gray, Thomas	Ode on a Distant Prospect of Eton College	26
Letts, M. W.	The Spires of Oxford	30
Longfellow, Henry Wadsworth	To the Avon	32
Masefield, John	London Town	33
Shakespeare, William	England	35
Thomson, James	Rule, Britannia	36
Upson, Arthur	The Avon and the Thames	38
Wordsworth, William	I Wandered Lonely as a Cloud	40
Wordsworth, William	Inside of King's College Chapel, Cambridge	42
Wordsworth, William	Upon Westminster Bridge, September 3, 1802	43

SCOTLAND
Burns, Robert	Highland Mary	47
Burns, Robert	My Heart's in the Highlands	49

		PAGE
Burns, Robert	*Ye Banks and Braes*	50
Fleming, Elizabeth S.	*The Chain of Princes Street*	51
Longfellow, Henry Wadsworth	*Robert Burns*	53
Noyes, Alfred	*Edinburgh*	56
Scott, Sir Walter	*Melrose Abbey*	58
Scott, Sir Walter	*The Trossachs*	61
Wilkinson, Marguerite	*Heather*	68

BELGIUM AND HOLLAND

Byron, Lord	*Waterloo*	71
Field, Eugene	*Nightfall in Dordrecht*	74
Longfellow, Henry Wadsworth	*The Belfry of Bruges*	76
McCrae, John	*In Flanders Fields*	80
Mitchell, S. Weir	*Near Amsterdam*	81

FRANCE

Aldrich, Thomas Bailey	*An Old Castle*	85
Blunt, Wilfrid Scawen	*The Venus of Milo*	88
Bradby, Godfrey Fox	*Versailles*	90
Carman, Bliss	*The Wingèd Victory*	94
Coates, Florence Earle	*The Angelus*	97
de Lisle, Rouget	*La Marseillaise*	98
Gautier, Théophile	*Notre Dame*	100
Kilmer, Joyce	*Trees*	103
Leitch, Mary Sinton	*Charlemagne*	104
Longfellow, Henry Wadsworth	*To the River Rhone*	106
McGiffert, Gertrude Huntington	*Gargoyles: Strasbourg Cathedral*	107
Nadaud, Gustave	*Carcassonne*	108
Patterson, Antoinette De Coursey	*In Old Rouen*	110
Slattery, Charles Lewis	*In the Galleries of the Louvre*	111
Slattery, Charles Lewis	*The Book-Stalls on the Seine*	112

GERMANY

Aldrich, Thomas Bailey	*The Lorelei*	115
Byron, Lord	*Drachenfels*	117
Byron, Lord	*To the Rhine*	119
Holland, Josiah Gilbert	*Albert Dürer's Studio*	121
Longfellow, Henry Wadsworth	*Nuremberg*	123

Contents

	PAGE
Longfellow, Henry Wadsworth............The Three Kings......	127
Longfellow, Henry Wadsworth............Walter von der Vogelweid.............	130
Meredith, George........Pictures of the Rhine...	133
Speyer, Leonora........Bagpipe Player: Nuremberg Fountain.......	137

SWITZERLAND
Aldrich, Thomas Bailey...An Alpine Picture.....	141
Byron, Lord............Lake Leman..........	142
Byron, Lord............The Prisoner of Chillon.	145
Kenyon, John...........Monument at Lucerne..	158
Wordsworth, William....The Simplon Pass.....	160

SPAIN
Longfellow, Henry Wadsworth..............Castles in Spain.......	163
Lowell, James Russell....Aladdin.............	167
Shorter, Dora Sigerson....The Little Bells of Sevilla............	168
Turner, W. J...........Evening: Spain........	170
Wylie, Elinor...........Castilian.............	172

ITALY
PART I—GENERAL
Binyon, Laurence......Umbria..............	175
Byron, Lord..........Petrarch's Tomb.......	177
Byron, Lord..........Prison of Tasso.......	178
Byron, Lord..........Stanzas to the Po......	180
Hare, A. W...........Italy................	182
Hildreth, Charles Lotin.Implora Pace.........	186
Johnson, Robert Underwood.............Browning at Asolo.....	187
Landor, Walter Savage..Milton in Italy........	189
Lang, Andrew........San Terenzo..........	190
Longfellow, Henry Wadsworth.........Italian Scenery........	191
Lushington, Henry.....To King Victor Emmanuel............	195
Mifflin, Lloyd.........Dawn in Arqua.......	198
Phelps, Ruth Shepard...Skies Italian..........	199
Rodd, Sir Rennell.....At Fano.............	200
Rogers, Samuel.......Verona	203
Santayana, George.....Ode: The Mediterranean..............	204

Contents

Savage-Armstrong,
G. F. .... *A Divine Barrier* 206
Shelley, Percy Bysshe ... *Passage of the Apennines* 207

PART II—ITALIAN LAKES
Catullus .... *Sirmio: Lago di Garda* .. 211
Landor, Walter Savage .. *To Saint Charles Borromeo* 213
Longfellow, Henry
Wadsworth .... *Cadenabbia* 215
Wordsworth, William .. *The Lake of Como* 217

PART III—MILAN
De Vere, Aubrey ...... *The Cathedral of Milan* 223
Symonds, John Addington .... *Lines Written on the Roof of Milan Cathedral* 225
Wordsworth, William .. *The Last Supper* 227

PART IV—ASSISI
Longfellow, Henry
Wadsworth .... *The Sermon of St. Francis* 231

PART V—GENOA
De Vere, Aubrey ...... *Genoa* 235
Faber, F. W. .... *Genoa* 236
Gibson, William ...... *Genoa* 239

PART VI—VENICE
Aldrich, Thomas Bailey *The Piazza of St. Mark at Midnight* 243
Byron, Lord .... *Ode on Venice* 245
Byron, Lord .... *Venice: A Fragment* 251
de Musset, Alfred ...... *Venice* 253
De Vere, Aubrey ...... *Venice by Day* 255
De Vere, Aubrey ...... *Venice in the Evening* .. 256
Houghton, Lord .... *Lido* 258
Landor, Walter Savage .. *To Venice* 261
Longfellow, Henry
Wadsworth .... *The Venetian Gondolier* 262
Longfellow, Henry
Wadsworth .... *Venice* 264

Contents

	PAGE
Moore, Thomas......*Mourn Not for Venice*..	265
Read, Thomas Buchanan *Venice*..............	268
Symonds, John Addington..............*For One of Gian Bellini's Little Angels*.......	273
Symonds, John Addington..............*The Invitation to the Gondola*...........	275
Symonds, John Addington................*Venice*...............	276
Todhunter, John.......*In a Gondola*.........	277
Wordsworth, William..*On the Extinction of the Venetian Republic*...	282

PART VII—PISA

Gibson, William......*Pisa*................	287
Shelley, Percy Bysshe...*Evening: Ponte a Mare, Pisa*..............	288

PART VIII—FLORENCE

Browning, Robert.....*Andrea del Sarto*......	293
Byron, Lord..........*Approach to Florence*..	303
Byron, Lord..........*Santa Croce*..........	304
Clarke, George Herbert..*Santa Maria del Fiore*..	307
De Vere, Aubrey......*Giotto's Campanile*.....	309
Fabbri, Cora..........*In Florence*...........	310
Longfellow, Henry Wadsworth.........*Giotto's Tower*........	313
Longfellow, Henry Wadsworth.........*Il Ponte Vecchio di Firenze*............	314
Longfellow, Henry Wadsworth.........*The Old Bridge at Florence*............	315
Lowell, James Russell..*Masaccio*............	317
Rosetti, Dante Gabriel..*Spring*..............	319
Shelley, Percy Bysshe...*Ode to the West Wind*..	320
Shelley, Percy Bysshe...*On the Medusa of Leonardo da Vinci in the Florentine Gallery*...	323
Trench, Richard Chenevix...............*On the Perseus and Medusa of Benvenuto Cellini, at Florence*...	326
Wilde, Oscar.........*By the Arno*..........	327
Wordsworth, William..*At Florence*..........	329

Contents

PAGE

PART IX—ROME

Baillie, Joanna	The Catacombs	333
Byron, Lord	Rome	335
De Vere, Aubrey	St. Peter's by Moonlight	336
du Bellay, Joachim	The Ruins of Rome	337
Holmes, Oliver Wendell	After a Lecture on Shelley	339
Johnson, Robert Underwood	The Name Writ in Water	341
Landor, Walter Savage	To Shelley	342
Landor, Walter Savage	Two Graves	343
Longfellow, Henry Wadsworth	Belisarius	344
Longfellow, Henry Wadsworth	Jugurtha	347
Moore, Thomas	The Conspiracy of Rienzi	349
Poe, Edgar Allan	The Coliseum	353
Rogers, Samuel	I am in Rome	356
Shelley, Percy Bysshe	Fragment on Keats	358
Shelley, Percy Bysshe	Keats	359
Symons, Arthur	Villa Borghese	361
Wilde, Oscar	Rome Unvisited	362
Wilde, Oscar	The Grave of Keats	364
Woodberry, George Edward	Shelley's House	365
Wordsworth, William	At Rome	367
Wordsworth, William	Near Rome, In Sight of St. Peter's	368
Wordsworth, William	The Pillar of Trajan	369

PART X—NAPLES

Flexner, Hortense	Street of Good Fortune—Pompeii	375
Longfellow, Henry Wadsworth	Amalfi	376
Longfellow, Henry Wadsworth	Monte Cassino	379
Symonds, John Addington	At Amalfi	383
Symonds, John Addington	At Castellamare	385
Trench, Richard Chenevix	Sorrento: A Fragment	387

EPILOGUE

Carman, Bliss	The Enchanted Traveller	392
Guest, Edgar A	On Traveling	393

		PAGE
Ketchum, Arthur	*Traveller's Joy*	394
Longfellow, Henry Wadsworth	*Travels by the Fireside*	396
Southey, Robert	*The Traveller's Return*	398
Van Dyke, Henry	*America for Me*	399

ILLUSTRATIONS

Temple of Vesta, the so-called Temple of the Sybil, Tivoli.............................*Frontispiece*

Facing Page

Thirlmere and Helvellyn, English Lake District...... 14
Burns' Cottage, Alloway....................... 46
A Canal, Dordrecht, Holland.................. 70
The Louvre, Paris............................ 84
Burg Stolzenfels on the Rhine.................. 114
Matterhorn and Riffelsee...................... 140
Court of the Lions in the Alhambra, Granada....... 162
Oria, Lago di Lugano......................... 174

GENERAL

A PASSER-BY

Whither, O splendid ship, thy white sails crowding,
   Leaning across the bosom of the urgent West,
That fearest nor sea rising, nor sky clouding,
   Whither away fair rover, and what thy quest?
   Ah! soon, when Winter has all our vales oppressed,
When skies are cold and misty, and hail is hurling,
   Wilt thou glide on the blue Pacific, or rest
In a summer haven asleep, thy white sails furling.

I there before thee, in the country that well thou knowest,
   Already arrived, am inhaling the odorous air:
I watch thee enter unerringly where thou goest,
   And anchor queen of the strange shipping there,
   Thy sails for awnings spread, thy masts bare:
Nor is aught from the foaming reef to the snow-capped grandest
   Peak, that is over the feathery palms, more fair
Than thou, so upright, so stately and still thou standest.

And yet, O splendid ship, unhailed and nameless,
   I know not if, aiming a fancy, I rightly divine
That thou hast a purpose joyful, a courage blameless,
   Thy port assured in a happier land than mine.
   But for all I have given thee, beauty enough is thine,
As thou, aslant with trim tackle and shrouding,
   From the proud nostril curve of a prow's line
In the offing scatterest foam, thy white sails crowding.

                              ROBERT BRIDGES.

NIGHT AT SEA

A brooding silence of stars, and a path of light
Where the ship wakes fleeting fires in the sea's calm night.
The swift typhoon may leap from a sudden cloud
And these waves turn cruel as hate and white as a shroud,
But to-night the sombre sweetness of sea and sky
Is hushed as the touch of your lips when we said good-bye.

AMELIA JOSEPHINE BURR.

TO THE OCEAN

From *Childe Harold's Pilgrimage*

There is a pleasure in the pathless woods,
There is a rapture on the lonely shore,
There is society where none intrudes
By the deep Sea, and music in its roar:
I love not Man the less, but Nature more,
From these our interviews, in which I steal
From all I may be, or have been before,
To mingle with the Universe, and feel
What I can ne'er express, yet can not all conceal.

Roll on, thou deep and dark blue Ocean, roll!
Ten thousand fleets sweep over thee in vain;
Man marks the earth with ruin, his control
Stops with the shore; upon the watery plain
The wrecks are all thy deed, nor doth remain
A shadow of man's ravage, save his own,
When, for a moment, like a drop of rain,
He sinks into thy depths with bubbling groan,
Without a grave, unknelled, uncoffined, and unknown.

His steps are not upon thy paths, thy fields
Are not a spoil for him,—thou dost arise
And shake him from thee; the vile strength he wields
For earth's destruction thou dost all despise,
Spurning him from thy bosom to the skies,
And send'st him, shivering in thy playful spray
And howling, to his Gods, where haply lies
His petty hope in some near port or bay,
And dashest him again to earth:—there let him lay.

The armaments which thunderstrike the walls
Of rock-built cities, bidding nations quake
And monarchs tremble in their capitals,
The oak leviathans, whose huge ribs make
Their clay creator the vain title take
Of lord of thee and arbiter of war,—
These are thy toys, and, as the snowy flake,
They melt into thy yeast of waves, which mar
Alike the Armada's pride or spoils of Trafalgar.

Thy shores are empires, changed in all save thee;—
Assyria, Greece, Rome, Carthage, what are they?
Thy waters washed them power while they were free,
And many a tyrant since; their shores obey
The stranger, slave, or savage; their decay
Has dried up realms to deserts:—not so thou;
Unchangeable save to thy wild waves' play,
Time writes no wrinkle on thine azure brow;
Such as creation's dawn beheld, thou rollest now.

Thou glorious mirror, where the Almighty's form
Glasses itself in tempests; in all time,
Calm or convulsed,—in breeze, or gale, or storm,
Icing the pole, or in the torrid clime
Dark-heaving;—boundless, endless, and sublime,—
The image of Eternity,—the throne
Of the Invisible; even from out thy slime
The monsters of the deep are made; each zone
Obeys thee; thou goest forth, dread, fathomless, alone.

To the Ocean

And I have loved thee, Ocean! and my joy
Of youthful sports was on thy breast to be
Borne, like thy bubbles, onward. From a boy
I wantoned with thy breakers,—they to me
Were a delight; and if the freshening sea
Made them a terror, 'twas a pleasing fear;
For I was as it were a child of thee,
And trusted to thy billows far and near,
And laid my hand upon thy mane,—as I do here.

Lord Byron.

WANDERLUST

Beyond the East the sunrise, beyond the West the sea,
And East and West the wanderlust that will not let me be;
It works in me like madness, dear, to bid me say good-by!
For the seas call and the stars call, and oh, the call of the sky!

I know not where the white road runs, nor what the blue hills are,
But man can have the sun for friend, and for his guide a star;
And there's no end of voyaging when once the voice is heard,
For the river calls and the road calls, and oh, the call of a bird!

Yonder the long horizon lies, and there by night and day
The old ships draw to home again, the young ships sail away;
And come I may, but go I must, and if men ask you why,
You may put the blame on the stars and the sun and the white road and the sky!

GERALD GOULD.

HE NEVER TOOK A VACATION

He never took a vacation, he hadn't the time, he said.
It was off to the "grind" in the morning,
It was home, and the papers and bed.
'Twas the desk, or the office, or counter,
Where he fought out his battles with men,
He would work just a few years longer,
Then quit, "take it easy," and then—?

So he toiled and he moiled and struggl'd,
Nor knew that the gods of gain
Drank deep of the wine he proffer'd
The blood of his heart and brain;
Nor knew while he piled up his millions,
And gathered his bags of gold,
His friends said at forty "he's aging,"
At fifty they said "he is old."

He never took a vacation, and at sixty they read his will.
His day for "retiring from business"
Death wrote in a codicil;
And pinn'd on the door of his office
Was a notice which grimly read,
"Out of town—on a long vacation
Indefinite" it said.

JOHN WARREN HARPER.

SEA-FEVER

I must go down to the seas again, to the lonely sea and the sky,
And all I ask is a tall ship and a star to steer her by,
And the wheel's kick and the wind's song and the white sail's shaking,
And a grey mist on the sea's face and a grey dawn breaking.

I must go down to the seas again, for the call of the running tide
Is a wild call and a clear call that may not be denied;
And all I ask is a windy day with the white clouds flying,
And the flung spray and the blown spume, and the sea-gulls crying.

I must go down to the seas again to the vagrant gypsy life,
To the gull's way and the whale's way where the wind's like a whetted knife;
And all I ask is a merry yarn from a laughing fellow-rover,
And quiet sleep and a sweet dream when the long trick's over.

JOHN MASEFIELD.

DAWN ON MID-OCEAN

The first light of coming day brings hope to many a tired and weary traveler but never more so than after a stormy night at sea. With the coming of dawn the instinctive fear of humanity for dangers that cannot be seen yields to the glories of the new morn just as the powers of darkness yield to the sunlight.

Veiled are the heavens, veiled the throne,
    The sacred spaces of the vast
And virgin sea make sullen moan
    Into the Void whence God has passed.

With His right hand He wakened it,
    The sorrowing Deep, to sweet dismay,—
And sighed; with His left hand He lit
    The stars in heaven, and took His way,

Leaving this loveliness behind:
    The inconsolable Vacancy
Bears witness in the veiled night and blind
    To some departed Mystery.

Disconsolate for One withdrawn,
    Moan the vague mouths. One cold and clear
Star, like a lamp, in the pale dawn
    Trembles for passion: God was here!

JOHN HALL WHEELOCK.

ENGLAND

THIRLMERE AND HELVELLYN, ENGLISH LAKE DISTRICT

ON THE TOMBS IN WESTMINSTER ABBEY

In this great mortuary of historic personages one must spend many sober and rather melancholy hours wandering amid shadowed aisles and dimly lighted chapels to realize completely what Westminster Abbey means to the British people. Parts of the present structure date from 1065. Like the Santa Croce of Florence, it is a Pantheon of genius, but no temple of fame in any other country can equal England's minster which "wears the triple crown of noble architecture, venerable age and hallowed memories, and through each aisle and chapel of this national mausoleum flows the majestic strain of English history none the less real because invisible."

Mortality, behold and fear!
What a change of flesh is here!
Think how many royal bones
Sleep within this heap of stones;
Here they lie had realms and lands,
Who now want strength to stir their hands;
Where from their pulpits seal'd with dust
They preach, "In greatness is no trust."
Here's an acre sown indeed
With the richest royall'st seed
That the earth did e'er suck in,
Since the first man died for sin;
Here the bones of birth have cried,
"Though gods they were, as men they died."
Here are sands, ignoble things,
Dropt from the ruin'd sides of kings.
Here's a world of pomp and state,
Buried in dust, once dead by fate.

FRANCIS BEAUMONT.

HOME THOUGHTS FROM ABROAD

Oh, to be in England
Now that April's there,
And whoever wakes in England
Sees, some morning, unaware,
That the lowest boughs and the brushwood sheaf
Round the elm-tree bole are in tiny leaf,
While the chaffinch sings on the orchard bough
In England—now!

And after April, when May follows
And the white-throat builds, and all the swallows!
Hark, where my blossomed pear-tree in the hedge
Leans to the field and scatters on the clover
Blossoms and dewdrops—at the bent spray's edge—
That's the wise thrush: he sings each song twice over,
Lest you should think he never could recapture
The first fine careless rapture!
And though the fields look rough with hoary dew,
All will be gay when noontide wakes anew
The buttercups, the little children's dower
—Far brighter than this gaudy melon-flower!

ROBERT BROWNING.

THE ROLLING ENGLISH ROAD

There is a subtle charm for many Americans in "Old England." One cannot find another spot on this old globe where such profound literary and historic memories arise to greet us at every little village or crossroad. Say what you will, it is the Mother Country. Here there is no alien speech and we do not feel ourselves strangers.

England's panoramic stage and theatre have been so small that interests and attractions have crowded one upon the other in profusion. Monotony is impossible.

While the roads of other lands are white with dust England's roads roll through hedge-marked fields fresh and moist with summer showers. The "tight little isle" has been spared many of the disasters of Europe by the "silver streak" that separates it from the continent, and the verdure of its fields is in strange harmony with the soft light that filters from its cloudy sky. The roads roll along well-groomed hillsides but there are no lofty mountains. As Mrs. Browning has said: "God's finger touched but did not press in making England."

Before the Roman came to Rye or out of Severn strode,
The rolling English drunkard made the rolling English road.
A reeling road, a rolling road, that rambles round the shire,
And after him the parson ran, the sexton and the squire;
A merry road, a mazy road, and such as we did tread,
The night we went to Birmingham by way of Beachy Head.

I knew no harm of Bonaparte and plenty of the Squire,
And for to fight the Frenchman I did not much desire;

But I did bash their bagginets because they came arrayed
To straighten out the crooked road an English drunkard made,
When you and I went down the lane with ale-mugs in our hands,
The night we went to Glastonbury by way of Goodwin Sands.

His sins they were forgiven him; or why do flowers run
Behind him; and the hedges all strengthening in the sun?
The wild thing went from left to right and knew not which was which,
But the wild rose was above him when they found him in the ditch.
God pardon us, nor harden us; we did not see so clear
The night we went to Bannockburn by way of Brighton Pier.

My friends, we will not go again or ape an ancient rage,
Or stretch the folly of our youth to be the shame of age,
But walk with clearer eyes and ears this path that wandereth,
And see undrugged in evening light the decent inn of death;
But there is good news yet to hear and fine things to be seen,
Before we go to Paradise by way of Kensal Green.

G. K. CHESTERTON.

ENGLAND

How often to the European traveler from our own shores the cry of "Land in sight" means a lighthouse on some western point in England's coast line. The news brings every passenger to the ship's rail. Commonplace though it may be, there is after all a veritable romance for even the most blasé.

The ruined castles and rolling roads, the green fields and thatched cottages mean home to some, and for those returning from a distant land the lines following bring a deeper sense of the happiness of being once more in their native land.

> No lovelier hills than thine have laid
>   My tired thoughts to rest:
> No peace of lovelier valleys made
>   Like peace within my breast.
>
> Thine are the woods whereto my soul,
>   Out of the noontide beam,
> Flees for a refuge green and cool
>   And tranquil as a dream.
>
> Thy breaking seas like trumpets peal;
>   Thy clouds—how oft have I
> Watched their bright towers of silence steal
>   Into infinity!
>
> My heart within me faints to roam
>   In thought even far from thee:
> Thine be the grave whereto I come,
>   And thine my darkness be.

WALTER DE LA MARE.

ELEGY WRITTEN IN A COUNTRY CHURCHYARD

Many a King and Emperor, statesman and philanthropist, will be forgotten long before the quiet scholar of Pembroke Hall. Thomas Gray planned many a great poem, but actually finished only one or two. When he died he left many memoranda, and two score or more fragments of fine things, but what else? And yet we, travelers from a distant land, come to his tomb because he left us the "Elegy Written in a Country Churchyard." At his own request, he was buried near the Church at Stoke Poges. It is fitting that he who has sung so touchingly of the dead sleeping here, should find near them his last resting place. As we go through the park on the way to the church, it is well to recall the verse that Gray originally wrote for the Elegy, but later discarded:

> "There scatter'd oft, the earliest of the year,
> By hands unseen are showers of violets found.
> The redbreast loves to build and warble there,
> And little footsteps lightly print the ground."

Who can really appreciate the poem without knowing the quaint place which inspired it? "Those rugged elms," "that yew tree's shade," "the frail memorials," "with uncouth rhimes and shapeless sculpture," are here. We can still look upon "the ivy-mantled tower," even though we cannot hear the "moping owl" "to the moon complain." Even today, in this quiet English countryside, "all the air a solemn stillness holds"; those who will wait till eventide, will know why the poet wrote: "The lowing herd winds slowly o'er the lea." Read the poem underneath the yew tree and you will not grudgingly admit that you have enjoyed one of the most delightful visits England can vouchsafe you.

The curfew tolls the knell of parting day,
    The lowing herd winds slowly o'er the lea,
The ploughman homeward plods his weary way,
    And leaves the world to darkness and to me.

Now fades the glimmering landscape on the sight,
    And all the air a solemn stillness holds,

Elegy Written in a Country Churchyard

Save where the beetle wheels his droning flight,
   And drowsy tinklings lull the distant folds;

Save that from yonder ivy-mantled tower
   The moping owl does to the moon complain
Of such as, wand'ring near her secret bower,
   Molest her ancient solitary reign.

Beneath those rugged elms, that yew-tree's shade,
   Where heaves the turf in many a mouldering heap,
Each in his narrow cell for ever laid,
   The rude Forefathers of the hamlet sleep.

The breezy call of incense-breathing Morn,
   The swallow twitt'ring from the straw-built shed,
The cock's shrill clarion, or the echoing horn,
   No more shall rouse them from their lowly bed.

For them no more the blazing hearth shall burn,
   Or busy housewife ply her evening care;
No children run to lisp their sire's return,
   Or climb his knee the envied kiss to share.

Oft did the harvest to their sickle yield,
   Their furrow oft the stubborn glebe has broke;
How jocund did they drive their team afield!
   How bowed the woods beneath their sturdy stroke!

Let not Ambition mock their useful toil,
   Their homely joys, and destiny obscure;
Nor Grandeur hear, with a disdainful smile,
   The short and simple annals of the poor.

Elegy Written in a Country Churchyard

The boast of heraldry, the pomp of power,
   And all that beauty, all that wealth e'er gave,
Await alike th' inevitable hour.
    The paths of glory lead but to the grave.

Nor you, ye Proud, impute to these the fault,
   If Mem'ry o'er their tomb no trophies raise,
Where thro' the long-drawn aisle and fretted vault
    The pealing anthem swells the note of praise.

Can storied urn or animated bust
   Back to its mansion call the fleeting breath?
Can Honour's voice provoke the silent dust,
    Or Flatt'ry soothe the dull cold ear of Death?

Perhaps in this neglected spot is laid
   Some heart once pregnant with celestial fire;
Hands, that the rod of empire might have swayed,
    Or waked to ecstasy the living lyre.

But Knowledge to their eyes her ample page
   Rich with the spoils of time did ne'er unroll;
Chill Penury repressed their noble rage,
    And froze the genial current of the soul.

Full many a gem, of purest ray serene
   The dark unfathomed caves of ocean bear;
Full many a flower is born to blush unseen,
    And waste its sweetness on the desert air.

Some village-Hampden, that with dauntless breast
   The little tyrant of his fields withstood;
Some mute inglorious Milton here may rest,
    Some Cromwell guiltless of his country's blood.

Elegy Written in a Country Churchyard

Th' applause of listening senates to command,
　　The threats of pain and ruin to despise,
To scatter plenty o'er a smiling land,
　　And read their history in a nation's eyes,

Their lot forbad; nor circumscribed alone
　　Their growing virtues, but their crimes confined;
Forbad to wade through slaughter to a throne,
　　And shut the gates of mercy on mankind,

The struggling pangs of conscious truth to hide,
　　To quench the blushes of ingenuous shame,
Or heap the shrine of Luxury and Pride
　　With incense kindled at the Muse's flame.

Far from the madding crowd's ignoble strife,
　　Their sober wishes never learned to stray;
Along the cool sequestered vale of life
　　They kept the noiseless tenor of their way.

Yet ev'n these bones from insult to protect
　　Some frail memorial still erected nigh,
With uncouth rhimes and shapeless sculpture decked,
　　Implores the passing tribute of a sigh.

Their name, their years, spelt by th' unlettered Muse,
　　The place of fame and elegy supply;
And many a holy text around she strews,
　　That teach the rustic moralist to die.

For who, to dumb Forgetfulness a prey,
　　This pleasing anxious being e'er resigned,
Left the warm precincts of the cheerful day,
　　Nor cast one longing ling'ring look behind?

On some fond breast the parting soul relies,
  Some pious drops the closing eye requires;
E'en from the tomb the voice of Nature cries,
  E'en in our ashes live their wonted fires.

For thee, who mindful of th' unhonoured Dead
  Dost in these lines their artless tale relate,
If chance, by lonely contemplation led,
  Some kindred spirit shall inquire thy fate,

Haply some hoary-headed swain may say,
  'Oft have we seen him at the peep of dawn
'Brushing with hasty steps the dews away
  'To meet the sun upon the upland lawn.

'There at the foot of yonder nodding beach,
  'That wreathes its old fantastic roots so high,
'His listless length at noontide would he stretch,
  'And pore upon the brook that babbles by.

'Hard by yon wood, now smiling as in scorn,
  'Mutt'ring his wayward fancies he would rove,
'Now drooping, woeful wan, like one forlorn,
  'Or crazed with care, or crossed in hopeless love.

'One morn I missed him on the customed hill,
  'Along the heath and near his fav'rite tree;
'Another came; nor yet beside the rill,
  'Nor up the lawn, nor at the wood was he;

'The next with dirges due in sad array
  'Slow thro' the church-way path we saw him borne.
'Approach and read (for thou can'st read) the lay,
  'Graved on the stone beneath yon aged thorn.'

The Epitaph

Here rests his head upon the lap of Earth
  A Youth to Fortune and to Fame unknown.
Fair Science frowned not on his humble birth,
  And Melancholy marked him for her own.

Large was his bounty, and his soul sincere,
  Heav'n did a recompence as largely send;
He gave to Misery all he had, a tear,
  He gained from Heav'n ('twas all he wished) a friend.

No farther seek his merits to disclose,
  Or draw his frailties from their dread abode,
(There they alike in trembling hope repose,)
  The bosom of his Father and his God.

THOMAS GRAY.

ODE ON A DISTANT PROSPECT OF ETON COLLEGE

From the north terrace of Windsor Castle the traveler may look out over one of the many beautiful countrysides to be found along the Thames. Half a mile away on the other side of the river, beyond the roofs of the little city, is Eton College, best known of all English schools.

We can see little of the school, but among the fine mellow red brick buildings the stately chapel stands out.

On our excursion to or from Windsor we should stop for a while at the school and wander about the quadrangles and through the classrooms now covered with the names of over 15,000 boys. The name of Shelley is there but it is to another poet we turn for a description of the panorama before us.

Ye distant spires, ye antique towers,
    That crown the watry glade,
Where grateful Science still adores
    Her Henry's holy Shade;
And ye, that from the stately brow
    Of Windsor's heights the expanse below
Of grove, of lawn, of mead survey,
    Whose turf, whose shade, whose flowers among
Wanders the hoary Thames along
    His silver-winding way.

Ah happy hills, ah pleasing shade,
    Ah fields beloved in vain,
Where once my careless childhood strayed,
    A stranger yet to pain!
I feel the gales that from ye blow,
    A momentary bliss bestow,
As waving fresh their gladsome wing
    My weary soul they seem to soothe,
And, redolent of joy and youth,
    To breathe a second spring.

Ode on a Distant Prospect of Eton College

Say, Father Thames, for thou hast seen
    Full many a sprightly race
Disporting on thy margent green
    The paths of pleasure trace,
Who foremost now delight to cleave
    With pliant arm, thy glassy wave?
The captive linnet which enthrall?
    What idle progeny succeed
To chase the rolling circle's speed
    Or urge the flying ball?

While some on earnest business bent
    Their murmuring labours ply
'Gainst graver hours, that bring constraint
    To sweeten liberty;
Some bold adventurers disdain
    The limits of their little reign,
And unknown regions dare descry;
    Still as they run they look behind,
They hear a voice in every wind,
    And snatch a fearful joy.

Gay hope is theirs by fancy fed,
    Less pleasing when possesst;
The tear forgot as soon as shed,
    The sunshine of the breast;
Theirs buxom health of rosy hue,
    Wild wit, invention ever-new,
And lively cheer of vigour born;
    The thoughtless day, the easy night,
The spirits pure, the slumbers light,
    That fly th' approach of morn.

Ode on a Distant Prospect of Eton College

Alas, regardless of their doom,
   The little victims play!
No sense have they of ills to come,
   Nor care beyond to-day:
Yet see how all around 'em wait
   The Ministers of human fate,
The black Misfortune's baleful train!
   Ah, show them where in ambush stand,
To seize their prey, the murtherous band!
   Ah, tell them, they are men!

These shall the fury Passions tear,
   The vultures of the mind,
Disdainful Anger, pallid Fear,
   And Shame that sculks behind;
Or pining Love shall waste their youth,
   Or Jealousy with rankling tooth,
That inly gnaws the secret heart,
   And Envy wan, and faded Care,
Grim-visaged comfortless Despair,
   And Sorrow's piercing dart.

Ambition this shall tempt to rise,
   Then whirl the wretch from high,
To bitter Scorn a sacrifice
   And grinning Infamy.
The stings of Falsehood those shall try,
   And hard Unkindness' altered eye,
That mocks the tear it forced to flow;
   And keen Remorse with blood defiled,
And moody Madness laughing wild
   Amid severest woe.

Ode on a Distant Prospect of Eton College

Lo, in the vale of years beneath
  A grisly troop are seen,
The painful family of Death,
  More hideous than their queen.
This racks the joints, this fires the veins,
  That every laboring sinew strains,
Those in the deeper vitals rage;
  Lo, Poverty, to fill the band,
That numbs the soul with icy hand,
  And slow-consuming Age.

To each his sufferings; all are men,
  Condemned alike to groan,
The tender for another's pain,
  The unfeeling for his own.
Yet ah! why should they know their fate?
  Since sorrow never comes too late,
And happiness too swiftly flies.
  Thought would destroy their paradise.
No more; where ignorance is bliss,
  'Tis folly to be wise.

THOMAS GRAY.

THE SPIRES OF OXFORD

Ten centuries, if you will, are found chronicled in the stones of Oxford. The thread of its story runs unbroken through social, political and religious revolutions. Perhaps nowhere else in all England, unless it be at Cambridge, can the mind and eye of the traveler find so much antiquity as here beneath the spires of Oxford.

Generation after generation has seen this historic pile enlarged and improved in accordance with varying tastes and needs. As seen from a distance the grouping of its spires and towers is renowned for its beauty. The verdant "quads" and sequestered gardens add much to the charm of this "home of lost causes."

> I saw the spires of Oxford
>   As I was passing by,
> The grey spires of Oxford
>   Against a pearl-grey sky;
> My heart was with the Oxford men
>   Who went abroad to die.
>
> The years go fast in Oxford,
>   The golden years and gay;
> The hoary colleges look down
>   On careless boys at play,
> But when the bugles sounded—War!
>   They put their games away.
>
> They left the peaceful river,
>   The cricket field, the quad,
> The shaven lawns of Oxford
>   To seek a bloody sod.
> They gave their merry youth away
>   For country and for God.

The Spires of Oxford

God rest you, happy gentlemen,
  Who laid your good lives down,
Who took the khaki and the gun
  Instead of cap and gown.
God bring you to a fairer place
  Than even Oxford town.

W. M. LETTS.

TO THE AVON

We walk slowly down the chancel of Old Trinity Church at Stratford-on-Avon and stand looking down upon the epitaph whose awful imprecation has protected undisturbed the long sleep of the Bard of Avon.

> "Good friend for Jesus' sake forbear
> To dig the dust enclosed here;
> Blest be the man that spares these stones
> And curst be he that moves my bones."

J. L. Stoddard once came this way and, after leaving this hallowed shrine, walked across the old churchyard to the Avon, whose murmur mingles in harmony with the music of the church organ. "I strolled," he said, "beside the River Avon, which like a silver ribbon, threads its way for miles between green meadows carpeted with velvet turf and gemmed with flowers. The very trees seem fond of this historic stream, for they bend over it, gaze into its dark depths, and with their countless fingers touch caressingly its limpid waves. Surely beside this stream of Shakespeare all national differences can be forgotten. Upon the Avon's banks Americans and English form but one historic family, bowing alike in filial admiration for the king of poets and claiming as their common heritage the noble English language, which the great Bard of Stratford has so glorified."

> Flow on, sweet river! like his verse
> Who lies beneath this sculptured hearse;
> Nor wait beside the churchyard wall
> For him who cannot hear thy call.
>
> Thy playmate once; I see him now
> A boy with sunshine on his brow,
> And hear in Stratford's quiet street
> The patter of his little feet.

HENRY WADSWORTH LONGFELLOW.

LONDON TOWN

Oh London Town's a fine town, and London sights are rare,
And London ale is right ale, and brisk's the London air,
And busily goes the world there, but crafty grows the mind,
And London Town of all towns I'm glad to leave behind.

Then hey for croft and hop-yard, and hill, and field, and pond,
With Bredon Hill before me and Malvern Hill beyond,
The hawthorn white i' the hedgerow, and all the spring's attire
In the comely land of Teme and Lugg, and Clent, and Clee, and Wyre.

Oh London girls are brave girls, in silk and cloth o' gold,
And London shops are rare shops where gallant things are sold,
And bonnily clicks the gold there, but drowsily blinks the eye,
And London Town of all towns I'm glad to hurry by.

Then, hey for covert and woodland, and ash and elm and oak,
Tewkesbury inns, and Malvern roofs, and Worcester chimney smoke.
The apple trees in the orchard, the cattle in the byre,
And all the land from Ludlow town to Bredon church's spire.

Oh London tunes are new tunes, and London books are wise,
And London plays are rare plays, and fine to country eyes,
But wretchedly fare the most there and merrily fare the few,
And London Town of all towns I'm glad to hurry through.

So hey for the road, the west road, by mill and forge and fold,
Scent of the fern and song of the lark by brook, and field, and wold,
To the comely folk at the hearth-stone and the talk beside the fire,
In the hearty land, where I was bred, my land of heart's desire.

JOHN MASEFIELD.

ENGLAND

From *Richard II*

This royal throne of kings, this sceptr'd isle,
This earth of majesty, this seat of Mars,
This other Eden, demi-paradise;
This fortress, built by nature for herself,
Against infection and the hand of war;
This happy breed of men, this little world;
This precious stone set in the silver sea,
Which serves it in the office of a wall,
Or as a moat defensive to a house,
Against the envy of less happier lands;
This blessed plot, this earth, this realm, this England.

WILLIAM SHAKESPEARE.

RULE, BRITANNIA

"Rule, Britannia" is perhaps not among the finest poems of England but it is full of the patriotic pride and spirit that makes England one of the world's greatest nations. Wherever the British flag waves this song is known. It was first sung in 1740 at a masque given for the Prince and Princess of Wales.

When Britain first, at Heaven's command,
    Arose from out the azure main,
This was the charter of the land,
    And guardian angels sung this strain:
Rule, Britannia, rule the waves!
    Britons never will be slaves.

The nations not so blest as thee
    Must, in their turns, to tyrants fall,
Whilst thou shalt flourish, great and free,
    The dread and envy of them all.

Still more majestic shalt thou rise,
    More dreadful from each foreign stroke;
As the loud blast that tears the skies,
    Serves but to root thy native oak.

Thee haughty tyrants ne'er shall tame;
    All their attempts to bend thee down
Will but arouse thy generous flame,
    But work their woe, and thy renown.

To thee belongs the rural reign;
    Thy cities shall with commerce shine;
All thine shall be the subject main,
    And every shore it circles, thine.

The Muses, still with Freedom found,
　　Shall to thy happy coast repair:
Blest Isle! with matchless beauty crowned,
　　And manly hearts to guard the fair.
Rule, Britannia, rule the waves,
　　Britons never will be slaves.

　　　　　　　　　　　　JAMES THOMSON.

THE AVON AND THE THAMES

"Avon why runnest thou away so fast?
Rest thee before that Chancel where repose
The bones of him whose spirit moves the world.
I have beheld thy birthplace, I have seen
Thy tiny ripples where they played amid
The golden cups and ever waving blades.
I have seen mighty rivers . . . . .
. . . .
Worthier art thou of worship, and I bend
My knees upon thy bank and call thy name
And hear, or think I hear, thy voice reply."
                                WALTER SAVAGE LANDOR.

Surely the Avon and the Thames speak to the traveler if he takes the time to listen and if he has his heart and soul attuned to the music of the romance and history that rises from the places enshrined along their banks.

"Welcome, ye English speaking pilgrims, ye
Whose hands around the world are joined by him
Who makes his speech the language of the sea,
Till winds of Ocean waft from rim to rim
The Breath of Avon."
                                THEODORE WATTS-DUNSTON.

On that island of the Thames at Runnymede where King John signed the Great Charter there is still a pleasant meadow where rushes grow in the clear water of the running river and where its banks are green with grass and trees. Far down this same river stands the famous Tower of London.

If, in all Albion's storied sweep,
   No other wave were seen,
The Avon and the Thames would keep
   Her romance gardens green.

Two silver cords are those she wears,
   Fast by her side to hold
Her book of songs, her book of prayers,
   As did the dames of old.

The Avon and the Thames

Fine lyric lore the first book reads,
  Of woodland wanderings;
The other, ancient, holy deeds
  And orisons of kings.

Mitres and crowns continually
  Allure the chanting Thames;—
The Avon lilts to any lea
  For cowslip diadems.

The Thames, at Oxford turned the sage,
  The Prince at Windsor grown,
Betakes himself in pilgrimage
  To Lambeth's reverend throne.

But Avon, gentle Avon, goes
  Far from such loud renown,
Beneath old Warwick's porticos
  To quiet Stratford town.

And there—sweet home of high romance!—
  It loiters, giving praise
For him whose consecrating glance
  Sought once its leafy ways.

Gold reveries, silken dreams, beside
  Its marge their glamour blend,
Till, slipping to the Severn's tide,
  It smiles an envied end.

While Thames and Avon onward sing,
  Their music's spell shall fall,
The one's on warrior, priest and king,
  The other's upon all.

ARTHUR UPSON.

I WANDERED LONELY AS A CLOUD

Those who go to the English Lake District are "on the edge of a country—a famous and beautiful country—which has given a school of poetry to England, and to which crowds of visitors come every year, where Wordsworth lived and died, and where all at one time Southey, Coleridge, DeQuincey, Arnold of Rugby, his poet son, Matthew Arnold, and Miss Martineau, lived and worked, drawing their inspiration from the quiet beauty of the mountains and building up work that England has not let die." Whether we sojourn at Windermere, Ambleside, Keswick or Derwentwater, the lover of nature's poets makes a pilgrimage to the little Grasmere Churchyard of St. Oswald and Dove Cottage for:

"In Grasmere's Vale, whose nestling dimple lake
Laughs to the hills which seem to wed the sky,
Sweet Alice dwelt, a wild flower of the brake,
That lovelier grew as Spring and Spring went by.

"The day died out in purple on the lake,
A warm light brooded over stirless flowers,
They laid her mid the blossoms of the brake,
The wild blooms she had loved in childhood's hours."

Not far from Dove Cottage, where William and Dorothy Wordsworth lived from 1799 to May 1829, he wrote "I Wandered Lonely as a Cloud."

I wandered lonely as a cloud
That floats on high o'er vales and hills,
When all at once I saw a crowd,
A host, of golden daffodils;
Beside the lake, beneath the trees,
Fluttering and dancing in the breeze.

I Wandered Lonely as a Cloud

Continuous as the stars that shine
And twinkle on the milky way,
They stretched in never-ending line
Along the margin of a bay:
Ten thousand saw I at a glance,
Tossing their heads in sprightly dance.

The waves beside them danced; but they
Out-did the sparkling waves in glee:
A poet could not but be gay,
In such jocund company:
I gazed—and gazed—but little thought
What wealth the show to me had brought.

For oft when on my couch I lie
In vacant or in pensive mood,
They flash upon that inward eye
Which is the bliss of solitude;
And then my heart with pleasure fills,
And dances with the daffodils.

WILLIAM WORDSWORTH.

INSIDE OF KING'S COLLEGE CHAPEL, CAMBRIDGE

Although at a distance the profiles of Oxford and Cambridge are almost the same, King's College Chapel at Cambridge makes up for any possible deficiency in the outline. The chapel is the glory of Cambridge and England. Of the perpendicular English Gothic, the lofty ceiling with its delicate fan tracery reminds one of huge white scallop shells. The Tudor rose and portcullis are carved in every nook. With the sunshine streaming through the richly painted east and west windows the interior becomes a gorgeous vision of light and glory, of vivid and superb colors.

Tax not the royal Saint with vain expense,
With ill-matched aims the Architect who planned—
Albeit labouring for a scanty band
Of white-robed Scholars only—this immense

And glorious work of fine intelligence!
Give all thou canst; high Heaven rejects the lore
Of nicely-calculated less or more;
So deemed the man who fashioned for the sense

These lofty pillars, spread that branching roof
Self-poised, and scooped into ten thousand cells
Where light and shade repose, where music dwells

Lingering—and wandering on as loth to die;
Like thoughts whose very sweetness yieldeth proof
That they were born for immortality.

WILLIAM WORDSWORTH.

UPON WESTMINSTER BRIDGE
September 3, 1802

The visitor to the great metropolis of London should if possible stand on Westminster Bridge as Wordsworth did and read these lines that make up one of his finest sonnets. Few poems are more often quoted. One morning in the summer of 1802 the poet was going over Westminster Bridge on the way to Dover. The great city was still sleeping and the early sun made the scene one of such grandeur that the following poem took form as he traveled on towards his destination.

Earth has not anything to show more fair:
Dull would he be of soul who could pass by
A sight so touching in its majesty:
This City now doth, like a garment, wear

The beauty of the morning; silent, bare,
Ships, towers, domes, theatres, and temples lie
Open unto the fields, and to the sky;
All bright and glittering in the smokeless air.

Never did sun more beautifully steep
In his first splendour valley, rock, or hill;
Ne'er saw I, never felt, a calm so deep!

The river glideth at his own sweet will:
Dear God! the very houses seem asleep;
And all that mighty heart is lying still!

WILLIAM WORDSWORTH.

SCOTLAND

BURNS' COTTAGE, ALLOWAY

HIGHLAND MARY

What tender recollections are awakened in the hearts of those who have stood beside the brook where Burns and Highland Mary, holding a Bible between them, pledged a solemn vow of everlasting faithfulness.

This stream of running water was the emblem of eternity, yet how little did they realize that their parting was forever. A few days later Mary died and today, in the west kirkyard of Greenock near Crawford Street, she lies beneath a monument upon which is delicately sculptured in relief the figures of the lovers clasping hands in that last farewell.

Above her resting place is inscribed:

<blockquote>
Erected over the Grave of
HIGHLAND MARY
1842
"<i>My Mary, dear departed shade,
Where is thy place of blissful rest?</i>"
</blockquote>

No other name is needed, for who does not know "Highland Mary," the girl Burns loved? In the Burns monument on that lovely hillside of Ayr is the Bible on which the two lovers pledged their love and loyalty. On one of the faded pages is Burns' autograph and beneath lies a tress of Highland Mary's hair.

Of their parting Burns says: "We met by appointment on the second Sunday of May in a sequestered spot on the Ayr, where we spent the day in taking farewell before she should embark for the West Highlands to prepare for our projected change of life."

Ye banks and braes and streams around
    The castle o' Montgomery,
Green be your woods, and fair your flowers,
    Your waters never drumlie!
There simmer first unfauld her robes,
    And there the langest tarry;
For there I took the last fareweel
    O' my sweet Highland Mary.

How sweetly bloom'd the gay green birk,
    How rich the hawthorn's blossom,
As underneath their fragrant shade
    I clasp'd her to my bosom!
The golden hours on angel wings
    Flew o'er me and my dearie;
For dear to me as light and life
    Was my sweet Highland Mary.

Wi' mony a vow, and lock'd embrace,
    Our parting was fu' tender;
And, pledging aft to meet again,
    We tore oursels asunder;
But Oh! fell death's untimely frost,
    That nipt my flower sae early!
Now green's the sod, and cauld's the clay,
    That wraps my Highland Mary!

O pale, pale now, those rosy lips,
    I aft have kiss'd sae fondly!
And closed for aye the sparkling glance,
    That dwelt on me sae kindly!
And mouldring now in silent dust,
    That heart that lo'ed me dearly!
But still within my bosom's core
    Shall live my Highland Mary.

                              ROBERT BURNS.

MY HEART'S IN THE HIGHLANDS

My heart's in the Highlands, my heart is not here;
My heart's in the Highlands a-chasing the deer;
Chasing the wild deer, and following the roe,
My heart's in the Highlands, wherever I go.
Farewell to the Highlands, farewell to the North,
The birth-place of valour, the country of worth;
Wherever I wander, wherever I rove,
The hills of the Highlands for ever I love.

Farewell to the mountains, high cover'd with snow;
Farewell to the straths and green valleys below;
Farewell to the forests and wild-hanging woods;
Farewell to the torrents and loud-pouring floods.
My heart's in the Highlands, my heart is not here;
My heart's in the Highlands a-chasing the deer;
Chasing the wild deer, and following the roe,
My heart's in the Highlands, wherever I go.

ROBERT BURNS.

YE BANKS AND BRAES

"The songs of the Ploughman Poet have by their beauty and charm woven a spell throughout the world." Literary pilgrims from every land seek the little towns, the rich pastoral lands, the heather, and the lochs of the country that inspired him. Ayrshire, small and restricted as it is, sufficed for the field of his endeavor. He never forgot Scottish moorland, stream or mountain.

Bobbie Burns' poems live in the hearts of Scotsmen the world over, but who does not feel a literary kinship in the charm of Ayrshire when he reads the poems inspired by the stream that was so intimately associated with the life of the poet?

Ye banks and braes o' bonnie Doon,
    How can ye bloom sae fresh and fair?
How can ye chant, ye little birds,
    And I sae weary fu' o' care?
Thou'lt break my heart, thou warbling bird,
    That wantons thro' the flowering thorn:
Thou minds me o' departed joys,
    Departed never to return.

Aft hae I rov'd by bonnie Doon,
    To see the rose and woodbine twine;
And ilka bird sang o' its love,
    And fondly sae did I o' mine.
Wi' lightsome heart I pu'd a rose,
    Fu' sweet upon its thorny tree;
And my fause lover stole my rose,
    But ah! he left the thorn wi' me.

                                ROBERT BURNS.

THE CHAIN OF PRINCES STREET

Edinburgh is the "Queen of the North" and it is for many of us, as it was for Scott, "mine own romantic town."

The traveler who climbs to the summit of Calton Hill finds a prospect widening before him that is filled with beauty and charm. He sees the outline of Arthur's Seat, and the ruined arches of Holyrood's Gothic chapel, almost embraced by the dark battlements of Holyrood Cástle itself, —the castle where Mary Queen of Scots lived and where Rizzio was murdered.

Too often the view may be dimmed by gusts of rain sweeping across the hilltop, but "Old Misty" shows even then the outline of the distant quarters of the town, the heights crowned by the Castle and the lengthening profile of Princes Street.

Well has Princes Street been called the "noblest street in Europe." Its variety, its picturesque setting, its monuments and beautiful architectural effects make it a rival of any of the world's famous city streets. A century and a half ago it was a wide expanse of meadow land where the citizens of "Old Reekie" enjoyed a country walk. When the "Old Town" with its wynds and closes became too cramped for the increasing population, a new town was planned. In the scheme for the "New Town", beyond Nor' Loch Princes Street was to be called St. Giles Street, but when the plans were shown to George III and he saw that the principal street was to bear a name suggesting to Londoners all that was mean and squalid he cried, "Hey—hey—what—what—call your chief street St. Giles Street? Never do, never do!" And so today we walk down the street named after the younger members of the royal family.

> "If I were Queen of all the land,
> To ask whate'er I might,
> I'd wear the chain of Princes Street,
> Of Princes Street at night.
>
> "(Strung on a strand of silver wire
> Between the earth and sky,
> The golden lights of Princes Street
> Will haunt me till I die.)

"I'd wear it on a purple gown,
   With fur of twilight gray,
And set it swaying, shimmering,
   At closing of the day.

"And as I went my way serene,
   The people would bow down,
And say, 'There goes the bonny Queen
   Of Edinburgh Town!'"

ELIZABETH S. FLEMING.

ROBERT BURNS

Just as Stratford-on-Avon and Shakespeare form one idea, so Ayr and Burns are enshrined together in the hearts of the English-speaking people. The land over which the spirit of the poet still hovers is well called the Burns Country. Within the compass of a summer day's journey lie Dumfries, Mount Oliphant, Lochlea and the charming village of Kirkoswald, where many eventful years of his life were passed.

The visitor to Ayr rides but a short distance from the Burns monument in the public square to the cottage,—the "auld clay biggin" of two rooms. It requires little effort of the imagination to call up a picture of the humble solitary cottage of a century and a half ago, in which the poet was born. Here the peasant father devoted the evening hours, after a day of toil in the nearby fields, to teaching the future poet the elements of an education. This devotion deserves the tribute of later generations.

> I see amid the fields of Ayr
> A ploughman, who in foul and fair,
>   Sings at his task
> So clear, we know not if it is
> The laverock's song we hear, or his,
>   Nor care to ask.
>
> For him the ploughing of those fields
> A more ethereal harvest yields
>   Than sheaves of grain;
> Songs flush with purple bloom the rye,
> The plover's call, the curlew's cry,
>   Sing in his brain.
>
> Touched by his hand, the wayside weed
> Becomes a flower; the lowliest reed
>   Beside the stream
> Is clothed with beauty; gorse and grass
> And heather, where his footsteps pass,
>   The brighter seem.

He sings of love, whose flame illumes
The darkness of lone cottage rooms;
   He feels the force,
The treacherous undertow and stress
Of wayward passions, and no less
   The keen remorse.

At moments, wrestling with his fate,
His voice is harsh, but not with hate;
   The brushwood, hung
Above the tavern door, lets fall
Its bitter leaf, its drop of gall
   Upon his tongue.

But still the music of his song
Rises o'er all, elate and strong;
   Its master-chords
Are Manhood, Freedom, Brotherhood,
Its discords but an interlude
   Between the words.

And then to die so young and leave
Unfinished what he might achieve!
   Yet better sure
Is this, than wandering up and down
An old man in a country town,
   Infirm and poor.

For now he haunts his native land
As an immortal youth; his hand
   Guides every plough;
He sits beside each ingle-nook,
His voice is in each rushing brook,
   Each rustling bough.

His presence haunts this room to-night,
A form of mingled mist and light
  From that far coast.
Welcome beneath this roof of mine!
Welcome! this vacant chair is thine,
  Dear guest and ghost!
            HENRY WADSWORTH LONGFELLOW.

EDINBURGH

"Where the huge castle holds its state
And all the steep slopes down,
Whose ridgy back heaves to the sky
Piles deep and massy, close and high,
Mine own romantic town."

The origin of Edinburgh or Edwinsburgh is lost in a hoary antiquity. The most striking and dominant feature of the landscape is the great frowning fortress-castle which offered shelter and protection long before the town came into existence. Many a romance and legend enwraps "the city that claims the Heart of Midlothian." From Calton Hill, if perchance you are one of the favored, you may see just at the "Cat Nick" the profile of Arthur's head against the rocks of Salisbury Crags,—a profile not unlike the Arthur of Gustave Doré.

Edinburgh, "a city of song," has seen many poets born and bred within her gates and has in turn inspired many others. Scott, Hume, Burns and Robert Louis Stevenson are a few of those who have helped to invest the grand old city with a deeper and more lasting interest. As the years pass, there are many who grieve to see how the "Edinborough of the past" is becoming but a memory to haunt the dreams of those who love her as she deserves.

City of mist and rain and blown grey spaces,
   Dashed with wild wet colour and gleam of tears,
Dreaming in Holyrood halls of the passionate faces
   Lifted to one Queen's face that has conquered
     the years,
Are not the halls of thy memory haunted places?
   Cometh there not as a moon (where the blood-
     rust sears
Floors a-flutter of old with silks and laces),
   Gliding, a ghostly Queen, thro' a mist of tears?

Edinburgh

Proudly here, with a loftier pinnacled splendour,
    Throned in his northern Athens, what spells remain
Still on the marble lips of the Wizard, and render
    Silent the gazer on glory without a stain!
Here and here, do we whisper, with hearts more tender,
    Tusitala wandered thro' mist and rain;
Rainbow-eyed and frail and gallant and slender,
    Dreaming of pirate-isles in a jewelled main.

Up the Canongate climbeth, cleft asunder
    Raggedly here, with a glimpse of the distant sea
Flashed through a crumbling alley, a glimpse of wonder,
    Nay, for the City is throned on Eternity!
Hark! from the soaring castle a cannon's thunder
    Closeth an hour for the world and an aeon for me,
Gazing at last from the martial heights whereunder
    Deathless memories roll to an ageless sea.

ALFRED NOYES.

MELROSE ABBEY

From *Lay of the Last Minstrel*

We cannot look upon the ruins of Melrose without picturing its former beauty here along the bank of the Tweed. Such great churches were the "flowering of religious faith and architectural genius, of a holy imagination." "Masters in live stone" were these men who built them as if they were a living speech. Not only were these Abbeys the expressions of a great faith, but also an outward manifestation of the life of the people. The spires of these churches, rising in their midst above their homes, offered testimony to the unity and inspiration of their lives. "It stood for that strength which is embodied law and obedience; it illustrated the only lasting beauty—that of structure, proportion, and order; it was a visible aspiration and prayer, its ascending lines carrying the imagination on to an invisible perfection; for it was the evidence of things not seen." No one loved Melrose more than Sir Walter Scott, and its beauty is nowhere more faithfully described than in his "Lay of the Last Minstrel."

THE CLOISTERS

Now, slow and faint, he led the way,
Where, cloistered round, the garden lay;
The pillared arches were over their head,
And beneath their feet were the bones of the dead.
Spreading herbs and flowerets bright
Glistened with the dew of night;
Nor herb nor floweret glistered there
But was carved in the cloister-arches as fair.

The best view of the Abbey is obtained from the churchyard, but,

THE CHANCEL

By a steel-clenched postern door
   They entered now the chancel tall;
The darkened roof rose high aloof
   On pillars lofty and light and small:

The keystone that locked each ribbed aisle
Was a fleur-de-lys or a quatre-feuille;
The corbels were carved grotesque and grim;
And the pillars, with clustered shafts so trim,
With base and with capital flourished around,
Seemed bundles of lances which garlands had bound.

THE EAST ORIEL

The moon on the east oriel shone
Through slender shafts of shapely stone,
   By foliaged tracery combined;
Thou wouldst have thought some fairy's hand
'Twixt poplars straight the osier wand
   In many a freakish knot had twined,
Then framed a spell when the work was done,
And changed the willow wreaths to stone.

The Abbey is said to contain the grave of a leading personage in the "Lay of the Last Minstrel,"

The wondrous Michael Scott;
A wizard of such dreaded fame,
That when, in Salamanca's cave,
Him listed his magic wand to wave,
The bells would ring in Notre-Dame!

It was he also who spoke

The words that cleft Eildon Hills in three,
And bridled the Tweed with a curb of stone.

"It may be added that, as a fitting memorial to the author who loved the Abbey so well, Mr. G. M. Kemp, in designing the beautiful Scott Monument in Edinburgh, took all its details from Melrose Abbey."

If thou wouldst view fair Melrose aright,
Go visit it by the pale moonlight;

Melrose Abbey

For the gay beams of lightsome day
Gild but to flout the ruins gray.
When the broken arches are black in night,
And each shafted oriel glimmers white;
When the cold light's uncertain shower
Streams on the ruined central tower;
When buttress and buttress, alternately,
Seem framed of ebon and ivory;
When silver edges the imagery,
And the scrolls that teach thee to live and die;
When distant Tweed is heard to rave,
And the owlet to hoot o'er the dead man's grave,
Then go—but go alone the while—
Then view Saint David's ruined pile;
And, home returning, soothly swear
Was never scene so sad and fair!

SIR WALTER SCOTT.

THE TROSSACHS

From *The Lady of the Lake*

A few hours' journey from the Burns' country or Edinburgh brings the traveler into the heart of Scott's land. Here we need no other guides than copies of "Marmion" and "The Lady of the Lake" and a memory filled with the history and legends in the Waverly Novels.

Along the shores of Loch Katrine one may still see the smooth white beach upon which Scott bestowed the name "The Silver Strand." Here was the meeting place of Fitz-James and Ellen, the Lady of the Lake. Picturesque mountains form the horizon and one can see the peaks that recall the scenes associated with Fitz-James and Roderick Dhu.

Scott opens his story of "The Lady of the Lake" with the description of a stag hunt. Night comes on and the hunter, fearing to spend it alone in the wild passes of the Trossachs, winds his horn in the hope of calling his scattered followers—

> "When lo! forth starting at the sound,
> From underneath an aged oak
> That slanted from the islet rock,
> A damsel guider of its way,
> A little skiff shot to the bay.
>
> . . . .
> The boat had touched this silver strand,
> Just as the hunter left his stand,
> And stood concealed amid the brake,
> To view this Lady of the Lake."

Only Scott can describe the wild natural beauty of the Trossachs. Without the touch of the "great magician" the romantic history of these lakes and passes would long since have been forgotten. His poem serves as a perfect guide to Ellen's Isle where James Fitz-James spends the night and is rowed ashore next morning while Ellen watches his going.

Scott carries the traveler into a realm of fancy and by his genius fills this land with renewed interest. His word picture of the famous pass of the Trossachs and the song of the huntsman make the poems live again if we read them within sight of the places they describe.

CANTO I.

XII.

Boon nature scattered, free and wild,
Each plant or flower, the mountain's child.
Here eglantine embalmed the air,
Hawthorn and hazel mingled there;
The primrose pale and violet flower
Found in each cliff a narrow bower;
Fox-glove and nightshade, side by side,
Emblems of punishment and pride,
Grouped their dark hues with every stain
The weather-beaten crags retain.
With boughs that quaked at every breath,
Grey birch and aspen wept beneath;
Aloft, the ash and warrior oak
Cast anchor in the rifted rock;
And, higher yet, the pine-tree hung
His shattered trunk, and frequent flung,
Where seemed the cliffs to meet on high,
His boughs athwart the narrowed sky.
Highest of all, where white peaks glanced,
Where glistening streamers waved and danced,
The wanderer's eye could barely view
The summer heaven's delicious blue;
So wondrous wild, the whole might seem
The scenery of a fairy dream.

XIII.

Onward, amid the copse 'gan peep
A narrow inlet, still and deep,
Affording scarce such breadth of brim
As served the wild duck's brood to swim.
Lost for a space, through thicket veering,
But broader when again appearing,

Tall rocks and tufted knolls their face
Could on the dark-blue mirror trace;
And farther as the hunter strayed,
Still broader sweep its channels made.
The shaggy mounds no longer stood,
Emerging from entangled wood,
But, wave-encircled, seemed to float,
Like castle girdled with its moat;
Yet broader floods extending still
Divide them with their parent hill,
Till each, retiring, claims to be
An islet in an inland sea.

XIV.

And now, to issue from the glen,
No pathway meets the wanderer's ken,
Unless he climb with footing nice
A far-projecting precipice.
The broom's tough roots his ladder made,
The hazel saplings lent their aid;
And thus an airy point he won,
Where, gleaming with the setting sun,
One burnished sheet of living gold,
Loch Katrine lay beneath him rolled,
In all her length far winding lay,
With promontory, creek, and bay,
And islands that, empurpled bright,
Floated amid the livelier light,
And mountains that like giants stand
To sentinel enchanted land.
High on the south, huge Benvenue
Down to the lake in masses threw
Crags, knolls, and mounds, confusedly hurled
The fragments of an earlier world;

A wildering forest feathered o'er
His ruined sides and summit hoar,
While on the north, through middle air,
Ben-an heaved high his forehead bare.

xv.

From the steep promontory gazed
The stranger, raptured and amazed;
And, 'What a scene were here,' he cried,
'For princely pomp, or churchman's pride!
On this bold brow, a lordly tower;
In that soft vale, a lady's bower;
On yonder meadow far away,
The turrets of a cloister grey;
How blithely might the bugle-horn
Chide on the lake the lingering morn!
How sweet at eve the lover's lute
Chime when the groves were still and mute!
And, when the midnight moon should lave
Her forehead in the silver wave,
How solemn on the ear would come
The holy matins' distant hum,
While the deep peal's commanding tone
Should wake, in yonder islet lone,
A sainted hermit from his cell,
To drop a bead with every knell—
And bugle, lute, and bell, and all,
Should each bewildered stranger call
To friendly feast, and lighted hall.

. . . .

Canto III.

II.

The Summer dawn's reflected hue
To purple changed Loch Katrine blue;
Mildly and soft the western breeze
Just kissed the lake, just stirred the trees,
And the pleased lake, like maiden coy,
Trembled but dimpled not for joy:
The mountain-shadows on her breast
Were neither broken nor at rest;
In bright uncertainty they lie,
Like future joys to Fancy's eye.
The water-lily to the light
Her chalice reared of silver bright;
The doe awoke, and to the lawn,
Begemmed with dew-drops, led her fawn;
The gray mist left the mountain-side,
The torrent showed its glistening pride;
Invisible in leckèd sky,
The lark sent down her revelry;
The blackbird and the speckled thrush
Good-morrow gave from brake and bush;
In answer cooed the cushat dove
Her notes of peace and rest and love.

. . . .

Canto I.

XXXI

Song.

'Soldier, rest! thy warfare o'er,
　Sleep the sleep that knows not breaking;
Dream of battled fields no more,
Days of danger, nights of waking.

In our isle's enchanted hall,
    Hands unseen thy couch are strewing,
Fairy strains of music fall,
    Every sense in slumber dewing.
Soldier, rest! thy warfare o'er,
Dream of fighting fields no more:
Sleep the sleep that knows not breaking
Morn of toil, nor night of waking.

'No rude sound shall reach thine ear,
    Armor's clang, or war-steed champing,
Trump nor pibroch summon here
    Mustering clan, or squadron tramping.
Yet the lark's shrill fife may come
    At the day-break from the fallow,
And the bittern sound his drum,
    Booming from the sedgy shallow.
Ruder sounds shall none be near,
Guards nor warders challenge here,
Here's no war-steed's neigh and champing,
Shouting clans, or squadrons stamping.'

XXXII.

She paused,—then, blushing, led the lay,
To grace the stranger of the day.
Her mellow notes awhile prolong
The cadence of the flowing song,
Till to her lips in measured frame
The minstrel verse spontaneous came.

Song (continued)

'Huntsman, rest! thy chase is done,
    While our slumbrous spells assail ye,
Dream not, with the rising sun,
Bugles here shall sound reveille.

Sleep! the deer is in his den;
   Sleep! thy hounds are by thee lying:
Sleep! nor dream in yonder glen
   How thy gallant steed lay dying.
Huntsman, rest! thy chase is done;
Think not of the rising sun,
For at dawning to assail ye
Here no bugles sound reveille.'
SIR WALTER SCOTT.

HEATHER

"O Caledonia! stern and wild!
Meet nurse for a poetic child!
Land of brown heath and shaggy wood,
Land of the mountain and the flood."
                    SCOTT, *Lay of the Last Minstrel.*

It may be that four-fifths of Scotland is unfit for cultivation but it seems that the Creator has made some compensation, for He gave to its people sons like Scott, Stevenson and Burns, and landscapes where mountains, moors, and lochs are filled with romance, legend, folklore and adventure. He also covered her hillside with heather, that serves sooner or later to draw every son of Scotland back to his native land.

All my life long I had longed to see heather
   In the land of my kinsmen far over the sea—
Now here is heather like a wide purple ocean
   Rolling its tides toward me,

Dark, dipping waves of it, deeper than amethyst
   When the gold day was begun—
Long, curving swells of it, dusky and lovely,
   Here on the downs in the sun;

Or in a gray mist, sombre and wonderful,
   Like a great twilight outspread
Far over earth that would meet with the heavens
   Purple and wild overhead.

Now I am shaken by great storms of beauty
   Wetting my eyelids with joy of my eyes;
Now is my soul like a wind-stricken sea bird
   Troubling the deep with her cries!
                    MARGUERITE WILKINSON.

BELGIUM AND HOLLAND

A CANAL, DORDRECHT, HOLLAND

WATERLOO
From *Childe Harold's Pilgrimage*

It was the summer of 1812. There was revelry in the Belgian Capital. Ponsonby's Dragoons were playing "The Girl I Left Behind Me." "There is at this present moment," said the Duke of Richmond to his Lady, "more love-making to the square inch in Brussels, ma'am, than in any city on the continent." And yet, there was a feeling in the air that something was about to happen.

No one knew where "Bony" was but they were sure he was about to strike. They did not know that his final orders would be "Sauve qui peut, tout est perdu."

Before driving out through the Forest of Soignes to the Mt. St. Jean one may well read the poem in which Byron expresses the emotions he felt while viewing the field where Wellington and Napoleon fought for supremacy. Then some evening at home, by the fireside, read in Thackeray's *Vanity Fair* his graphic chapter on Waterloo.

There was a sound of revelry by night,
And Belgium's capital had gathered then
Her Beauty and her Chivalry, and bright
The lamps shone o'er fair women and brave men;
A thousand hearts beat happily; and when
Music arose with its voluptuous swell,
Soft eyes looked love to eyes which spake again,
And all went merry as a marriage bell;—
But hush! hark! a deep sound strikes like a rising knell!

Did ye not hear it?—No; 'twas but the wind,
Or the car rattling o'er the stony street;
On with the dance! let joy be unconfined;
No sleep till morn, when Youth and Pleasure meet
To chase the glowing Hours with flying feet—
But hark!—that heavy sound breaks in once more,
As if the clouds its echo would repeat;
And nearer, clearer, deadlier than before!
Arm! Arm! it is—it is—the cannon's opening roar!

Within a windowed niche of that high wall
Sate Brunswick's fated chieftain; he did hear
That sound the first amidst the festival,
And caught its tone with Death's prophetic ear;
And when they smiled because he deemed it near,
His heart more truly knew that peal too well
Which stretched his father on a bloody bier,
And roused the vengeance blood alone could quell:
He rushed into the field, and, foremost fighting, fell.

Ah! then and there was hurrying to and fro,
And gathering tears, and tremblings of distress,
And cheeks all pale, which but an hour ago
Blushed at the praise of their own loveliness;
And there were sudden partings, such as press
The life from out young hearts, and choking sighs
Which ne'er might be repeated; who could guess
If ever more should meet those mutual eyes,
Since upon night so sweet such awful morn could rise!

And there was mounting in hot haste: the steed,
The mustering squadron, and the clattering car,
Went pouring forward with impetuous speed,
And swiftly forming in the ranks of war;
And the deep thunder peal on peal afar;
And near, the beat of the alarming drum
Roused up the soldier ere the morning star;
While thronged the citizens with terror dumb,
Or whispering, with white lips,—"The foe! They come! They come!"

And wild and high the "Cameron's gathering" rose!
The war-note of Lochiel, which Albyn's hills
Have heard, and heard, too, have her Saxon foes:—

Waterloo

How in the noon of night that pibroch thrills,
Savage and shrill! But with the breath which fills
Their mountain-pipe, so fill the mountaineers
With the fierce native daring which instils
The stirring memory of a thousand years,
And Evan's, Donald's fame rings in each clansman's ears!

And Ardennes waves above them her green leaves,
Dewy with nature's tear-drops as they pass,
Grieving, if aught inanimate e'er grieves,
Over the unreturning brave,—alas!
Ere evening to be trodden like the grass
Which now beneath them, but above shall grow
In its next verdure, when this fiery mass
Of living valour, rolling on the foe
And burning with high hope, shall moulder cold and low.

Last noon beheld them full of lusty life,
Last eve in Beauty's circle proudly gay,
The midnight brought the signal-sound of strife,
The morn the marshalling in arms,—the day
Battle's magnificently stern array!
The thunder-clouds close o'er it, which when rent
The earth is covered thick with other clay,
Which her own clay shall cover, heaped and pent,
Rider and horse,—friend, foe,—in one red burial blent!

LORD BYRON.

NIGHTFALL IN DORDRECHT

Look at the map of Holland and note the two rivers, the Maas and the Waal, as they flow together from Gorcum. Where they again separate into two branches you will find Dordrecht. It was at this point that one of the typical robber barons of the Middle Ages, the Count of Holland, built a tower, or thure, at the trecht, or crossing, in order that he might levy toll on every passing ship Thus arose the name Thurtrecht or Dordrecht, the tower-ferry. Few cities have a more important place in the commercial, political and religious history of Brave Little Holland. It numbers, too, among its painters Nicolas Maes and Albrecht Cuyp.

The mill goes toiling slowly around
    With steady and solemn creak,
And my little one hears in the kindly sound
    The voice of the old mill speak.
While round and round those big white wings
    Grimly and ghost-like creep,
My little one hears that the old mill sings:
    "Sleep, little tulip, sleep!"

The sails are reefed and the nets are drawn,
    And over his pot of beer
The fisher against the morrow's dawn
    Lustily maketh cheer.
He mocks at the winds that caper along,
    From the far off clam'rous deep;
But we, we love their lullaby song,
    Of "Sleep, little tulip, sleep."

Old dog Fritz in slumber sound
    Groans on the stony mart:
To-morrow how proudly he'll trot you round,
    Hitched to our new milk-cart!

Nightfall in Dordrecht

And you shall help me blanket the kine
    And fold the gentle sheep
And set the herring a-soak in brine,—
    But now, little tulip, sleep!

A Dream-one comes to blanket the eyes
    That wearily droop and sink;
While the old mill buffets the frowning skies,
    And scolds at the stars that blink.
Over your face the misty wings
    Of that beautiful Dream-one sweep,
And rocking your cradle, she softly sings:
    "Sleep, little tulip, sleep!"

EUGENE FIELD.

THE BELFRY OF BRUGES

Cities in northern countries delight in assuming the names of older and often better known cities in southern climes as though the name itself brought added culture or romance. Bruges was long called the "Venice of the North" because, like Venice, it was built on many islands.

In Charlemagne's time Baldwin of the Iron Arm built a watch-tower and castle at Brügge, the bridge over the Reye, where he might keep watch for the Norsemen and be ready to sally forth to give them battle. As trade routes gradually developed more bridge-money or tolls poured in to the lord of the castle and from this small beginning grew the city of the bridges, or Bruges. By the fifteenth century ships from Genoa and Venice were unloading their precious cargoes at her quays.

In the market place, the center of trade activity of the mediaeval city, was the old belfry. The lofty and majestic tower, adorned with fine stone, has played no small part in the eventful history of Bruges. Such towers were ever a notable feature in Flemish cities. Their sweet toned bells called the citizen to worship, to sorrow, to joy or action, and few poets have excelled our own Longfellow in recalling the voices of these time-honored bells and chimes.

In the market-place of Bruges stands the belfry old and brown;
Thrice consumed and thrice rebuilded, still it watches o'er the town.

As the summer morn was breaking, on that lofty tower I stood,
And the world threw off the darkness, like the weeds of widowhood.

Thick with towns and hamlets studded, and with streams and vapors gray,
Like a shield embossed with silver, round and vast the landscape lay.

The Belfry of Bruges

At my feet the city slumbered. From its chimneys, here and there,
Wreaths of snow-white smoke, ascending, vanished, ghost-like, into air.

Not a sound rose from the city at that early morning hour,
But I heard a heart of iron beating in the ancient tower.

From their nests beneath the rafters sang the swallows wild and high;
And the world, beneath me sleeping, seemed more distant than the sky.

Then most musical and solemn, bringing back the olden times,
With their strange, unearthly changes rang the melancholy chimes,

Like the psalms from some old cloister, when the nuns sing in the choir;
And the great bell tolled among them, like the chanting of a friar.

Visions of the days departed, shadowy phantoms filled my brain;
They who live in history only seemed to walk the earth again;

All the Foresters of Flanders,—mighty Baldwin Bras de Fer,
Lyderick du Bucq and Cressy, Philip, Guy de Dampierre.

I beheld the pageants splendid that adorned those
    days of old;
Stately dames, like queens attended, knights who
    bore the Fleece of Gold;

Lombard and Venetian merchants with deep-
    laden argosies;
Ministers from twenty nations; more than royal
    pomp and ease.

I beheld proud Maximilian, kneeling humbly on
    the ground;
I beheld the gentle Mary, hunting with her hawk
    and hound;

And her lighted bridal-chamber, where a duke slept
    with the queen,
And the armèd guard around them, and the sword
    unsheathed between.

I beheld the Flemish weavers, with Namur and
    Juliers bold,
Marching homeward from the bloody battle of the
    Spurs of Gold;

Saw the fight at Minnewater, saw the White Hoods
    moving west,
Saw great Artevelde victorious scale the Golden
    Dragon's nest.

And again the whiskered Spaniard all the land
    with terror smote;
And again the wild alarum sounded from the
    tocsin's throat;

The Belfry of Bruges

Till the bell of Ghent responded o'er lagoon and dike of sand,
"I am Roland! I am Roland! there is victory in the land!"

Then the sound of drums aroused me. The awakened city's roar
Chased the phantoms I had summoned back into their graves once more.

Hours had passed away like minutes; and, before I was aware,
Lo! the shadow of the belfry crossed the sun-illumined square.

HENRY WADSWORTH LONGFELLOW.

IN FLANDERS FIELDS

Among the poems and songs the World War gave us, none is better known or of finer spirit than "In Flanders Fields." Since the Armistice a visit to Paris means a trip to the Battlefields around Rheims and Verdun. Long after the visible ravages of war have healed, the great fields of snow white crosses will bring back to our hearts poignant grief for those who must remain forever in Flanders fields. Who would not, while standing in one of the war cemeteries, swear renewed devotion to the cause of Universal Peace?

In Flanders fields the poppies blow
Between the crosses, row on row,
   That mark our place; and in the sky
   The larks, still bravely singing, fly
Scarce heard amid the guns below.

We are the Dead. Short days ago
We lived, felt dawn, saw sunset glow,
   Loved and were loved, and now we lie
     In Flanders fields.

Take up our quarrel with the foe:
To you from failing hands we throw
   The torch; be yours to hold it high.
   If ye break faith with us who die
We shall not sleep, though poppies grow
     In Flanders fields.

JOHN MCCRAE.

NEAR AMSTERDAM
After Albert Cuyp

Not far from where the Y empties into the Zuider Zee is Amsterdam, largest of the cities of Holland. It is well called the Northern Venice for its canals vie in number with its streets and often the traveler gets glimpses here and there of real Venetian vistas.

Out from this city as a center many interesting excursions may be taken through the countryside made famous by Franz Hals, Rembrandt, Vermeer, de Hooch, Ruisdael, Cuyp, and Hobbema. On a visit to Maarken or Volendam one steps off the boat into the midst of a scene recalling the Middle Ages, so strange and fantastic are the costumes of the wooden-shoe folk in these villages on the Zuider Zee.

Some day in no distant future huge "polders" will be redeemed from this inland sea and the trip by fishing smack to Maarken will be a thing of the past.

Sober gray skies and ponderous clouds,
    With gaps between of pallid blues;
Bluff breezes stirring the brown canal;
    A broad, flat meadow's myriad hues

Of soft and changeful breadths of green,
    Barred with the silvery grass that bows
By straight canals, and dotted o'er
    With black and white of basking cows;

And distant sails of hidden ships
    The ceaseless windmills show or hide,
Through languid willows white they gleam,
    And over red-tiled houses glide.

Two sturdy lads with wooden shoes
    Go clumping down the reed-fringed dyke,
And tow a broad-bowed boat, where dreams
    The quaint, sweet virgin of Van Eyck.

And slipt from out the revel high,
  Where gay Franz Hals has bid him sit,
Above the bridge, his lazy pipe
  Smokes placidly the stout De Witt.

S. WEIR MITCHELL.

FRANCE

THE LOUVRE, PARIS

AN OLD CASTLE

Whether the traveler is wending his way along the legend-haunted valley of the Rhine, or visiting the hill-towns of Italy, the grey forbidding walls of an old castle will bring to mind many a story of the past. The romance of its countless corridors, the ghost of an old robber baron, perhaps the long forgotten song of a troubadour, will come back to haunt the threshold of his memory.

In Kenilworth, Roslyn, Warwick, Chillon or Pergine the verses of the American poet may lend added romance to the grim old ruin.

> The gray arch crumbles,
> And totters and tumbles;
> The bat has built in the banquet hall;
> In the donjon-keep
> Sly mosses creep;
> The ivy has scaled the southern wall.
> No man-at-arms
> Sounds quick alarms
> A-top of the cracked martello tower;
> The drawbridge-chain
> Is broken in twain—
> The bridge will neither rise nor lower.
> Not any manner
> Of broidered banner
> Flaunts at a blazoned herald's call.
> Lilies float
> In the stagnant moat;
> And fair they are, and tall.
>
> Here, in the old
> Forgotten springs,
> Was wassail held by queens and kings;
> Here at the board
> Sat clown and lord.

An Old Castle

Maiden fair and lover bold,
Baron fat and mistrel lean,
The prince with his stars,
The knight with his scars,
The priest in his gabardine.

Where is she
Of the fleur-de-lys,
And that true knight who wore her gages?
Where are the glances
That bred wild fancies
In curly heads of my lady's pages?
Where are those
Who, in steel or hose,
Held revel here, and made them gay?
Where is the laughter
That shook the rafter—
Where is the rafter, by the way?
Gone is the roof,
And perched aloof
Is an owl, like a friar of Orders Gray.
(Perhaps 'tis the priest
Come back to feast—
He had ever a tooth for capon, he!
But the capon's cold,
And the steward's old,
And the butler's lost the larder-key!)
The doughty lords
Sleep the sleep of swords;
Dead are the dames and damozels;
The king in his crown
Hath laid him down,
And the Jester with his bells.

All is dead here:
Poppies are red here,
Vines in my lady's chamber grow—
If 'twas her chamber
Where they clamber
Up from the poisonous weeds below.
All is dead here,
Joy is fled here;
Let us hence. 'Tis the end of all—
The gray arch crumbles,
And totters, and tumbles,
And Silence sits in the banquet hall.

THOMAS BAILEY ALDRICH.

THE VENUS OF MILO

Down that long corridor of the Louvre we gaze for our long anticipated view of the marble form of the goddess that for centuries lay beneath the furrows of the "little Melian farm." During those centuries of darkness its surface became roughened and its lines softened, but a spirit within always seems on the point of breaking through the constraining marble.

The mystery of the immortal statue is still unsolved. Just a mutilated fragment of a glorious body, we consider it a sacrilege to replace the missing arms or to repair some of the great damage that resulted from that tragic struggle on the beach at Melos. Turkish sailors, while dragging the precious marble along the strand towards their vessel, were attacked by the French soldiers. The wooden sled upon which it was being drawn collapsed and the statue fell upon its back. "The sailors dragged the statue just as it had fallen over the harsh stones of the beach." A few of the pieces that had broken off were collected and the Goddess of Beauty, after a year of wandering about the Mediterranean, reached Paris to become the priceless gem of a vast and famous collection.

Victor Hugo, in a satiric pamphlet, mocked at his "narrow hipped" countrywomen, and declared that he now knew how a beautiful woman should look.

Kings and artists, scholars and poets have bowed down before this Goddess. Her arms are missing, the lovely skin scratched and scarred, a great scar on her right shoulder, but she has won the admiration of all mankind.

Alfred de Musset, Théophile Gautier, Paul de Saint Victor have written about her. As a dying wish, Heinrich Heine asked to be taken in his invalid chair to gaze once more upon "Notre Dame de Beauté."

"As I entered the hall," he writes, "where the most blessed goddess of beauty, our dear lady of Melos, stands on her pedestal, I well-nigh broke down, and fell at her feet sobbing piteously, so that even a heart of stone must be softened. And the goddess gazed at me compassionately, yet withal so comfortless, as who should say: 'Seest thou not that I have no arms and cannot help thee?' "

The Venus of Milo

What art thou? Woman? Goddess? Aphrodite?
Yet never such as thou from the cold foam
Of ocean, nor from cloudy heaven might come,
Who wast begotten on her bridal night
In passionate Earth's womb by Man's delight,
When Man was young. I cannot trace in thee
Time's handiwork. Say, rather, where is he
For whom thy face was red which is so white?
Thou standest ravished, broken, and thy face
Is writ with ancient passions. Thou art dumb
To my new love. Yet, whatsoe'er of good,
Of crime, of pride, of passion, or of grace
In woman is, thou, woman, hast in sum.
Earth's archetypal Eve. All Womanhood.
      WILFRID SCAWEN BLUNT.

VERSAILLES

Some three centuries ago Versailles was a tiny village; "a muddy pond in which uncouth pigs wallow, pothouses for waggoners, where the wine trickles down the tables; three or four inns, their creaking signboards swinging in the wind; and an old feudal castle turned into a farm." This was the condition of the former estate of Lord Hugo de Versaliis, when here in America William Penn was about to lay out the streets of Philadelphia.

Hunting was good and after the chase Louis XIII found it more convenient to rest here than to return to Saint Germain. From this early hunting lodge, "the little House of Cards," arose the glory and grandeur of Versailles. With Louis XIV began "Le Grand Siècle" and the century of the "Roi Soleil." Under a régime of almost eternal festivals and magnificence, only a palace like Versailles was a fitting residence for the king and his court. What mattered it then if on one side of the shield all was gold, and on the other, the single word, bankruptcy. Hating Paris, Louis lavished prodigal wealth upon the building of this great château which, long ago, was called the French Thebes.

Few places are more historical. Even during the present generations the German Empire and the French Republic have sprung into existence within its great halls. The ghosts of DuBarry, La Pompadour, Madame de Maintenon, Marie Antoinette and many other royal favorites must still wander through these corridors in atonement for the millions squandered on their amusements.

The park today is almost the same as when Le Nôtre completed it. There one finds the Grand Trianon, the Petit Trianon and the hamlet where the Queen and her maids lived a romantic and pastoral life with a dairy, a chapel and a curate's house.

Sadly neglected, the walls are slowly tumbling down, the shrubbery is growing wilder, and the water in the streams and ponds is stagnant. There is still promise of a better day for the old pleasure ground.

Versailles

Here, in the palace gardens, where the stately fountains play,
And a quiet sunshine bathes the land in the balm of an April day,
It is pleasant to sit and dream awhile of the things that have passed away.

For if much has changed, there is much remains; and half of the trees that grow
Were planted here in the Bourbon days, when a king was a king, you know;
And they watched them, all the women and men who walked here long ago;

Duke and Marquis and Abbé, who lounged on the terrace stair,
With a stately bow to the wise and great, and a nod to Molière;
And dainty dames with the tarnished names, and the smiles and the powdered hair.

Ah! life was life in the palace then, and the world was a gallant place,
With the polished ways and the pungent phrase and the ruffles, and swords, and lace,
And sin was hardly a thing to shun when it beckoned with such a grace.

Music and wit and laughter, and pleasure enthroned in state,
And the gardens bright with a fairy light at many a summer fête;
And ruin and famine and death and Hell not half a mile from the gate!

Hell, and they couldn't see it! Death, and they only played!
For a serf—why a serf was born to serve, and a monarch to be obeyed;
Till the tumbrels came and the guillotine: but at least they were not afraid.

Shadows among the shadows, they flit through the chequered ways,
And the long, straight walks, where the elm-trees grow, and the time-worn statues gaze
Silent and cold, and gray and old, like the ghosts of forgotten days.

Kindly, blundering Louis, and beautiful Antoinette,
With the royal face, and the human heart, and the tears—could we but forget!
Down there is the little Trianon; perhaps we shall see her yet!

Poor girl-queen! It's hard to be great; and you tried, and we can but try:
But what you took for the Truth and France was only a painted lie:
Did you know it at last, and understand, when the time had come to die?

Nay, I trust you did: for if Truth brings pain, I hold it is better far,
Were it only once, for a moment's space, like the flash of a falling star,
To pierce the cloud that has dimmed our eyes, and to see things as they are.

Versailles

For a 'sunshine king' is a costly thing when monarch and man are blind,
And somebody reaps the whirlwind when others have sowed the wind,
And if death and famine stalk through the land, it isn't enough to be kind.

King and Queen, who were boy and girl, long since, ere the die was cast,
Was it all a riddle too hard to solve? Poor souls! You have wept and passed,
And after the din and the strife and sin there is peace, we hope, at the last.

And now the Tricolour triumphs where once the Lilies reigned;
Its red is red with a sea of blood, and the white—ah! the white is stained,
But a giant lie has been swept away, and France and the world have gained.

GODFREY FOX BRADBY.

THE WINGÈD VICTORY

Ascending the *Escalier Daru* at the Louvre, that great treasure house of things beautiful and rare, we are confronted by the majestic Victory of Samothrace, "one of the noblest examples of Greek art, wrought immediately before it had spent its creative force and began to direct a subtle and technical mastery to serve private luxury and pomp." Erected on the Island of Samothrace by Demetrius, one of Alexander's generals, it commemorated a naval victory in the year 306 B.C. over Ptolemy, his former companion in arms.

Today the Victory stands upon a large pedestal representing the prow of a ship. With her wings directed backward as though about to be folded from flight, she presents an amazing suggestion of motion. The mastery displayed in the draperies has never been surpassed. It offers a fine example of the use of draperies; though quite artificial in form, it still suggests the flexibility and texture of cloth, as well as the motion of the figure.

Although mutilated, the vigorous forward thrust of the body, the clinging garments, and the majesty of its poise, make it a great achievement in sculpture. "Irresistible in her transparent drapery, she cleaves the sea air as the prow of the ship shears the blue wave in two long streaks of flashing foam."

Thou dear and most high Victory,
Whose home is the unvanquished sea,
Whose fluttering wind-blown garments keep
The very freshness, fold, and sweep
They wore upon the galley's prow,
By what unwonted favor now
Hast thou alighted in this place,
Thou Victory of Samothrace?

O thou to whom in countless lands
With eager hearts and striving hands
Strong men in their last need have prayed,
Greatly desiring, undismayed,

The Wingèd Victory

And thou hast been across the fight
Their consolation and their might,
Withhold not now one dearer grace,
Thou Victory of Samothrace!

Behold, we, too, must cry to thee,
Who wage our strife with Destiny,
And give for Beauty and for Truth
Our love, our valor and our youth.
Are there no honors for these things
To match the pageantries of kings?
Are we more laggard in the race
Than those who fell at Samothrace?

Not only for the bow and sword,
O Victory, be thy reward!
The hands that work with paint and clay
In Beauty's service, shall not they
Also with mighty faith prevail?
Let hope not die, nor courage fail,
But joy come with thee pace for pace,
As once long since in Samothrace.

Grant us the skill to shape the form
And spread the color living-warm,
(As they who wrought aforetime did),
Where love and wisdom shall lie hid,
In fair impassioned types, to sway
The cohorts of the world to-day,
In Truth's eternal cause, and trace
Thy glory down from Samothrace.

With all the ease and splendid poise
Of one who triumphs without noise,
Wilt thou not teach us to attain
Thy sense of power without strain,
That we a little may possess
Our souls with thy sure loveliness,—
That calm the years cannot deface,
Thou Victory of Samothrace?

Then in the ancient, ceaseless war
With infamy, go thou before!
Amid the shoutings and the drums
Let it be learned that Beauty comes,
Man's matchless Paladin to be,
Whose rule shall make his spirit free
As thine from all things mean or base.
Thou Victory of Samothrace.

BLISS CARMAN.

THE ANGELUS

Jean François Millet

In the summer of 1849 Millet, with his wife and children, journeyed in a rumbling omnibus from Paris to Fontainebleau. Next day, under the guidance of a woodcutter, they set out to find the "place that ends in *zon*." "Mon Dieu, Mon Dieu, que c'est beau," he was heard to say over and over again as he first gazed upon Barbizon.

Diaz, Rousseau, Corot, and Barye, the sculptor, came here and soon Père Gannes' hostelry became the rendezvous of a colony of painters. Years after, he boasted that he had sheltered beneath his roof the best artists of his time.

At the entrance to the Forest of Fontainebleau is a monument to Millet's memory, but the primeval rocks scattered round about and the great trees "form the fittest possible monument to an artist who was rooted like a rock in this soil, and whose place in the history of art is established with equal firmness forever."

Not far from Paris, in fair Fontainebleau,
   A lovely memory-haunted hamlet lies,
   Whose tender spell makes captive, and defies
Forgetfulness. The peasants come and go—
Their backs too used to stoop, and patient sow
   The harvest which their narrow need supplies—
   Even as when, Earth's pathos in his eyes,
Millet dwelt here, companion of their woe.

Ah, Barbizon! With thorns, not laurels, crowned,
He looked thy sorrows in the face, and found—
   Vital as seed warm-nestled in the sod—
The hidden sweetness at the heart of pain;
Trusting thy sun and dew, thy wind and rain—
   At home with Nature, and at one with God!

                    FLORENCE EARLE COATES.

LA MARSEILLAISE

"Think of the city of Paris where all the best of the realms of nature and art in the whole earth are open to daily contemplation, a world-city where the crossing of every bridge or every square recalls a great past, and where at every street corner a piece of history has been unfolded." He who knows Paris may know France but the visitor must hear the grandest story of liberty ever written before he really understands the spirit and patriotism of the French. "La Marseillaise" was originally written in French by Captain Rouget de Lisle, a French officer at Strasbourg, in 1792, and was first called "The Hymn of the Army of the Rhine." The author was a captain of the Rhine army and he wrote the song for his soldiers to sing as they marched. Later it was re-named "La Marseillaise" because it was first brought to Paris by soldiers who came from Marseilles. Enthusiastic fighters in the days of the Revolution, they soon made this song so popular that it became the national anthem of the Republic.

Arise, ye children of the nation,
The day of glory now is here!
See the hosts of dark oppression,
Their blood-stained banners rear;
Their blood-stained banners rear;
Do ye not heed? roaring the tyrants go,
Scattering homes and peace;
Our sons, our comrades face the foe,
The wounds of war increase.
    To arms, ye warriors all!
    Your bold battalions call!
    March on, ye free!
    Death shall be ours, or glorious liberty!

That sacred love—the love of country,
Spurs on afresh our eager arms,
And for conquest and for freedom,
We dare the vast alarms!
We dare the vast alarms!
Speedily then, crowning heroic deeds,
Triumph shall lift each head.
And our One Flag fly proudly o'er
The living and the dead!
   To arms, ye etc. . . . .

ROUGET DE LISLE.

NOTRE DAME

This aged queen of French cathedrals shows the countless defacements and mutilations that man has left upon the still sublime and majestic building. Its façade, with the three receding portals, is one of the finest pages in the history of architecture. It lacks the eleven steps which once raised it above the level of the ground; the statues which filled the niches over the doors and the row of twenty-eight ancient kings that adorned the gallery of the first story and the stained glass of gorgeous hue have been replaced, but every stone is a page in the history of France. It is the most perfect expression of early Gothic art, wherein the builders lavished all their artistic powers in a sympathetic expression of their outlook on life and eternity.

From the time Julius Caesar addressed his legionaires on this island, two milleniums of history have been enacted here and few spots have more historic memories. It has been associated with every important act during the reigns of all the kings of France. Here Charles IX celebrated the glories of St. Bartholomew, and Napoleon and his Empress, with a Pope as sponsor, received their imperial crowns.

Often at evening, when the summer sun,
Floats like a gold balloon above the roofs,
I climb this silent tower of Notre Dame—
My sole companion Hugo's deathless book—
For here all limits vanish, here my soul
Breathes and expands, and knows a wider life.
Here in the lustrous, shimmering sunset hour
Painter and poet both might find new words,
New colours, seeing opened in the sky
The jewel-casket of Ithuriel—
Sapphires, cornelians, opals! Pictures here
Are seen, so gorgeous and so rich in hue
That Titian's and Rubens' colouring
Grows pale in memory; and here are built
Misty cathedrals, wonderfully arched,
Mountains of smoke, fantastic colonnades—

Notre Dame

All doubled in the mirror of the Seine. . . .
Now comes a breeze which moulds the tattered
  clouds
Into a thousand new and changing forms,
Mysterious and vague; the passing day,
As if for his good-night, reclothes the church
In vesture of a richer, purer tint.
Her tall twin-towers—those canticles in stone—
Drawn with great strokes upon the fiery sky,
Seem like two mighty arms upraised in pray'r
To God by Paris ere she sinks to sleep.
But ah! when in the darkness you have climbed
The slender spiral staircase, when at last
You see again the blue sky overhead,
The void above you, the abyss below,
Then are you seized by dizziness and fear
Sublime, to feel yourself so close to God.
E'en as a branch beneath a perching bird,
The tower shrinks 'neath the pressure of your feet,
Trembles and thrills; th' intoxicated sky
Waltzes and reels around you; the abyss
Opens its jaws: the imp of dizziness,
Flapping you with his wings, leaps mockingly,
And all the parapets shudder and shake.
Weathercocks, spires, and pointed roofs move past
Your dazzled eyes, outlined in silhouette
Against the whirling sky, and in the gulf
Where the apocalyptic raven wheels,
Far down, lies Paris, howling—yet unheard!
O, how the heart beats now! To dominate
With feeble human eye from this great height
A city so immense! With one swift glance
To embrace this mighty whole, standing so near
To Heaven, and beholding, even as
A soaring mountain-eagle, far, far down

In the depth of the crater's heart, the writhing smoke,
The boiling lava! . . .
And yet, O Notre Dame, though Paris robed
In flame-like vesture is so beautiful,
Her beauty vanishes if one should leave
Thy towers and reach the level earth again.
All fades and changes then; nought grand is left
Save only thee. . . . For O, within thy walls
The Lord God makes His Dwelling! Through thy dark
And shadowy places Heaven's angels move,
And light thee with reflections from their wings.
O, world of poetry in this world of prose!
At sight of thee a knocking at the heart
Is felt, a perfect faith makes pure the soul.
When evening damascenes thee with her gold,
And in the dingy square thou, gleaming, stand'st
Like a huge monstrance on a purple daïs,
I can believe that by a miracle
Between thy towers the Lord might show Himself. . . .
How small our bourgeois monuments appear
Beside thy Gallic majesty! No dome,
No spire, however proud, can vie with thee—
Thou seem'st indeed to strike against the sky!
Who could prefer, e'en in pedantic taste,
These poor bare Grecian styles, these Panthéons,
These antique fripperies, perishing with cold,
And scarcely knowing how to stand upright,
To the demure, straight folds of thy chaste robe? . . .

THÉOPHILE GAUTIER.
(Translated by Eva M. Martin)

TREES

Rheims and some of the other small northern French towns were not on the Grand Tour before the World War, but who today does not know Soisson and Berry-au-Bac? Should you, while on the battlefield trip, stop at the American cemetery, walk up the main drive past several rows of snow white crosses and then turn in to the right. You will find there the grave of Joyce Kilmer. Stop reverently for a moment and read one of the finest and best known poems of this youthful American poet.

> I think that I shall never see
> A poem lovely as a tree.
>
> A tree whose hungry mouth is prest
> Against the earth's sweet flowing breast;
>
> A tree that looks at God all day,
> And lifts her leafy arms to pray;
>
> A tree that may in Summer wear
> A nest of robins in her hair;
>
> Upon whose bosom snow has lain;
> Who intimately lives with rain.
>
> Poems are made by fools like me
> But only God can make a tree.
>
> JOYCE KILMER.

CHARLEMAGNE

When Charles was crowned Emperor of the Romans by Pope Leo III in old St. Peter's, the age of the barbarians was ended by the greatest of them. He was, it is true, the heir of an old barbarian monarchy, but he was also founder of a new empire. Already the story of his conquests reads like the epitome of a lost romance.

His outposts extended from Russia to Spain. His expeditions in Spain have been immortalized in the French epic, "La Chanson de Roland." Lombard kings and princes yielded submission and such conflicts placed him at the head of the one great power west of the Elbe and Adriatic. He exalted the church but enslaved her. In his character as Emperor he became "the fountain of justice, the guardian of public order, the protector of peaceful industry and commerce."

"Woe to thee, Rome, and woe to the people of Rome. The great and glorious Charles is taken from you. Woe to thee, Italy, and to all thy fair cities. Many are the afflictions that Frankland has known, but never knew she such a sorrow as when at Aachen she laid in the earth the august and eloquent Charles." Such were the words written by an unknown monk.

(Charlemagne was buried sitting upright on his throne, robed and crowned, his sword at his side.)

He sits beneath the dust of conquered worlds
Clothed in imperial robes, his restless sword—
The terror once of Arab, Saxon, Moor—
Held in that last cold grasp of lifeless clay.
How must that spirit, tortured by the sight
Of crumbling empires, struggle to break free!
How must that hand, once glorious in the strife,
That death alone could conquer, strain to lift
The sword and save the kingdom from its doom!
And yet he moves not! On his shadow throne,

While muffled sounds of kingdoms falling strike
His earth-clogged ears, he reigns among the shad-
 ows
Until with wide unblinded eyes he see
All thrones and crowns lie broken in the dust.
>   MARY SINTON LEITCH.

TO THE RIVER RHONE

Long before rivers like the Rhone were regulated, the annual flooding of the alluvial plains made it necessary for man to build his habitations high above the level of the river. Destructive floods and avalanches were common in the valleys of such a powerful unembanked river. Today frequent wayside crosses mark the spots where travelers have met death.

From its "frozen cataract" at the foot of the Rhone Glacier, the turbulent milk-white torrent rushes past Brieg and Visp emptying finally into Lake Geneva, from which it again emerges clear as crystal. Along its course are priceless vestiges of the past. At Geneva was the bridge—its ancient foundations still remain—that Caesar was forced to demolish before he could check the onslaught of the Helvetians against his Roman legions.

At Lyons, where the Saône joins its waters with the Rhone, the river begins its lower course. The tourist, if he wishes, may travel the distance from Lyons to Avignon by steamer, but the more hurried summer visitor makes the journey by train. Either way lies through a land rich in historic lore.

The house of Petrarch at Vaucluse, the remains of provincial Rome at Nîmes and Arles, the memorial of the Babylonian Captivity of the Papacy at Avignon, and the echoes of the Troubadours of Old Provence make the Rhone a river of interesting and lasting memories.

Thou Royal River, born of sun and shower
  In chambers purple with the Alpine glow,
  Wrapped in the spotless ermine of the snow
And rocked by tempests!—at the appointed hour
Forth, like a steel-clad horseman from a tower,
  With clang and clink of harness dost thou go
  To meet thy vassal torrents, that below
Rush to receive thee and obey thy power.
And now thou movest in triumphal march,
  A king among the rivers! On thy way
  A hundred towns await and welcome thee;
Bridges uplift for thee the stately arch,
  Vineyards encircle thee with garlands gay,
  And fleets attend thy progress to the sea!

                HENRY WADSWORTH LONGFELLOW.

GARGOYLES
STRASBOURG CATHEDRAL

On the site of a church built by Clovis in A.D. 510, stands the great Cathedral of Strasbourg. In its towers, spires, finials and flying buttresses we find illustrations of the rise, perfect development and decline of Gothic art. From the lofty platform one looks off across the valley of the Rhine and the old city where Gutenberg gave printing to the world and where Rouget de Lisle composed the "Marseillaise" for France.

Like the little sins great souls ignore,
The little sins we love them for,
They cluster slyly with grimace and grin,
Mocking the reverent peace within.

In unbridled mischief, a naughty brood,
Defying the great cathedral's mood,
'Twixt flying buttresses they stare
At the holy ones who go for prayer.
With horn and hoof, with leer and sneer—
Impudent creatures—they peep and peer.

Grotesque, uncouth, down far below
The sky-wrought spire they never know
How petty their part in the soaring whole
And plume themselves with complacent soul,
And nod and wink in conscious pride,
As strangers spy them side by side.

Not demons accurst, nor a sin-bred crew,
But the vagrant fancies some old priest knew;
Gay imps that chased his prayers from the throne—
Now doomed forever to dwell in stone.

GERTRUDE HUNTINGTON MCGIFFERT.

CARCASSONNE

This old city, unsurpassed in its lovely setting, stands crowded behind walls and towers on its hill beside the river Aude. It is a "piece of unspoiled mediaevalism, like a fly imprisoned in amber."

> "I can scarce believe the tale,
> Borne to me on every gale;
> You have been to Carcassonne?
> Looked the stately towers upon?
>
> "All men go to Arcady,
> Soon or late they breathe its air,
> Learn its language, pray its prayer;
> Linger there till dreams are done,
> Yet few go to Carcassonne."

From this old stronghold of the Visigoths one gets his first view of the Pyrenees and when the weather is clear the days close amid never-to-be-forgotten sunsets.

> "I'm growing old, I've sixty years;
> I've labored all my life in vain.
> In all that time of hopes and fears,
> I've failed my dearest wish to gain.
> I see full well that here below
> Bliss unalloyed there is for none:
> My prayer would else fulfilment know—
> Never have I seen Carcassonne!
>
> "You see the city from the hill,
> It lies beyond the mountains blue;
> And yet to reach it one must still
> Five long and weary leagues pursue,
> And, to return, as many more.
> Had but the vintage plenteous grown—
> But, ah! the grape withheld its store.
> I shall not look on Carcassonne!

"They tell me every day is there
    Not more or less than Sunday gay;
In shining robes and garments fair
    The people walk upon their way.
One gazes there on castle walls
    As grand as those of Babylon,
A bishop and two generals!
    What joy to dwell in Carcassonne!

"The vicar's right: he says that we
    Are ever wayward, weak, and blind;
He tells us in his homily
    Ambition ruins all mankind;
Yet could I there two days have spent,
    While still the autumn sweetly shone,
Ah, me! I might have died content
    When I had looked on Carcassonne.

"Thy pardon, Father, I beseech,
    In this my prayer if I offend;
One something sees beyond his reach
    From childhood to his journey's end.
My wife, our little boy, Aignan,
    Have travelled even to Narbonne;
My grandchild has seen Perpignan;
    And I—have not seen Carcassonne!"

So crooned, one day, close by Limoux,
    A peasant, double-bent with age.
"Rise up, my friend," said I; "with you
    I'll go upon this pilgrimage."
We left, next morning, his abode,
    But (Heaven forgive him!) half-way on
The old man died upon the road.
    He never gazed on Carcassonne.

GUSTAVE NADAUD.

(Translated by John R. Thompson).

IN OLD ROUEN

Richer in mediaeval architecture than any other French city, this ancient capital of France is most interesting. The 13th Century cathedral with its "tour de Beurre," so called because it was built with the funds secured from Lenten indulgences to eat butter, is full of historic associations. The Tombs of Rollo of Normandy, the effigy of Richard the Lion-heart, the monument of Cardinal d'Amboise and Diane de Poitiers are reminders of days of long ago. And then the many curious old houses,—how strange and alluring! But it is the Place de la Pucelle with its statue of Joan of Arc and the Place du Vieux-Marche where she was burned at the stake, that give the following verses their appeal.

In Old Rouen, where past and present meet,
A mighty duke once reigned—a girl was burned;
And still their shades in boulevard and street
Or some dim crypt or tower may be discerned.

And one has outlines very blurred and faint,
And one has gathered glory, from the years;—
Ah, it is not the Conqueror, but the Saint,
Who holds a world's remembrance—through its tears.

ANTOINETTE DE COURSEY PATTERSON.

IN THE GALLERIES OF THE LOUVRE

Few buildings are more remarkable for vast extent and magnificence than the Louvre, and no other has such a priceless collection of art treasures. The Victory of Samothrace, the Venus de Milo, the Rubens, the Rembrandts, the Slaves of Michael Angelo, the Mona Lisa and masterpieces in painting and sculpture of the great artists of all ages are here to hold the lover of art enthralled.

Among the pictures in these palace halls
One scene which holds me fast with charméd grace
Is of a poor Dutch room, with chimney-place.
There by a window, through which twilight falls,

Sits blesséd Mary, whom her Child enthralls
With His sweet smile and with His fond embrace:
The glowing hearth lights up her joyous face;
From heaven calm sleep, with crooning song, she calls.

Is this Dutch scene the home of Christ the King—
The Infant of far-distant Palestine?
Yea, Holy Child, for all the earth is Thine;
'Round ev'ry mother's neck Thy fingers cling;

And what Thy loving mother sang to Thee
Is sung by mothers through eternity.

CHARLES LEWIS SLATTERY.

THE BOOK-STALLS ON THE SEINE

An interesting place to shop for some long-desired volume is among the Book-Stalls on the Seine. Here, when the weather is fair and daylight makes reading possible, you will find many an old Parisian or a tourist book-lover poring over some dusty tome, hoping sooner or later to make a find.

When you're in Paris next, just after rain—
Whene'er the sun comes out (Give God the praise!)—
Go down and watch their varied owners raise
The covers of the book-stalls on the Seine.

Then watch some stooping scholar, who would fain,
Among worn texts of Greek and Latin plays,
Discover what he's longed for all his days,—
A book so rare he doubts if one remain.

He's scanned two hundred titles line by line,
And failed again. But Look! His eyes shine bright:
He's found it! Published by . . . yes, all is right:
The date is fifteen hundred thirty-nine.

And thus you know that Paris is the home
Of Abélard and Bernard—and not Rome.

CHARLES LEWIS SLATTERY.

GERMANY

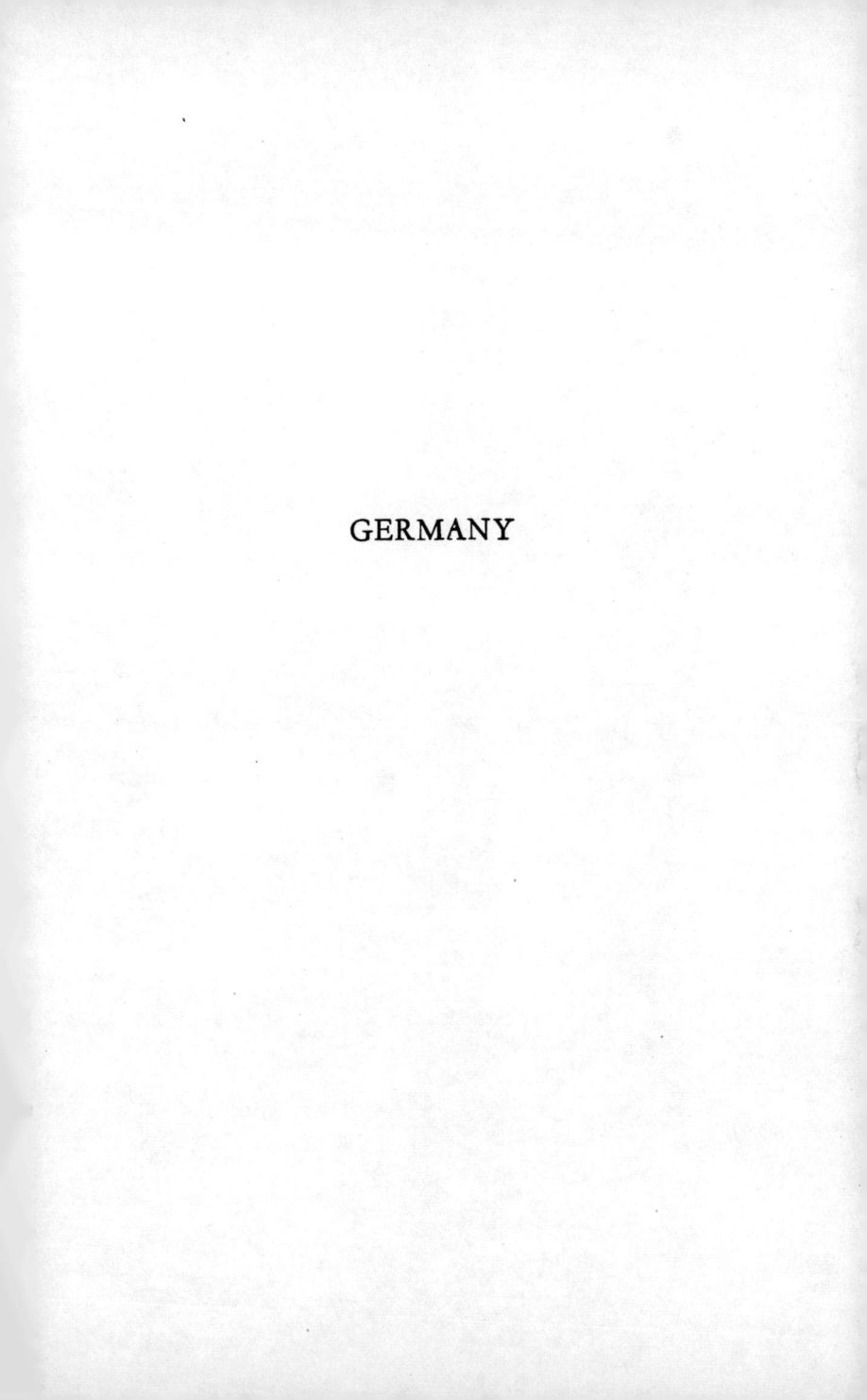

BURG STOLZENFELS ON THE RHINE

THE LORELEI

Few can understand the Spirit of Germany without a trip down the Rhine, for along this beautiful river the Germany of peaceful legend and romantic ruins is at her best. From the time of the half-savage Celts, who first took possession of this mighty valley, to the present day, the swift current of the Rhine has been the spectator of many an historic event. Caesar led his legions across its waters; Titus, Trajan, Hadrian and Julian came this way and built fortresses along its banks. Like an immense chain, Roman colonies protected the frontier of the Empire. The chain broke when Rome weakened and the northern hordes became too powerful, and the banks of the river were strewed with ruined Roman fortresses, just as today they are strewed with feudal castles.

In the words of Hugo, "The Rhine is unique; it combines the qualities of every river. Like the Rhone it is rapid; broad like the Loire; encased, like the Meuse; serpentine, like the Seine; limpid and green, like the Somme; historic, like the Tiber; royal, like the Danube; mysterious, like the Nile; spangled with gold, like an American river; and like a river of Asia, abounding with phantoms and fables."

Everyone on the Rhine steamer has purchased a map of the river with its pictures of castles and interesting towns along the way. As we journey down the river the boom of the cannon gives warning that we are passing the famous Lorelei Rock.

Some have been reading the stories of Bishop Hatto and the Mouse Tower, the Drachenfels, Ehrenbreitstein, and the soldier of the Legion from Fair Bingen, but we already know the story of the maiden with the golden hair who lured brave mariners towards her lofty eyrie. As the oft-repeated echoes die away and the steamer leaves the Rock far behind, we will once more wish to turn to our poem and read it.

Yonder we see it from the steamer's deck,
The haunted Mountain of the Lorelei—
The hanging crags sharp-cut against a sky
Clear as a sapphire without flaw or fleck.

'Twas here the Siren lay in wait to wreck
The fisher-lad. At dusk, as he rowed by,
Perchance he heard her tender amorous cry,
And, seeing the wondrous whiteness of her neck,
Perchance would halt, and lean towards the shore;
Then she by that soft magic which she had
Would lure him, and in gossamers of her hair,
Gold upon gold, would wrap him o'er and o'er,
Wrap him, and sing to him, and drive him mad,
Then drag him down to no man knoweth where.

THOMAS BAILEY ALDRICH.

DRACHENFELS
From *Childe Harold's Pilgrimage*

Opposite Bonn, the "city of the Muses," the Rhine voyageurs see the mighty summits of the Seven Mountains. On one of these rocky points the crumbling walls of an old knight's castle are to be seen. Of the many legends heard along this romantic waterway, none is more touching than the legend of the Drachenfels where a terrible dragon of hideous form left his den each day and raged up and down the mountain side.

A Christian maiden among the neighboring peoples was the object of jealous dissension between two barbarian chieftains. The tribal priest, in order to prevent the threatened struggle, demanded that she be dedicated to the Dragon in honor of Woden.

As the sacrificial procession neared the rock, so often stained by human blood, the younger chieftain followed the maiden with sympathetic gaze as she was led forward by the fanatical priest.

When the first rays of the morning sun gilded the eastern sky, the dragon pulled his scaly body from his den. A shudder of death crept over the maiden as, with trembling hand, she tore a golden crucifix from her breast.

To the utter wonderment of the people, the monster threw himself headlong into the dark waters below. The younger of the two chieftains looked on with amazement and bowed his head. The old priest asked the maiden what had saved her, and her reply was: "This picture of Christ has crushed the Dragon and saved me. The salvation of the world and the welfare of man lies in Him. May it soon lighten your spirit and those of all these people around."

A Christian temple long marked this spot and a powerful people ruled the countries along the great river.

The castled crag of Drachenfels
Frowns o'er the wide and winding Rhine,
Whose breast of waters broadly swells
Between the banks which bear the vine,
And hills all rich with blossomed trees,
And fields which promise corn and wine,
And scatter'd cities crowning these,

Whose far white walls along them shine,
Have strew'd a scene, which I should see
With double joy wert *thou* with me.

And peasant girls, with deep blue eyes,
And hands which offer early flowers,
Walk smiling o'er this paradise;
Above, the frequent feudal towers
Through green leaves lift their walls of gray;
And many a rock which steeply lowers,
And noble arch in proud decay,
Look o'er this vale of vintage-bowers;
But one thing want these banks of Rhine,—
Thy gentle hand to clasp in mine!

I send the lilies given to me;
Though long before thy hand they touch,
I know that they must wither'd be,
But yet reject them not as such;
For I have cherished them as dear,
Because they yet may meet thine eye,
And guide thy soul to mine even here,
When thou behold'st them drooping nigh,
And know'st them gathered by the Rhine,
And offer'd from my heart to thine!

The river nobly foams and flows,
The charm of this enchanted ground,
And all its thousand turns disclose
Some fresher beauty varying round:
The haughtiest breast its wish might bound
Through life to dwell delighted here;
Nor could on earth a spot be found
To nature and to me so dear,
Could thy dear eyes in following mine
Still sweeten more these banks of Rhine!

Lord Byron.

TO THE RHINE

From *Childe Harold's Pilgrimage*

Adieu to thee, fair Rhine! How long delighted
The stranger fain would linger on his way!
Thine is a scene alike where souls united
Or lonely Contemplation thus might stray;
And could the ceaseless vultures cease to prey
On self-condemning bosoms, it were here,
Where Nature, nor too sombre nor too gay,
Wild but not rude, awful yet not austere,
Is to the mellow Earth as Autumn to the year.

Adieu to thee again! a vain adieu!
There can be no farewell to scene like thine;
The mind is colour'd by thy every hue;
And if reluctantly the eyes resign
Their cherish'd gaze upon thee, lovely Rhine!
'Tis with the thankful glance of parting praise;
More mighty spots may rise, more glaring shine,
But none unite in one attaching maze
The brilliant, fair, and soft,—the glories of old days,

The negligently grand, the fruitful bloom
Of coming ripeness, the white city's sheen,
The rolling stream, the precipice's gloom,
The forest's growth, and Gothic walls between,
The wild rocks shaped as they had turrets been,
In mockery of man's art; and these withal
A race of faces happy as the scene,
Whose fertile bounties here extend to all,
Still springing o'er thy banks, though Empires near them fall.

But these recede. Above me are the Alps,
The palaces of Nature, whose vast walls
Have pinnacled in clouds their snowy scalps,
And throned Eternity in icy halls
Of cold sublimity, where forms and falls
The avalanche—the thunderbolt of snow!
All that expands the spirit, yet appalls,
Gather around these summits, as to show
How earth may pierce to Heaven, yet leave vain man below.

LORD BYRON.

ALBERT DÜRER'S STUDIO

In the Dürerplatz of Nuremberg, on the Pegnitz, is the house of Albrecht Dürer where a notable collection of the great northern artist's work has been assembled. In St. John's Churchyard the visitor to this quaint old city will find the grave of Dürer and Hans Sachs, the cobbler-poet.

The art treasures which still remain in the city and the historical buildings which it still possesses, justify the name which scholars have given to it: "Casket of German Gems." There is no finer jewel among them than the studio of Albrecht Dürer.

In the house of Albert Dürer
   Still is seen the studio
Where the pretty Nurembergers
   (Cheeks of rose and necks of snow)
Sat to have their portraits painted,
   Thrice a hundred years ago.

Still is seen the little loop-hole
   Where Frau Dürer's jealous care
Watched the artist at his labor,
   And the sitter in her chair,
To observe each word and motion
   That should pass between the pair.

Handsome, hapless Albert Dürer
   Was as circumspect and true
As the most correct of husbands,
   When the dear delightful shrew
Has him, and his sweet companions,
   Every moment under view.

But I trow that Albert Dürer
   Had within his heart a spot
Where he sat, and painted pictures
   That gave beauty to his lot,

And the sharp, intrusive vision
  Of Frau Dürer entered not.

Ah! if brains and hearts had loop-holes,
  And Frau Dürer could have seen
All the pictures that his fancy
  Hung upon their walls within,
How minute had been her watching,
  And how good he would have been!
JOSIAH GILBERT HOLLAND.

NUREMBERG

The subtle flavor of this little gem of mediaevalism is exquisite and indefinable. It is a "quaint old Town of Art and Song." As the home of the Meistersinger in the Middle Ages, it has appealing memories for music lovers. With its high gables, stone balconies and curious carvings, it retains much of the appearance of a mediaeval city. No city of the Middle Ages was more famous for its artistic handicrafts. It was the home of Hans Sachs, the cobbler-poet; Adam Kraft, the stone mason; Albrecht Dürer, engraver and painter; and Peter Vischer, brass founder. What city won greater fame for its casting of metals, goldsmith work, pewter, stained glass, curious clocks and holy shrines? Outside the town along the green meadows of the Pegnitz, *Die Meistersinger von Nürnberg* held festivals, the tradition of which became the source of Wagner's famous opera.

In the valley of the Pegnitz, where across broad meadow-lands
Rise the blue Franconian mountains, Nuremberg, the ancient, stands.

Quaint old town of toil and traffic, quaint old town of art and song,
Memories haunt thy pointed gables, like the rooks that round them throng:

Memories of the Middle Ages, when the emperors, rough and bold,
Had their dwelling in thy castle, time-defying, centuries old;

And thy brave and thrifty burghers boasted, in their uncouth rhyme,
That their great imperial city stretched its hand through every clime.

In the courtyard of the castle, bound with many an iron band,
Stands the mighty linden planted by Queen Cunigunde's hand;

On the square the oriel window, where in old heroic days
Sat the poet Melchior singing Kaiser Maximilian's praise.

Everywhere I see around me rise the wondrous world of Art:
Fountains wrought with richest sculpture standing in the common mart;

And above cathedral doorways saints and bishops carved in stone,
By a former age commissioned as apostles to our own.

In the church of sainted Sebald sleeps enshrined his holy dust,
And in bronze the Twelve Apostles guard from age to age their trust;

In the church of sainted Lawrence stands a pix of sculpture rare,
Like the foamy sheaf of fountains, rising through the painted air.

Here, when Art was still religion, with a simple, reverent heart,
Lived and labored Albrecht Dürer, the Evangelist of Art;

Hence in silence and in sorrow, toiling still with busy hand,
Like an emigrant he wandered, seeking for the Better Land,

Emigravit is the inscription on the tombstone where he lies;
Dead he is not, but departed,—for the artist never dies.

Fairer seems the ancient city, and the sunshine seems more fair,
That he once has trod its pavement, that he once has breathed its air!

Through these streets so broad and stately, these obscure and dismal lanes,
Walked of yore the Mastersingers, chanting rude poetic strains.

From remote and sunless suburbs came they to the friendly guild,
Building nests in Fame's great temple, as in spouts the swallows build.

As the weaver plied the shuttle, wove he too the mystic rhyme,
And the smith his iron measures hammered to the anvil's chime;

Thanking God, whose boundless wisdom makes the flowers of poesy bloom
In the forge's dust and cinders, in the tissues of the loom.

Here Hans Sachs, the cobbler-poet, laureate of the
    gentle craft,
Wisest of the Twelve Wise Masters, in huge folios
    sang and laughed.

But his house is now an ale-house, with a nicely
    sanded floor,
And a garland in the window, and his face above
    the door;

Painted by some humble artist, as in Adam Pusch-
    man's song,
As the old man gray and dove-like, with his great
    beard white and long.

And at night the swart mechanic comes to drown
    his cark and care,
Quaffing ale from pewter tankards, in the master's
    antique chair.

Vanished is the ancient splendor, and before my
    dreamy eye
Wave these mingled shapes and figures, like a faded
    tapestry.

Not thy Councils, not thy Kaisers, win for thee the
    world's regard;
But thy painter, Albrecht Dürer, and Hans Sachs
    thy cobbler bard.

Thus, O Nuremberg, a wanderer from a region far
    away,
As he paced thy streets and courtyards, sang in
    thought his careless lay:

Gathering from the pavement's crevice, as a flow-
    eret of the soil,
The nobility of labor,—the long pedigree of toil.

HENRY WADSWORTH LONGFELLOW.

THE THREE KINGS

Overlooking the Rhine, and the city of Cologne, with its impressive turrets and towers, stands the great Cathedral, glory of the modern city and one of the grandest Gothic churches ever built.

Six hundred years in building, it now has within its walls many sacred relics and religious treasures. Among the most venerated of these is the golden shrine of the Magi. Since the 12th Century it has enclosed the sacred bones, brought by the Empress Helena from Constantinople to Milan and later transferred by Frederick Barbarossa to Cologne. Today a gold mark opens the treasure house to travelers from all corners of the earth and they are permitted to gaze at the resting place of the Three Wise Men who followed the Star in the East.

Three Kings came riding from far away,
   Melchior and Gaspar and Baltasar;
Three Wise Men out of the East were they,
   And they travelled by night and they slept by day,
For their guide was a beautiful, wonderful star.

The star was so beautiful, large, and clear,
   That all the other stars of the sky
Became a white mist in the atmosphere,
   And by this they knew that the coming was near
Of the Prince foretold in the prophecy.

Three caskets they bore on their saddle-bows,
   Three caskets of gold with golden keys;
Three robes were of crimson silk with rows
   Of bells and pomegranates and furbelows,
Their turbans like blossoming almond-trees.

And so the Three Kings rode into the West,
   Through the dusk of night, over hill and dell,
And sometimes they nodded with beard on breast,
   And sometimes talked, as they paused to rest,
With the people they met at some wayside well.

"Of the child that is born," said Baltasar,
  "Good people, I pray you, tell us the news;
For we in the East have seen his star,
  And have ridden fast, and have ridden far,
To find and worship the King of the Jews."

And the people answered, "You ask in vain;
  We know of no King but Herod the Great!"
They thought the Wise Men were men insane,
  As they spurred their horses across the plain,
Like riders in haste, and who cannot wait.

And when they came to Jerusalem,
  Herod the Great, who had heard this thing,
Sent for the Wise Men and questioned them;
  And said: "Go down unto Bethlehem,
And bring me tidings of this new King."

So they rode away; and the star stood still,
  The only one in the gray of morn;
Yes, it stopped,—it stood still of its own free will,
  Right over Bethlehem on the hill,
The City of David, where Christ was born.

And the Three Kings rode through the gate and the guard,
  Through the silent street, till their horses turned
And neighed as they entered the great inn-yard;
  But the windows were closed, and the doors were barred,
And only a light in the stable burned.

And cradled there in the scented hay,
  In the air made sweet by the breath of kine,
The little child in the manger lay,
  The child, that would be King one day
Of a kingdom not human but divine.

His Mother Mary of Nazareth,
  Sat watching beside his place of rest,
Watching the even flow of his breath,
  For the joy of life and the terror of death
Were mingled together in her breast.

They laid their offerings at his feet:
  The gold was their tribute to a King,
The frankincense, with its odor sweet,
  Was for the Priest, the Paraclete,
The myrrh for the body's burying.

And the Mother wondered and bowed her head,
  And sat as still as a statue of stone;
Her heart was troubled yet comforted,
  Remembering what the Angel had said
Of an endless reign and of David's throne.

Then the Kings rode out of the city gate,
  With a clatter of hoofs in proud array;
But they went not back to Herod the Great,
  For they knew his malice and feared his hate,
And returned to their homes by another way.

HENRY WADSWORTH LONGFELLOW.

WALTER VON DER VOGELWEID

Among the Meistersinger, so well known to music lovers, none is more familiar than Walter von der Vogelweid, who claimed that he learned life's tuneful melodies from the birds. His poetry breathes of the deepest love of nature. A few lines from his sonnet of May has a lyric quality of joy that makes this 13th Century bard seem almost Wordsworthian:

> "Gentle May, thou showerest fairly,
>   Gifts afar and near;
> Clothest all the woods so rarely,
>   And the meadows here;
> O'er the heath new colors glow;
> Flowers and clover on the plain,
> Merry rivals, strive amain
> Which can fastest grow.
>
> "Lady! part me from my sadness,
>   Love me while 'tis May;
> Mine is but a borrowed gladness
>   If thou frown alway;
> Look around and smile anew!
> All the world is glad and free;
> Let a little joy from thee
> Fall to my lot too!"

At other times he was as serious as any of the Meistersinger and wrote many religious poems.

Vogelweid the Minnesinger,
  When he left this world of ours,
Laid his body in the cloister,
  Under Würtzburg's minster-towers.

And he gave the monks his treasures,
  Gave them all with this behest:
They should feed the birds at noontide
  Daily on his place of rest;

Saying, "From these wandering minstrels
  I have learned the art of song;
Let me now repay the lessons
  They have taught so well and long."

Thus the bard of love departed;
  And, fulfilling his desire,
On his tomb the birds were feasted
  By the children of the choir.

Day by day, o'er tower and turret,
  In foul weather and in fair,
Day by day, in vaster numbers,
  Flocked the poets of the air.

On the tree whose heavy branches
  Overshadowed all the place,
On the pavement, on the tombstone,
  On the poet's sculptured face,

On the cross-bars of each window,
  On the lintel of each door,
They renewed the War of Wartburg,
  Which the bard had fought before.

There they sang their merry carols,
  Sang their lauds on every side;
And the name their voices uttered
  Was the name of Vogelweid.

Till at length the portly abbot
  Murmured, "Why this waste of food?
Be it changed to loaves henceforward
  For our fasting brotherhood."

Then in vain o'er tower and turret,
  From the walls and woodland nests,
When the minster-bells rang noontide,
  Gathered the unwelcome guests.

Then in vain, with cries discordant,
  Clamorous round the Gothic spire,
Screamed the feathered Minnesingers
  For the children of the choir

Time has long effaced the inscriptions
  On the cloister's funeral-stones,
And tradition only tells us
  Where repose the poet's bones.

But around the vast cathedral,
  By sweet echoes multiplied,
Still the birds repeat the legend,
  And the name of Vogelweid.

HENRY WADSWORTH LONGFELLOW.

PICTURES OF THE RHINE

The days of summer find tourists from nearly every country of the globe making the Rhine Trip. Most of them get but a fleeting view of the majestic stream with its multitude of memories. There is the Rhine that so many thousands see and there is the Rhine that the patriotic German sees when he sings, "The Watch on the Rhine:"

"Der Rhein, der Rhein, der deutsche Rhein."

The river that Heinrich Heine was thinking about in his "Die Lorelei," or Thackeray, in his *Vanity Fair*, and *The Newcombs*, is a far different river from the one that the present day hurrying tourist sees and enjoys. He gets little more than a glimpse of the crumbling castles of the old-time robber barons who, from their lofty eyries, laid heavy toll upon every merchant who dared to come this way. Happy is the traveler who can linger awhile amid such a panorama of folklore and legends.

I

The spirit of Romance dies not to those
Who hold a kindred spirit in their souls:
Even as the odorous life within the rose
Lives in the scattered leaflets and controls
Mysterious adoration, so there glows
Above dead things a thing that cannot die;
Faint as the glimmer of a tearful eye,
Ere the orb fills and all the sorrow flows,
Beauty renews itself in many ways;
The flower is fading while the new bud blows;
And this dear land as true a symbol shows,
While o'er it like a mellow sunset strays
The legendary splendour of old days,
In visible, inviolate repose.

II

About a mile behind the viny banks,
How sweet it was, upon a sloping green,
Sunspread, and shaded with a branching screen,
To lie in peace half-murmuring words of thanks!
To see the mountains on each other climb,
With spaces for rich meadows flowery bright;
The winding river freshening the sight
At intervals, the trees in leafy prime;
The distant village-roofs of blue and white,
With intersections of quaint-fashioned beams
All slanting crosswise, and the feudal gleams
Of ruined turrets, barren in the light;—
To watch the changing clouds, like clime in clime;
Oh! sweet to lie and bless the luxury of time.

III

Fresh blows the early breeze, our sail is full;
A merry morning and a mighty tide.
Cheerily O! and past St. Goar we glide,
Half hid in misty dawn and mountain cool.
The river is our own! and now the sun
In saffron clothes the warning atmosphere;
The sky lifts up her white veil like a nun,
And looks upon the landscape blue and clear;—
The lark is up; the hills, the vines in sight;
The river broadens with his waking bliss
And throws up islands to behold the light;
Voices begin to rise, all hues to kiss;—
Was ever such a happy morn as this!
Birds sing, we shout, flowers breathe, trees shine with one delight!

IV

Between the two white breasts of her we love,
A dewy blushing rose will sometimes spring;
Thus Nonnenwerth like an enchanted thing
Rises mid-stream the crystal depths above.
On either side the waters heave and swell,
But all is calm within the little Isle;
Content it is to give its holy smile,
And bless with peace the lives that in it dwell.
Most dear on the dark grass beneath its bower
Of kindred trees embracing branch and bough,
To dream of fairy foot and sudden flower;
Or haply with a twilight on the brow,
To muse upon the legendary hour,
And Roland's lonely love and Hildegard's sad vow.

V

Hark! how the bitter winter breezes blow
Round the sharp rocks and o'er the half-lifted wave,
While all the rocky woodland branches rave
Shrill with the piercing cold, and every cave,
Along the icy water-margin low,
Rings bubbling with the whirling overflow;
And sharp the echoes answer distant cries
Of dawning daylight and the dim sunrise,
And the gloom-coloured clouds that stain the skies
With pictures of a warmth, and frozen glow
Spread over endless fields of sheeted snow;
And white untrodden mountains shining cold,
And muffled footpaths winding thro' the wold,
O'er which those wintry gusts cease not to howl and blow.

VI

Rare is the loveliness of slow decay!
With youth and beauty all must be desired,
But 'tis the charm of things long past away,
They leave, alone, the light they have inspired:
The calmness of a picture; Memory now
Is the sole life among the ruins grey,
And like a phantom in fantastic play
She wanders with rank weeds stuck on her brow,
Over grass-hidden caves and turret-tops,
Herself almost as tottering as they;
While to the steps of Time, her latest props
Fall stone by stone, and in the Sun's hot ray
All that remains stands up in rugged pride,
And bridal vines drink in his juices on each side.

GEORGE MEREDITH.

BAGPIPE PLAYER
Nuremberg Fountain

The visitor to Nuremberg, wandering midst its crooked and mediaeval streets, embowered by innumerable window flower boxes, finds at almost every turn turreted walls, and old mansions with picturesque gables and oriel windows.

These quaint sights and fountains like the Apollo, the Neptune, and the Schön Brunner in squares and market places, leave images that are ever pleasantly recalled to our memory by the magic name of Nuremberg.

He plays his little tune in water.
Each note spurts from the bronze pipe-holes;
The piper plays
Four sprays
That mix and make a chord their own,
Splashing to music held by the bowl of stone.

—I know this tune!
First played
In some deep German wood some drowsy June,
Where hoofed and hairy things drew near
To hear,
And nymphs were unafraid!—

Hans Sachs and Dürer passed this fountain,
And Peter Fischer, Luther's sculptor friend;
Passed . . . to their worthy end.
But did they mark the Goat-god's godless ditty?
Or did the dripping little knave
Play drier tunes for them
In the staid street of the red-gabled city?

LEONORA SPEYER.

SWITZERLAND

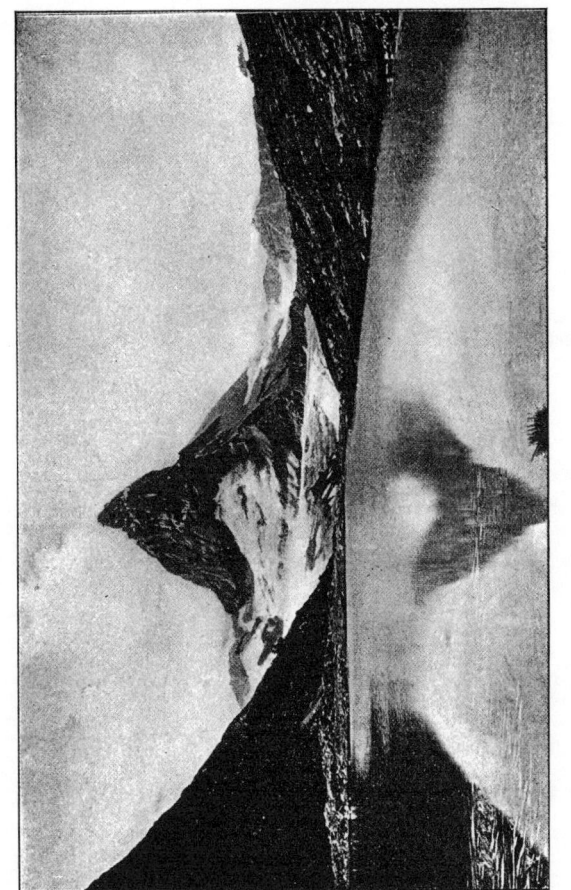

MATTERHORN AND RIFFELSEE

AN ALPINE PICTURE

To every European traveler, the first view of an Alpine peak is the announcement of a world he has long looked forward to visiting. The sight of these kingly mountains brings a thrill of exultation even to the indifferent and blasé.

As he comes nearer their world of ice and snow he realizes that, with all their beauty and grandeur, they have no mercy for those who would conquer their heights.

Stand here and look, and softly draw your breath
Lest the dread avalanche come crashing down!
How many leagues away is yonder town
Set flower-wise in the valley? Far beneath
Our feet lies summer; here a realm of death,
Where never flower has blossomed nor bird flown.
The ancient water-courses are all strown
With drifts of snow, fantastic wreath on wreath;
And peak on peak against the stainless blue
The Alps like towering campanili stand,
Wondrous, with pinnacles of frozen rain,
Silvery, crystal, like the prism in hue.
O tell me, love, if this be Switzerland—
Or is it but the frost-work on the pane?

THOMAS BAILEY ALDRICH.

LAKE LEMAN

From *Childe Harold's Pilgrimage*

There is an old legend that Neptune came one day to see Lake Leman, and, enraptured with the beauty of this little inland sea, gave to it, as he departed, his likeness in miniature. Many another charm has this Lake Geneva. In form it is a blue crescent forty-five miles in length and eight miles wide. Poets, novelists and scientists have praised it for its beauty and the purity of its waters. How surprising is the change in the appearance of the Rhone as it enters the lake, muddy and travel-stained from the long journey! As it leaves the lake at Geneva after its sojourn in the great mountain bowl, its waters are superbly blue and clear as crystal.

With it are associated many names of literary importance: Byron, Shelley and Madame de Staël have enjoyed its beauty; Gibbon wrote the concluding chapters of *The Decline and Fall of the Roman Empire* while living here. And then the stories of Rousseau, Voltaire and Calvin add further interest to the many associations found round about it.

Clear, placid Leman! thy contrasted lake,
With the wild world I dwelt in, is a thing
Which warns me with its stillness to forsake
Earth's troubled waters for a purer spring.
This quiet sail is as a noiseless wing
To waft me from distraction; once I loved
Torn ocean's roar, but thy soft murmuring
Sounds sweet as if a Sister's voice reproved,
That I with stern delights should e'er have been so moved.

It is the hush of night, and all between
Thy margin and the mountains, dusk, yet clear,
Mellow'd and mingling, yet distinctly seen,
Save darken'd Jura, whose capt heights appear
Precipitously steep; and drawing near,

There breathes a living fragrance from the shore,
Of flowers yet fresh with childhood; on the ear
Drops the light drip of the suspended oar,
Or chirps the grasshopper one good-night carol more.

He is an evening reveller, who makes
His life an infancy, and sings his fill;
At intervals, some bird from out the brakes
Starts into voice a moment, then is still.
There seems a floating whisper on the hill,
But that is fancy, for the starlight dews
All silently their tears of love instil,
Weeping themselves away, till they infuse
Deep into Nature's breast the spirit of her hues.

Ye stars! which are the poetry of heaven!
If in your bright leaves we would read the fate
Of men and empires,—'tis to be forgiven
That in our aspirations to be great,
Our destinies o'erleap their mortal state,
And claim a kindred with you; for ye are
A beauty and a mystery, and create
In us such love and reverence from afar
That fortune, fame, power, life, have named themselves star.

All heaven and earth are still—though not in sleep,
But breathless, as we grow when feeling most;
And silent, as we stand in thoughts too deep:—
All heaven and earth are still. From the high host
Of stars to the lull'd lake and mountain-coast,
All is concenter'd in a life intense,

Where not a beam nor air nor leaf is lost,
But hath a part of being, and a sense
Of that which is of all Creator and defence.

. . . .

The sky is changed!—and such a change! Oh night,
And storm, and darkness, ye are wondrous strong,
Yet lovely in your strength, as is the light
Of a dark eye in woman! Far along,
From peak to peak the rattling crags among
Leaps the live thunder! Not from one lone cloud,
But every mountain now hath found a tongue,
And Jura answers, through her misty shrouds,
Back to the joyous Alps, who call to her aloud!

And this is in the night:—Most glorious night!
Thou wert not sent for slumber! Let me be
A sharer in thy fierce and far delight,—
A portion of the tempest and of thee!
How the lit lake shines, a phosphoric sea,
And the big rain comes dancing to the earth!
And now again 'tis black,—and now, the glee
Of the loud hills shakes with its mountain-mirth,
As if they did rejoice o'er a young earthquake's birth.

LORD BYRON.

THE PRISONER OF CHILLON

Every visitor to Montreux on beautiful Lake Geneva spends some time in the Castle of Chillon made famous by Lord Byron's poem. "The Prisoner of Chillon" tells the story of three brothers who suffered imprisonment in the gloomy dungeon of the Castle in the cause of religion. Two of them died in prison and were buried beneath the stony floor of their dungeon. The third brother, who lived to recount their tragic history, eventually regained his freedom, but it came too late to be enjoyed.

We may wander with interest about the walls of this old castle of the Bernese feudal lords but how much more it will mean to us if we are familiar with the poem that made this place famous.

SONNET ON CHILLON

Eternal Spirit of the chainless Mind!
Brightest in dungeons, Liberty, thou art,
For there thy habitation is the heart—
The heart which love of thee alone can bind;
And when thy sons to fetters are consigned—
To fetters, and the damp vault's dayless gloom—
Their country conquers with their martyrdom,
And Freedom's fame finds wings on every wind.
Chillon! thy prison is a holy place,
And thy sad floor an altar; for 'twas trod,
Until his very steps have left a trace
Worn, as if thy cold pavement were a sod,
By Bonnivard!—May none those marks efface!
For they appeal from tyranny to God.

I

My hair is grey, but not with years,
    Nor grew it white
    In a single night,
As men's have grown from sudden fears.
My limbs are bowed, though not with toil,
   But rusted with a vile repose,

For they have been a dungeon's spoil,
    And mine has been the fate of those
To whom the goodly earth and air
Are banned and barred—forbidden fare.
    But this was for my father's faith,
I suffered chains and courted death.
That father perished at the stake
For tenets he would not forsake;
And for the same his lineal race
In darkness found a dwelling-place.
We were seven,—who now are one—
    Six in youth, and one in age,
Finished as they had begun,
    Proud of Persecution's rage:
One in fire, and two in field,
Their belief with blood have sealed—
Dying as their father died,
For the God their foes denied;
Three were in a dungeon cast,
Of whom this wreck is left the last.

II

There are seven pillars, of Gothic mould,
In Chillon's dungeons deep and old;
There are seven columns, massy and grey,
Dim with a dull imprisoned ray—
A sunbeam which hath lost its way,
And through the crevice and the cleft
Of the thick wall is fallen and left,
Creeping o'er the floor so damp,
Like a marsh's meteor-lamp.
And in each pillar there is a ring,
    And in each ring there is a chain:
That iron is a cankering thing,
    For in these limbs its teeth remain,

With marks that will not wear away
Till I have done with this new day,
Which now is painful to these eyes,
Which have not seen the sun so rise
For years—I cannot count them o'er;
I lost their long and heavy score
When my last brother drooped and died,
And I lay living by his side.

III

They chained us each to a column stone,
And we were three—yet, each alone;
We could not move a single pace;
We could not see each other's face,
But with that pale and livid light
That made us strangers in our sight;
And thus together; yet apart,
Fettered in hand, but joined in heart,
'Twas still some solace, in the dearth
Of the pure elements of earth,
To hearken to each other's speech,
And each turn comforter to each
With some new hope or legend old,
Or song heroically bold;
But even these at length grew cold.
Our voices took a dreary tone,
An echo of the dungeon-stone,
   A grating sound—not full and free,
   As they of yore were wont to be;
   It might be fancy—but to me
They never sounded like our own.

IV

I was the eldest of the three,
   And to uphold and cheer the rest
   I ought to do, and did, my best—
And each did well in his degree.

The youngest, whom my father loved,
Because our mother's brow was given
To him, with eyes as blue as heaven—
  For him my soul was sorely moved;
And truly might it be distressed
To see such bird in such a nest;
For he was beautiful as day
    (When day was beautiful to me
    As to young eagles, being free),—
  A polar day, which will not see
A sunset till its summer's gone—
  Its sleepless summer of long light,
The snow-clad offspring of the sun:
  And thus he was as pure and bright,
And in his natural spirit gay,
With tears for nought but others' ills;
And then they flowed like mountain rills,
Unless he could assuage the woe
Which he abhorred to view below.

v

The other was as pure of mind,
But formed to combat with his kind;
Strong in his frame, and of a mood
Which 'gainst the world in war had stood,
And perished in the foremost rank
  With joy; but not in chains to pine.
His spirit withered with their clank;
  I saw it silently decline—
  And so, perchance, in sooth, did mine:
But yet I forced it on, to cheer
Those relics of a home so dear.
He was a hunter of the hills,
  Had followed there the deer and wolf;
  To him this dungeon was a gulf,
And fettered feet the worst of ills.

VI

Lake Leman lies by Chillon's walls,
A thousand feet in depth below,
Its massy waters meet and flow;
Thus much the fathom-line was sent
From Chillon's snow-white battlement,
  Which round about the wave inthralls;
A double dungeon wall and wave
Have made—and like a living grave,
Below the surface of the lake
The dark vault lies wherein we lay;
We heard it ripple night and day;
  Sounding o'er our heads it knocked.
And I have felt the winter's spray
Wash through the bars when winds were high,
And wanton in the happy sky;
  And then the very rock hath rocked,
  And I have felt it shake, unshocked;
Because I could have smiled to see
The death that would have set me free.

VII

I said my nearer brother pined;
I said his mighty heart declined.
He loathed and put away his food;
It was not that 'twas coarse and rude;
For we were used to hunters' fare,
And for the like had little care.
The milk drawn from the mountain goat
Was changed for water from the moat;
Our bread was such as captives' tears
Have moistened many a thousand years,
Since man first pent his fellow-men
Like brutes, within an iron den.
But what were these to us or him?

These wasted not his heart or limb;
My brother's soul was of that mold
Which in a palace had grown cold,
Had his free breathing been denied
The range of the steep mountain's side.
But why delay the truth?—he died.
I saw, and could not hold his head,
Nor reach his dying hand—nor dead,—
Though hard I strove, but strove in vain,
To rend and gnash my bonds in twain.
He died—and they unlocked his chain,
And scooped for him a shallow grave
Even from the cold earth of our cave.
I begged them, as a boon, to lay
His corse in dust whereon the day
Might shine—it was a foolish thought;
But then within my brain it wrought,
That even in death his freeborn breast
In such a dungeon could not rest,
I might have spared my idle prayer—
They coldly laughed, and laid him there,
The flat and turfless earth above
The being we so much did love;
His empty chain above it leant—
Such murder's fitting monument!

VIII

But he, the favorite and the flower,
Most cherished since his natal hour,
His mother's image in fair face,
The infant love of all his race,
His martyred father's dearest thought,
My latest care, for whom I sought
To hoard my life, that his might be
Less wretched now, and one day free—

The Prisoner of Chillon

He too, who yet had held untired
A spirit natural or inspired—
He, too, was struck, and day by day
Was withered on the stalk away.
Oh, God! it is a fearful thing
To see the human soul take wing
In any shape, in any mood:
I've seen it rushing forth in blood;
I've seen it on the breaking ocean
Strive with a swoln, convulsive motion;
I've seen the sick and ghastly bed
Of Sin, delirious with its dread;
But these were horrors,—this was woe
Unmixed with such,—but sure and slow.
He faded, and so calm and meek,
So softly worn, so sweetly weak,
So tearless, yet so tender,—kind,
And grieved for those he left behind;
With all the while a cheek whose bloom
Was as a mockery of the tomb,
Whose tints as gently sunk away
As a departing rainbow's ray;
An eye of most transparent light,
That almost made the dungeon bright;
And not a word of murmur, not
A groan o'er his untimely lot—
A little talk of better days,
A little hope my own to raise;
For I was sunk in silence, lost
In this last loss, of all the most.
And then the sighs he would suppress
Of fainting nature's feebleness,
More slowly drawn, grew less and less.
I listened, but I could not hear—
I called, for I was wild with fear;

I knew 'twas hopeless, but my dread
Would not be thus admonishèd;
I called, and thought I heard a sound—
I burst my chain with one strong bound,
And rushed to him:—I found him not.
I only stirred in this black spot,
I only lived—*I* only drew
The accursèd breath of dungeon-dew;
The last, the sole, the dearest link
Between me and the eternal brink,
Which bound me to my failing race,
Was broken in this fatal place.
One on the earth, and one beneath—
My brothers—both had ceased to breathe.
I took that hand which lay so still—
Alas! my own was full as chill;
I had not strength to stir, or strive,
But felt that I was still alive—
A frantic feeling, when we know
That what we love shall ne'er be so.
   I know not why
   I could not die,
I had no earthly hope,—but faith,
And that forbade a selfish death.

IX

What next befell me then and there
 I know not well,—I never knew.
First came the loss of light and air,
 And then of darkness too.
I had no thought, no feeling—none:
Among the stones I stood a stone;
And was, scarce conscious what I wist,
As shrubless crags within the mist;
For all was blank, and bleak, and gray;

The Prisoner of Chillon

It was not night—it was not day;
It was not even the dungeon-light,
So hateful to my heavy sight;
But vacancy absorbing space,
And fixedness,—without a place;
There were no stars, no earth, no time,
No check, no change, no good, no crime—
But silence, and a stirless breath
Which neither was of life nor death—
A sea of stagnant idleness,
Blind, boundless, mute and motionless!

X

A light broke in upon my brain—
　It was the carol of a bird;
It ceased, and then it came again—
　The sweetest song ear ever heard;
And mine was thankful till my eyes
Ran over with the glad surprise,
And they that moment could not see
I was the mate of misery;
But then, by dull degrees, came back
My senses to their wonted track:
I saw the dungeon walls and floor
Close slowly round me as before;
I saw the glimmer of the sun
Creeping as it before had done;
But through the crevice where it came
That bird was perched, as fond and tame,
　And tamer than upon the tree—
A lovely bird, with azure wings,
And song that said a thousand things,
　And seemed to say them all for me!
I never saw its like before—
I ne'er shall see its likeness more.

It seemed, like me, to want a mate,
But was not half so desolate;
And it was come to love me when
None lived to love me so again,
And, cheering from my dungeon's brink,
Had brought me back to feel and think.
I know not if it late were free,
   Or broke its cage to perch on mine;
But knowing well captivity,
   Sweet bird! I could not wish for thine!
Or if it were, in wingèd guise,
A visitant from Paradise;
For—Heaven forgive that thought, the while
Which made me both to weep and smile!—
I sometimes deemed that it might be
My brother's soul come down to me;
But then at last away it flew,
And then 'twas mortal—well I knew;
For he would never thus have flown,
And left me twice so doubly lone—
Lone—as the corse within its shroud,
Lone—as a solitary cloud,
   A single cloud on a sunny day,
While all the rest of heaven is clear,
A frown upon the atmosphere,
That hath no business to appear
   When skies are blue, and earth is gay.

XI

A kind of change came in my fate—
My keepers grew compassionate.
I knew not what had made them so—
They were inured to sights of woe;
But so it was—my broken chain
With links unfastened did remain;

And it was liberty to stride
Along my cell from side to side,
And up and down, and then athwart,
And tread it over every part;
And round the pillars one by one,
Returning where my walk begun—
Avoiding only, as I trod,
My brothers' graves without a sod;
For if I thought with heedless tread
My step profaned their lowly bed,
My breath came gaspingly and thick,
And my crushed heart fell blind and sick.

XII

I made a footing in the wall:
   It was not therefrom to escape,
For I had buried one and all
   Who loved me in a human shape;
And the whole earth would henceforth be
A wider prison unto me;
No child, no sire, no kin had I,
No partner in my misery.
I thought of this, and I was glad,
For thought of them had made me mad;
But I was curious to ascend
To my barred windows, and to bend
Once more, upon the mountains high,
The quiet of a loving eye.

XIII

I saw them—and they were the same;
They were not changed, like me, in frame;
I saw their thousand years of snow
On high—their wide, long lake below,
And the blue Rhone in fullest flow;

I heard the torrents leap and gush
O'er channelled rock and broken bush;
I saw the white-walled distant town,
And whiter sails go skimming down;
And then there was a little isle,
Which in my very face did smile—
    The only one in view;
A small, green isle, it seemed no more,
Scarce broader than my dungeon-floor;
But in it there were three tall trees,
And o'er it blew the mountain breeze,
And by it there were waters flowing,
And on it there were young flowers growing
    Of gentle breath and hue.
The fish swam by the castle wall,
And they seemed joyous each and all;
The eagle rode the rising blast—
Methought he never flew so fast
As then to me he seemed to fly;
And then new tears came in my eye,
And I felt troubled, and would fain
I had not left my recent chain;
And when I did descend again,
The darkness of my dim abode
Fell on me as a heavy load;
It was as is a new-dug grave,
Closing o'er one we sought to save;
And yet my glance, too much oppressed,
Had almost need of such a rest.

XIV

It might be months, or years, or days—
    I kept no count, I took no note—
I had no hope my eyes to raise,
    And clear them of their dreary mote;

The Prisoner of Chillon

At last men came to set me free,
I asked not why, and recked not where;
It was at length the same to me,
Fettered or fetterless to be;
  I learned to love despair.
And thus, when they appeared at last,
And all my bonds aside were cast,
These heavy walls to me had grown
A hermitage—and all my own!
And half I felt as they were come
To tear me from a second home.
With spiders I had friendship made,
And watched them in their sullen trade;
Had seen the mice by moonlight play—
And why should I feel less than they?
We were all inmates of one place,
And I, the monarch of each race,
Had power to kill; yet, strange to tell!
In quiet we had learned to dwell.
My very chains and I grew friends,
So much a long communion tends
To make us what we are:—even I
Regained my freedom with a sigh.

LORD BYRON.

MONUMENT AT LUCERNE

TO THE SWISS GUARD MASSACRED AT THE ASSAULT ON THE TUILERIES, A. D. 1792

Within a huge niche hollowed out of the natural rock, near the glacier garden, Thorwaldsen carved the Lion of Lucerne. The prostrate figure of a great lion is indeed a fitting memorial of the fidelity and valor of the Swiss guards, who laid down their lives in defense of Louis XVI, during the attack upon the Tuileries in the opening days of the French Revolution. The handle of a spear protrudes from the side of the lion and his paws, even in the agony of death, reach out to protect the Bourbon shield and lily for which he has given his life. On the smooth rock surface below the figure are the names of the officers of the heroic guard.

"To the fidelity and bravery of the Swiss" is a fitting epitaph for such an impressive memorial.

When maddened France shook her King's palace floor,
   Nobly, heroic Swiss, ye met your doom.
Unflinching martyr to the oath he swore,
   Each steadfast soldier faced a certain tomb.

Not for your own, but others' claims ye died:
   The steep, hard path of fealty called to tread,
Threatened or soothed, ye never turned aside,
   But held right on, where fatal duty led!

Reverent we stand beside the sculptured rock,
   Your cenotaph,—Helvetia's grateful stone;
And mark in wonderment, the breathing block,
   Thorwaldsen's glorious trophy!—in your own.

Yon dying lion is your monument!
   Type of majestic suffering, the brave brute,
Human almost, in mighty languishment
   Lies wounded, not subdued; and, proudly mute,

Seems as for some great cause, resigned to die:
  And, hardly less than hero's parting breath,
Speaks to the spirit, through the admiring eye,
  Of courage, faith, and honorable death.
JOHN KENYON.

THE SIMPLON PASS

From *The Prelude*

The Simplon is one of the picturesque and popular Swiss-Italian passes. Today the hurrying tourist, going by train through the mighty Simplon Tunnel, passes through the very peaks and barriers which formerly prevented the mingling of Italians with the ultramontane peoples.

An occasional tourist finds the time to walk or drive from Brieg to Iselle, and he is rewarded by many an entrancing view of the Rhone as it flows towards Lake Geneva. He will hear the bubbling mountain rill and now and then catch glimpses of mist creeping along some shadowy glen. Then indeed will he know the charm and magic of the true Alpine landscape.

. . . Brook and road
Were fellow-travellers in this gloomy Pass,
And with them did we journey several hours
At a slow step. The immeasurable height
Of woods decaying, never to be decayed,
The stationary blasts of waterfalls,
And in the narrow rent, at every turn,
Winds thwarting winds bewildered and forlorn,
The torrents shooting from the clear blue sky,
The rocks that muttered close upon our ears,
Black drizzling crags that spake by the wayside
As if a voice were in them, the sick sight
And giddy prospect of the raving stream,
The unfettered clouds and region of the heavens,
Tumult and peace, the darkness and the light—
Were all like workings of one mind, the features
Of the same face, blossoms upon one tree,
Characters of the great Apocalypse,
The types and symbols of Eternity,
Of first, and last, and midst, and without end.

WILLIAM WORDSWORTH.

SPAIN

COURT OF THE LIONS IN THE ALHAMBRA, GRANADA

CASTLES IN SPAIN

We may almost divine the character of a country from its words of farewell. The "cheerio" of England, the "so long" or "good-bye" of America, the "au revoir" of France the "auf Wiedersehen" of Germany and the "vaya usted con Dios" (go with God) of Spain well suit the countries which have adopted them.

The religiously inclined will be at home in Spain. It is a country which boasts of the birthplace of Ignatius Loyola, the founder of the Jesuit Order, and of Tibidabo, the place where the devil tempted Christ with the kingdom of this earth. The country is full of sacred shrines and relics.

In Spain one finds in abundance the romantic, the poetical, the sentimental and the artistic, but, though nature has been prodigal in her soil and climate, the Spaniard has not always endeavored to conserve his wonderful heritage.

"There let the antiquarian pore over the stirring memorials of many thousand years, the vestiges of Phoenecian enterprise, of Roman magnificence, of Moorish elegance in that storehouse of ancient customs, that repository of all elsewhere long forgotten and passed by; there let him gaze upon those classical monuments, unequalled almost in Greece and Italy, and on those fairy Alladin palaces, the creatures of Oriental gorgeousness and imagination, with which Spain alone can enchant" the traveler.

> How much of my young heart, O Spain,
>   Went out to thee in days of yore!
> What dreams romantic filled my brain,
> And summoned back to life again
> The Paladins of Charlemagne
>   The Cid Campeador!
>
> And shapes more shadowy than these,
>   In the dim twilight half revealed;
> Phoenician galleys on the seas,
> The Roman camps like hives of bees,
> The Goth uplifting from his knees
>   Pelayo on his shield.

It was these memories perchance,
　From annals of remotest eld,
That lent the colors of romance
To every trivial circumstance,
And changed the form and countenance
　Of all that I beheld.

Old towns, whose history lies hid
　In monkish chronicle or rhyme,—
Burgos, the birthplace of the Cid,
Zamora and Valladolid,
Toledo, built and walled amid
　The wars of Wamba's time;

The long, straight line of the highway,
　The distant town that seems so near,
The peasants in the fields, that stay
Their toil to cross themselves and pray,
When from the belfry at midday
　The Angelus they hear;

White crosses in the mountain pass,
　Mules gay with tassels, the loud din
Of muleteers, the tethered ass
That crops the dusty wayside grass,
And cavaliers with spurs of brass
　Alighting at the inn;

White hamlets hidden in fields of wheat,
　White cities slumbering by the sea,
White sunshine flooding square and street,
Dark mountain ranges, at whose feet
The river beds are dry with heat,—
　All was a dream to me.

Castles in Spain

Yet something sombre and severe
  O'er the enchanted landscape reigned;
A terror in the atmosphere
As if King Philip listened near,
Or Torquemada, the austere,
  His ghostly sway maintained.

The softer Andalusian skies
  Dispelled the sadness and the gloom;
There Cadiz by the seaside lies,
And Seville's orange-orchards rise,
Making the land a paradise
  Of beauty and of bloom.

There Cordova is hidden among
  The palm, the olive, and the vine;
Gem of the South, by poets sung,
And in whose Mosque Almanzor hung
As lamps the bells that once had rung
  At Compostella's shrine.

But over all the rest supreme,
  The star of stars, the cynosure,
The artist's and the poet's theme,
The young man's vision, the old man's dream,—
Granada by its winding stream,
  The city of the Moor!

And there the Alhambra still recalls
  Aladdin's palace of delight:
Allah il Allah! through its halls
Whispers the fountain as it falls,
The Darro darts beneath its walls,
  The hills with snow are white.

Ah yes, the hills are white with snow,
  And cold with blasts that bite and freeze;
But in the happy vale below
The orange and pomegranate grow,
And wafts of air toss to and fro
  The blossoming almond-trees.

The Vega cleft by the Xenil,
  The fascination and allure
Of the sweet landscape chains the will;
The traveller lingers on the hill,
His parted lips are breathing still
  The last sigh of the Moor.

How like a ruin overgrown
  With flowers that hide the rents to time,
Stands now the Past that I have known;
Castles in Spain, not built of stone
But of white summer clouds, and blown
  Into this little mist of rhyme!

     HENRY WADSWORTH LONGFELLOW.

ALADDIN

When I was a beggarly boy,
   And lived in a cellar damp,
I had not a friend nor a toy,
   But I had Aladdin's lamp;
When I could not sleep for the cold,
   I had fire enough in my brain,
And builded, with roofs of gold,
   My beautiful castles in Spain!

Since then I have toiled day and night,
   I have money and power good store,
But I'd give all my lamps of silver bright
   For the one that is mine no more.
Take, Fortune, whatever you choose;
   You gave, and may snatch again;
I have nothing 'twould pain me to lose,
   For I own no more castles in Spain!

JAMES RUSSELL LOWELL.

THE LITTLE BELLS OF SEVILLA

Many monuments commemorate the history of the gay capital of Andalusia, Seville. Here Velasquez and Murillo were born, and here were laid the scenes of *Carmen, Don Juan*, and *Figaro*.

The city is in the heart of a country whose olive orchards, terraced hillsides, rocky gorges, and barren gray ranges are among the most picturesque and romantic places of Europe.

The melodious tones of the horses' little bells are often silenced by those of the great bells in the famous Giralda Tower of the Seville Cathedral,—that great Gothic masterpiece. The Tower, originally Arabian, is now a Christian bell tower. Still Arabian in appearance, it seems prouder of its vanquished builders than of the victors who have placed their cross upon it.

Are not, perhaps, the little bells on the harness of the horses also indicative of change,—the change from the "faith that doubts nothing" to the "reason that doubts everything;" the change from the old time church bell to the tiny tinkling ornament.

In our days when so much is sacrificed to comfort, "people no longer understand these sublime yearnings of the soul towards the Infinite, which were rendered by steeples, spires, bell-turrets, and ogives, stretching their arms of stone heavenward and joining them above the heads of the kneeling crowd, like gigantic hands clasped in an attitude of supplication."

The ladies of Sevilla go forth to take the air,
They loop their lace mantillas, a red rose in their hair;
Upon the road Delicias their little horses run,
And tinkle, tinkle, tinkle, the bells go every one.

Beside the Guadalquivir, by orange-scented way,
The ladies of Sevilla they come at cool of day;
They wave their fans coquettish, their black eyes gleam and glow,
And all their little carriage bells a-jingle, jingle, go.

The Little Bells of Sevilla

There, too the caballeros drive in the perfumed breeze,
Upon the road Delicias among the flowering trees;
Beneath their brown sombreros their dark eyes flame and flash,
And all their little horses' bells right merrily they crash.

Beside the Guadalquivir the hours are very fair,
The nightingale is tuning upon the scented air;
Oh, laughing Andalusia, beloved of the sun,
Your merry, merry little bells, they call me every one.

DORA SIGERSON SHORTER.

EVENING
SPAIN

And when night comes they will sing serenades
Under the open windows,
The lattices will not be shut,
The Moon will wander through the houses:
Spain herself with the voices of the past in her soul
Will sit in the shadows,
And kiss the petals of roses,
And drop them warm to her lovers below.

With the low thrumming of guitars,
With the gold throbbing of stars,
With the purple heaving of the seas,
With the glimmer of fading white walls
She drops her dusky hair over my soul;
O Spain, I am soul-drunken with thee,
I am intoxicated with the scent of thy garments,
I am a river delirious under the Moon
In whose bosom forests and stars and maidens
And innumerable worlds are singing.

With the low thrumming of guitars,
With white arms hanging from the lattices
From clouds of dim hair indistinguishable from
    the night
The souls of the serenaders are drunken,
Their voices murmur heavily like beetles
Wandering in a blur of flowers:
Spain is glimmering in those white arms,
The flowers float up in the dim darkness,
The shadows fill with her hair;
She has escaped into the palpitating night
Leaving a heap of scented garments—
In her dark room weeps the moonlight.

. . . .

Evening

The night is empty, emptier is the day,
That secret loveliness has passed away;
The sun is burning and the houses lie
Bare and untidy to the airless sky,
The sea is glass, a smooth and glittering pane,
The flies sleep in the dust. This is Spain.

W. J. TURNER.

CASTILIAN

Velasquez took a pliant knife
And scraped his palette clean;
He said, "I lead a dog's own life
Painting a king and queen."

He cleaned his palette with oily rags
And oakum from Seville wharves;
"I am sick of painting painted hags
And bad ambiguous dwarves.

"The sky is silver, the clouds are pearl,
Their locks are looped with rain.
I will not paint Maria's girl
For all the money in Spain."

He washed his face in water cold,
His hands in turpentine;
He squeezed out colour like coins of gold
And colour like drops of wine.

Each colour lay like a little pool
On the polished cedar wood;
Clear and pale and ivory-cool
Or dark as solitude.

He burnt the rags in the fireplace
And leaned from the window high;
He said, "I like that gentleman's face
Who wears his cap awry."

This is the gentleman, there he stands,
Castilian, sombre-caped,
With arrogant eyes, and narrow hands
Miraculously shaped.

ELINOR WYLIE.

ITALY
PART I
GENERAL

ORIA, LAGO DI LUGANO

UMBRIA

Northeast of Rome is the province of Umbria. The Tiber, on its way southward to the sea, winds through undulating plains, amid violet hills, on whose summits are scattered the cragged walls of mediaeval towns. Umbria's charm lies in its art, history and religious life. Perugia, Orvieto and Assisi are some of the names which recall the place these distant cities hold in the hearts of humanity.

Deep Italian day with a wide-washed splendour fills
Umbria green with valleys, blue with a hundred hills.
Dim in the south Soracte, a far rock faint as a cloud
Rumours Rome, that of old spoke over earth, "Thou art mine!"
Mountain shouldering mountain circles us forest-browed
Heaped upon each horizon in fair uneven line;
And white as on builded altars tipped with a vestal flame
City on city afar from the thrones of the mountains shine,
Kindling for us that name them, many a memoried fame,
Out of the murmuring ages, flushing the heart like wine.
Pilgrim-desired Assisi is there; Spoleto proud
With Rome's imperial arches, with hanging woods divine;
Monte Falco hovers above the hazy vale
Of sweet Clitumnus loitering under poplars pale;
O'er Foligno, Trevi clings upon Apennine.
And over this Umbrian earth—from where with bright snow spread

Towers abrupt Lernessa, huge, like a dragon's chine,
To western Ammiata's mist-apparelled head,
Ammiata that sailors watch on wide Tyrrhenian waves—
Lie in the jealous gloom of cold and secret shrine
Or Gorgon-sculptured chamber hewn in old rock caves,
Hiding their dreams from the light, the austere Etruscan dead.
O lone forests of oak and little cyclamens red
Flowering under shadowy silent boughs benign!
Streams that wander beneath us over a pebbly bed!
Hedges of dewy hawthorn and wild woodbine!
Now as the eastern ranges flush and the high air chills
Blurring meadowy vale, blackening heaths of pine,
Now as in distant Todi, loftily towered—a sign
To weary travellers—lights o'er hollow Tiber gleam,
Now our voices are stilled and our eyes are given to a dream,
As night, upbringing o'er us the ancient stars anew,
Stars that triumphing Caesar and tender Francis knew,
With fancied voices mild, august, immortal, fills
Umbria dim with valleys, dark with a hundred hills.

LAURENCE BINYON.

PETRARCH'S TOMB

From *Childe Harold's Pilgrimage*

Guarded by two lofty cypresses, silent and motionless in the quiet air, stands a tomb in the little village of Arqua. An epitaph below the bronze bust informs the traveler that the bones of Petrarch lie within. But not all, for three hundred years ago the tomb was broken open and an arm removed. Someone said that it was to be presented to Florence to compensate for the loss of one of her favorite sons.

The tomb alone would make Arqua immortal, but here also is the house and garden where "from the shade of a chestnut tree," Petrarch passed his last years amid the warmth and radiance of his beloved Italian sunshine.

"If from society we learn to live, 'tis solitude should teach us how to die."

There is a tomb in Arqua;—reared in air,
   Pillared in their sarcophagus, repose
The bones of Laura's lover; here repair
Many familiar with his well-sung woes,
The pilgrims of his genius. He arose
To raise a language, and his land reclaim
From the dull yoke of her barbaric foes;
Watering the tree which bears his lady's name
With his melodious tears, he gave himself to fame.

They kept his dust in Arqua, where he died;
The mountain-village where his latter days
Went down the vale of years; and 'tis their pride,—
An honest pride,—and let it be their praise,
To offer to the passing stranger's gaze
His mansion and his sepulchre; both plain
And venerably simple, such as raise
A feeling more accordant with his strain
Than if a pyramid formed his monumental fane.
                              LORD BYRON.

PRISON OF TASSO

From *Childe Harold's Pilgrimage*

In the center of this once brilliant capital of the illustrious Este family is the picturesque castello, the ancient stronghold of this famous Italian house. Ferrara, under the patronage of the ancient family from which so many of the royal families of Europe are descended, rose like a solitary jewel in the midst of the low-lying plains kept green and fertile by the waters of the Po.

Here Ariosto and Tasso resided and here may be seen portions of the "Orlando Furioso" and "Gerusaleme Liberata" as well as letters written by Tasso in prison. The great poet lived at 67 Via dell' Ariosto but his so-called prison for seven long years was in the hospital of St. Anna.

Ferrara, in thy wide and grass-grown streets,
Whose symmetry was not for solitude,
There seems as 'twere a curse upon the seats
Of former sovereigns, and the antique brood
Of Este, which for many an age made good
Its strength within thy walls, and was of yore
Patron or tyrant, as the changing mood
Of petty power impell'd, of those who wore
The wreath which Dante's brow alone had worn
  before.

And Tasso is their glory and their shame:
Hark to his strain and then survey his cell!
And see how dearly earn'd Torquato's fame,
And where Alfonso bade his poet dwell.
The miserable despot could not quell
The insulted mind he sought to quench, and
  blend
With the surrounding maniacs, in the hell
Where he plunged it. Glory without end
Scatter'd the clouds away, and on that name attend

The tears and praises of all time; while thine
Would rot in its oblivion—in the sink
Of worthless dust which from thy boasted line
Is shaken into nothing—but the link
Thou formest in his fortunes bids us think
Of thy poor malice, naming thee with scorn.
Alfonso! how thy ducal pageants shrink
From thee! if in another station born,
Scarce fit to be the slave of him thou madest to mourn:—

Thou! form'd to eat, and be despised, and die,
Even as the beasts that perish, save that thou
Hadst a more splendid trough and wider sty;
He! with a glory round his furrow'd brow,
Which emanated then, and dazzles now,
In face of all his foes, the Cruscan quire,
And Boileau, whose rash envy could allow
No strain which shamed his country's creaking lyre,
That whetstone of teeth,—monotony in wire!

Peace to Torquato's injured shade! 'twas his
In life and death to be the mark where Wrong
Aim'd with her poison'd arrows—but to miss.
O, victor unsurpass'd in modern song!
Each year brings forth its millions; but how long
The tide of generations shall roll on,
And not the whole combined and countless throng
Compose a mind like thine? Though all in one
Condensed their scatt'red rays, they would not form a sun.

LORD BYRON.

STANZAS TO THE PO

To the modern student of Europe, the Valley of the Po is the center of that diverging fan of railroad tracks that cross the Alps through the St. Gothard, the St. Bernard, the Simplon and other transalpine tunnels. In this valley, too, the rivers and the mountains have formed a plain on which many great cities have risen.

River, that rollest by the ancient walls,
    Where dwells the lady of my love, when she
Walks by the brink, and there perchance recalls
    A faint and fleeting memory of me;

What if thy deep and ample stream should be
    A mirror of my heart, where she may read
The thousand thoughts I now betray to thee,
    Wild as thy wave, and headlong as thy speed!

What do I say,—a mirror of my heart?
    Are not thy waters sweeping, dark, and strong?
Such as my feelings were and are, thou art;
    And such as thou art were my passions long.

Time may have somewhat tamed them,—not for ever;
    Thou overflow'st thy banks, and not for aye
Thy bosom overboils, congenial river!
    Thy floods subside, and mine have sunk away,

But left long wrecks behind, and now again,
    Borne on our old unchanged career, we move;
Thou tendest wildly onwards to the main,
    And I—to loving one I should not love.

The current I behold will sweep beneath
    Her native walls, and murmur at her feet;
Her eyes will look on thee, when she shall breathe
    The twilight air unharm'd by summer's heat.

She will look on thee,—I have looked on thee,
    Full of that thought: and from that moment, ne'er
Thy waters could I dream of, name, or see,
    Without the inseparable sigh for her!

Her bright eyes will be imaged in thy stream,—
    Yes! they will meet the wave I gaze on now:
Mine cannot witness, even in a dream,
    That happy wave repass me in its flow!

The wave that bears my tears returns no more:
    Will she return by whom that wave shall sweep?—
Both tread thy banks, both wander on thy shore,
    I by thy source, she by the dark blue deep.

But that which keepeth us apart is not
    Distance, nor depth of wave, nor space of earth,
But the distraction of a various lot,
    As various as the climates of our birth.

A stranger loves the lady of the land,
    Born far beyond the mountains, but his blood
Is all meridian, as if never fanned
    By the black wind that chills the polar flood.

My blood is all meridian; were it not,
    I had not left my clime, nor should I be,
In spite of tortures ne'er to be forgot,
    A slave again of love,—at least of thee.

'Tis vain to struggle—let me perish young—
    Live as I lived, and love as I have loved;
To dust if I return, from dust I sprung,
    And then, at least, my heart can ne'er be moved.

Lord Byron.

ITALY

". . . . a land
Which *was* the mightiest in its old command,
And *is* the loveliest, and must ever be
The master-mould of Nature's heavenly hand;
Wherein were cast the heroic and the free,
The beautiful, the brave, the lords of earth and sea.

"The commonwealth of Kings, the men of Rome!
And ever since, and now, fair Italy,
Thou art the garden of the world, the home
Of all Art yields, and Nature can decree;
Even in thy desert, what is like to thee?
Thy very weeds are beautiful, thy waste
More rich than other climes' fertility;
Thy wreck a glory, and thy ruin graced
With an immaculate charm which cannot be defaced."
                    Lord Byron, *Childe Harold's Pilgrimage.*

Few travelers now enter Italy as did the wayfarer of old, who climbed out of those northern countries by roads that zigzagged their way from the valleys of Switzerland or France; these roads took one to the mountain summits where winter reigns even in midsummer, and then on down to the sun-drenched plains of Lombardy. Today he rushes into sunny Italy through tunnel-pierced mountain barriers that shield the southern country from the fierce northern blasts.

Strike the loud harp: let the prelude be,
    Italy, Italy!
That chord again, again that note of glee:
    Italy, Italy!
Italy, O Italy! the very sound it charmeth:
Italy, O Italy! the name my bosom warmeth:
    High thoughts of self-devotions,
    Compassionate emotions,
    Soul-stirring recollections,
    With hopes, their bright reflexions,
Rush to my troubled heart at thought of thee,
My own illustrious, injured Italy.

Italy

   Dear queen of snowy mountains,
   And consecrated fountains,
Within whose rocky heaven-aspiring pale
   Beauty has fixt a dwelling
   All others so excelling,
To praise it right thine own sweet tones would fail—
   Hail to thee! Hail!
How rich art thou in lakes to poet dear,
And those broad pines amid the sunniest glade
   So reigning through the year,
Within the magic circle of their shade
   No sunbeam may appear!
   How fair thy double sea!
   In blue celestially
Glittering and circling!—But I may not dwell
   On gifts, which, decking thee too well,
Allured the spoiler. Let me fix my ken
   Rather upon thy godlike men,
The good, the wise, the valiant, and the free,
On history's pillars towering gloriously,
A trophy reared on high above thy strand,
   That every people, every clime,
   May mark and understand
What memorable courses may be run,
What golden never-failing treasures won,
     From time,
   In spite of chance,
   And worser ignorance,
If men be ruled by Duty's firm decree,
And Wisdom hold her paramount mastery.

What art thou now? Alas! Alas!
     Woe! Woe!
That strength and virtue thus should pass
   From men below!

That so divine, so beautiful a Maid
Should in the withering dust be laid,
As one that—Hush! who dares with impious breath
   To speak of death?
The fool alone and unbeliever weepeth.
   We know she only sleepeth;
      And from the dust,
   At the end of her correction,
Truth hath decreed her joyous resurrection:
   She shall arise, she must.
For can it be that wickedness has power
To undermine or topple down the tower
   Of virtue's edifice?
      And yet that vice
Should be allowed on sacred ground to plant
   A rock of adamant?
      It is of ice,
That rock, soon destined to dissolve away
Before the righteous sun's returning ray.

But who shall bear the dazzling radiancy,
   When first the royal Maid awaking
Darteth around her wild indignant eye,
   When first her bright spear shaking,
Fixing her feet on earth, her looks on sky,
She standeth like the Archangel prompt to vanquish,
Yet still imploring succour from on high?
O days of wearying hopes and passionate anguish,
      When will ye end?
Until that day he come, until I hear
      The Alps their mighty voices blend,
To swell and echo back the sound most dear
To patriot hearts, the cry of Liberty,
I must live on. But when the glorious Queen

As erst is canopied with Freedom's sheen,
When I have prest, with salutation meet,
And reverent love to kiss her honoured feet,
    I then may die,
  Die how well satisfied!
Conscious that I have watcht the second birth
Of her I've loved the most upon the earth;
    Conscious beside
That no more beauteous sight can here be given:
Sublimer visions are reserved for heaven.

                        A. W. Hare (1818).

IMPLORA PACE

How many times the traveler, wandering into some great cathedral, or Campo Santo, comes upon a sculptured tomb on which the epitaph has long since been obliterated by the ravages of time. Then it is that a poet's words bring a deeper emotion to the stranger's heart.

I stood within the cypress gloom
    Where old Ferrara's dead are laid,
And mused on many a sculptured tomb,
    Moss-grown and mouldering in the shade.

And there was one the eye might pass,
    And careless foot might tread upon,
A crumbling tablet in the grass,
    With weeds and wild vines overrun.

In the dim light I stooped to trace
    The lines the time-worn marble bore,
Of reverent praise or prayer for grace—
    "Implora Pace!"—nothing more.

Name, fame, and rank, if any were,
    Had long since vanished from the stone,
Leaving the meek, pathetic prayer,
    "Peace, I implore!" and this alone.

                        CHARLES LOTIN HILDRETH.

BROWNING AT ASOLO

Out of the much-traveled paths of the tourist is the pretty little town of Asolo. It does not surprise us to learn that the Cardinal Bembo was so pleased with the place that he coined the term "asolare" (to disport in the open air, or to amuse oneself at random). Browning named his last volume of poems "Asolando," because of his love for this very place.

This is the loggia Browning loved,
   High on the flank of the friendly town;
These are the hills that his keen eye roved,
   The green like a cataract leaping down
     To the plain that his pen gave new renown.

There to the West what a range of blue!—
The very background Titian drew
   To his peerless Loves! O tranquil scene!
Who than thy poet fondlier knew
   The peaks and the shore and the lore between?

See! yonder's his Venice—the valiant Spire,
   Highest one of the perfect three,
Guarding the others: the Palace choir,
The Temple flashing with opal fire—
   Bubble and foam of the sunlit sea.

Yesterday he was part of it all—
   Sat here, discerning cloud from snow
   In the flush of the Alpine afterglow,
   Or mused on the vineyard whose wine-stirred row
Meets in a leafy bacchanal.

Listen a moment—how oft did he!—
    To the bells from Fontalto's distant tower
Leading the evening in . . . ah, me!
Here breathes the whole soul of Italy
    As one rose breathes with the breath of the bower.

Sighs were meant for an hour like this
    When joy is keen as a thrust of pain.
Do you wonder the poet's heart should miss
This touch of rapture in Nature's kiss
    And dream of Asolo ever again?

"Part of it yesterday," we moan?
    Nay, he is part of it now, no fear.
What most we love we are that alone.
His body lies under the Minster stone,
    But the love of the warm heart lingers here.

ROBERT UNDERWOOD JOHNSON.

MILTON IN ITALY

Galileo found refuge in Florence after his trial at Rome; and John Milton, as a young man, went to nearby Arcetri in 1638 to visit the great astronomer, already grown blind.

"There it was that I found and visited Galileo, grown old, a prisoner of the Inquisition for thinking in astronomy otherwise than the Franciscan and the Dominican censures thought."

Milton's deep love for Italy is expressed in the following verse by Landor.

O Milton! couldst thou rise again and see
    The land thou lovedst in thy earlier day,
See, springing from her tomb, fair Italy
    (Fairer than ever) cast her shroud away,
That tightly-fastened, triple-folded shroud,
    Torn by her children off their mother's face!
Oh, couldst thou see her now, more justly proud
    Than of an earlier and a stronger race!

                                  WALTER SAVAGE LANDOR.

SAN TERENZO

On the nearer shore of the beautiful bay of Lerici is the little fishing village of San Terenzo with its castle. Few of the summer travelers in this land of sun and song pay much attention to the village, yet here our poet has found an inspiration for his well known verses.

Mid April seemed like some November day,
   When through the glassy waters, dull as lead,
   Our boat, like shadowy barques that bear the dead,
Slipped down the long shores of the Spezzian bay,
Rounded a point,—and San Terenzo lay
   Before us, that gay village, yellow and red,
   The roof that covered Shelley's homeless head,—
His house, a place deserted, bleak and gray.
The waves broke on the doorstep; fishermen
Cast their long nets, and drew, and cast again.
Deep in the ilex woods we wandered free,
   When suddenly the forest glades were stirred
   With waving pinions, and a great sea bird
Flew forth, like Shelley's spirit, to the sea!

                                      ANDREW LANG.

ITALIAN SCENERY

The modern railway train brings the traveler so quickly to Italy from the narrow valleys and tunnels of the Alpine barrier, that for a moment he is dazzled by the splendor of the bright sunlight. Yet has he not looked forward to the exquisite scenery with its haunting memories?

The Lombard plain, watered by historic rivers on whose banks have sprung up great cities, fills Italy's northern areas. Ensconced in its wooded hills and wide valleys are lakes graced with infinite charm. We wander along the winding shores of Como, Maggiore and Garda, or stand above the promontories of Bellagio or Orth and gaze upon a region so filled with quiet languor that we feel that here at last is the ideal refuge for the dreamer and the lover of peaceful haunts.

And then the rocky battlements of the Dolomites: to the lofty mountain scenery there is the added charm of sunshine. Its color, too, charms us—it is so varied at dawn, at twilight or when the moonlight falls upon the bastions and turrets of this strangely carved landscape.

The Venetian lagoons, with splendid palaces and noble churches upon their mud foundations, lend yet another picture to the many that Italy has for us.

Night rests in beauty on Mont Alto.
Beneath its shade the beauteous Arno sleeps
In Vallombrosa's bosom, and dark trees
Bend with a calm and quiet shadow down
Upon the beauty of that silent river.
Still in the west a melancholy smile
Mantles the lips of day, and twilight pale
Moves like a spectre in the dusky sky,
While eve's sweet star on the fast-fading year
Smiles calmly. Music steals at intervals
Across the water, with a tremulous swell,
From out the upland dingle of tall firs;
And a faint footfall sounds, where, dim and dark,
Hangs the gray willow from the river's brink,

O'ershadowing its current. Slowly there
The lover's gondola drops down the stream,
Silent, save when its dipping oar is heard,
Or in its eddy sighs the rippling wave.
Mouldering and moss-grown through the lapse of years,
In motionless beauty stands the giant oak;
Whilst those that saw its green and flourishing youth
Are gone and are forgotten. Soft the fount,
Whose secret springs the starlight pale discloses,
Gushes in hollow music; and beyond
The broader river sweeps its silent way,
Mingling a silver current with that sea,
Whose waters have no tides, coming nor going.
On noiseless wing along that fair blue sea
The halcyon flits; and, where the wearied storm
Left a loud moaning, all is peace again.

A calm is on the deep. The wings that came
O'er the dark sea-surge with a tremulous breathing,
And mourned on the dark cliff where weeds grew rank,
And to the autumnal death-dirge the deep sea
Heaved its long billows, with a cheerless song
Have passed away to the cold earth again,
Like a wayfaring mourner. Silently
Up from the calm sea's dim and distant verge,
Full and unveiled, the moon's broad disk emerges.
On Tivoli, and where the fairy hues
Of autumn glow upon Abruzzi's woods,
The silver light is spreading. Far above,
Encompassed with their thin, cold atmosphere,
The Apennines uplift their snowy brows,

Glowing with colder beauty, where unheard
The eagle screams in the fathomless ether,
And stays his wearied wing. Here let us pause.
The spirit of these solitudes—the soul
That dwells within these steep and difficult places—
Speaks a mysterious language to mine own,
And brings unutterable musing. Earth
Sleeps in the shades of nightfall, and the sea
Spreads like a thin blue haze beneath my feet;
Whilst the gray columns and the mouldering tombs
Of the Imperial City, hidden deep
Beneath the mantle of their shadows, rest.
My spirit looks on earth. A heavenly voice
Comes silently: "Dreamer, is earth thy dwelling
Lo! nursed within that fair and fruitful bosom,
Which has sustained thy being, and within
The colder breast of Ocean, lie the germs
Of thine own dissolution! E'en the air,
That fans the clear blue sky, and gives thee strength,
Up from the sullen lake of mouldering reeds,
And the wide waste of forest, where the osier
Thrives in the damp and motionless atmosphere,
Shall bring the dire and wasting pestilence,
And blight thy cheek. Dream thou of higher things:
This world is not thy home!" and yet my eye
Rests upon earth again. How beautiful,
Where wild Velino heaves its sullen waves
Down on high cliff of gray and shapeless granite,
Hung on the curling mist, the moonlight bow
Arches the perilous river! A soft light
Silvers the Albanian Mountains, and the haze
That rests upon their summits mellows down
The austerer features of their beauty. Faint
And dim-discovered glow the Sabine Hills;

And, listening to the sea's monotonous shell
High on the cliffs of Terracina stands
The castle of the royal Goth in ruins.

But night is in her wane: day's early flush
Glows like a hectic on her fading cheek,
Wasting its beauty. And the opening dawn
With cheerful lustre lights the royal city,
Where, with its proud tiara of dark towers,
It sleeps upon its own romantic bay.

HENRY WADSWORTH LONGFELLOW.

TO KING VICTOR EMMANUEL

Italian sculptors have left us equestrian statues of Victor Emmanuel in almost every public square in Italy. Seated on his famous charger, he looks down upon friend and stranger alike, and few know why he has merited such universal homage. The poet seeks to give us the reason.

Aye, let the Jesuits lie,
Pointing the moral of thy house's woes—
'Tis well the base be gladdened, when their foes,
The brave and gentle, die.

Aye—let them count the lives,
The dear ones, stricken sudden at thy side—
The mother, and the brother, and the bride—
'Lo! how our scorner thrives?'

Mock shepherds! texts like these
Suit well your lips: improve them to your folds,
Trainers and praisers of the hand that holds
Poerio's dungeon keys!

Yet onward, as before,
Victor Emmanuel! stricken, not in wrath—
Task nobler has none living; plain the path,
And upward; ask no more.

For full heroic strain
Of temper, level with heroic act,
Perchance but this a genial nature lacked—
The steeling touch of pain.

Be all the hour desires,
Soldier, inheritor of soldier blood,
O King! baptized to freedom in the flood
Of fatal battle fires,

Where 'mid the thousands slain
For Italy, her martyrs, not her last,
From sire to son the crown of Piedmont past,
Heirloom of noble pain.

A greater time is born:
A mightier cause at stake: the same, though other—
Ah, yes—he should be here to aid, the brother
Of dark Novara's morn!

Be Piedmont's flag unfurled
Where coiling trenches climb the stubborn height,
Where East with West joins battle—Wrong with Right,
To win or lose the world.

Fearless abroad, at home
Be resolute in truth, in boldness wise;
And scorning, teach thy people to despise
The unctuous threats of Rome.

Thy pole-star be yon shrine—
Where high Superga from the champaign springs
A vanquished exile sleeps 'mid victor kings,
Most honoured of his line.

A patriot's renown,
A people's tears, the laurel of the brave,
These Virtue gave him: Fortune took or gave
The Lombards' iron crown.

A Liberator's name
He left thee. When that columned crest shall see
The black train grow from out the gates for thee,
Leave to thy son the same.

So, where from fringing snow
Slope sunward the Riviera's olive-woods,
Or where past walls of Alps that feed his floods,
Sweeps through his plains the Po,

May Genoa, Turin, stand
Twin headstones of the corner: mighty rocks
Set in the desert, shading Freedom's flocks
Amid a weary land.

Win freely, ere thou die,
The calumnies that witness best to glory:
Be thine the foremost name in Savoy's story—
And let the Jesuits lie.

HENRY LUSHINGTON.

DAWN IN ARQUA

M. Pierre de Nothac had in mind the mountains of his native Auvergne when, on his pilgrimage to Arqua, he remarked: "My Limagne curves in lines like these on the horizon; the hills are less notable, but vines and dense foliage mingle there as here."

On the steep climb to the village the visitor stops at the fountain Petrarch caused to be built; and he drinks, as do all the villagers, of its clear, refreshing waters. The Latin inscription informs the wayfarer that "The spirit is present at the fountain. O pious guest! adore the waters whence drinking, Petrarch sang songs worthy of God."

Certainly Boccaccio praised the little hill town for preserving the bones of the illustrious old man. "As a Florentine," he said, "I envy Arqua which, hitherto obscure, will become famous among the nations. The sailor returning from distant shores will gaze with emotion at the Euganean Hills and will say to his companions: 'At the foot of these hills Petrarch is sleeping'!"

Sick of mere fame, and of Rome's Laureate leaf
  His Latin Epic brought him, up he went
To steep Arqueto, where he found content
Among the Euganean Hills—alas, too brief!
His was an irremediable grief:
That heart so loved, that head so opulent
Of gold, were long since dust . . . . Silent he bent
Above those Sonnets in that *Golden Sheaf*.
Far into midnight, lone he sat, and read—
The *Rimè* once again—oh, bitterest tears
By age, for love all unrequited, shed!—
Then in that volume slowly sank his head;
Thus, in the mountain cottage, bowed with years,
At early morn they found him, cold and dead.

                              LLOYD MIFFLIN.

SKIES ITALIAN

When once we feel the spirit of Italy as it stirs "the inner man" we then go in quest of some means of putting into words that thing which we cannot name—that feeling which for some people has changed their whole outlook on life.

Ruth Shepard Phelps has certainly felt that spirit, and in a few lines she has summed up in apt phrase the thing which so many of us want to say to the world when the spirit of Italy has come upon us.

"O woman-country!" Lisa's sweet still smile;
The tears of wasting Pia; the despair
Of young Pompilia, netted in foul snare;
Francesca's passion; something of the guile
Of her who wooed the Roman by the Nile;
Pale Juliet's moonlit beauty: these thy share,
These spells that like dim jewels star thy hair,
And hold a World thy lover this long while.

O Italy! the heart that knows not love
Half finds it, loving thee; the love-taught heart
Thrills newly by thy fountains. Ours thou art
Who cherish thee—it needs not that we prove
Us native to thy skies; nay, better be
Of young lands born, and born to yearn for thee!

RUTH SHEPARD PHELPS.

AT FANO

(To Robert Browning)

An ancient temple (fanum) of Fortune on an Adriatic beach north of Ancona, gave the town its name. Spanning one of the sunlit streets is the time-marked Arch of Augustus. It would be interesting to study this old memorial of the Roman emperor with its second story added by a builder four centuries later, but the lovers of Browning will seek the church of Saint Agostino. Within may be found the altar-piece of Guercino which inspired the poem, "The Guardian Angel."

Dearly honoured, great dead poet, still as living speak to me!
This is Fano, world-forgotten little Fano, by the sea:

I have come to see that angel which Guercino dreamed and drew,
Since whate'er you loved and honoured I would hold in honour too.

Like some sea-bird's nest the township clusters in its rampart wall,—
Such a twilight in the byways, such an autumn over all:

Gloomy streets with silent portals, all the pulse of life they hide,
Throbbing toward that one piazza where it centres into pride;

House and palace, as their wont is in these Adriatic ports,
Turn their backs on darkling alleys and their faces on the courts.

At Fano

Courts beyond each tunnelled entrance, where through vaulted arches seen
Glimpses flash of dancing sunlight, jets of fountain, glints of green.—

Here I found him, ever watchful for the work of love to do,
That white-winged one whose great glory you interpreted so true;

Still he folds the little fingers of that kneeling child to prayer,
On the grave which tells the story why it needs the angel's care;

Still above the forehead's glory arch the great wings wide unfurled
As alert to shield and succour all the orphans of the world.

Yet hath he but little honour in his home at Fano there
O'er the cold neglected altar in the chapel blanched and bare;

Few come here to read his message in the little nest of towers,—
Few that worship where he watches, none that deck his shrine with flowers.

Thence I passed out on the ramparts, high above the olive trees,
Skirting roofs and shadowy belfries, overlooking evening seas

Into such a rose of sunset, such a tender twilight hue
Where the orange sails came homeward on the Adriatic blue;

Oh, my poet, had you seen it, you had found the word to fit
That sweet world of peace at even' with God's love enfolding it!

There across the rose of sunset, through the perfect hush of things
Stole a gentle rhythmic motion that might be the beat of wings,—

Art thou free, at last, dear angel, art thou free to fly above,
Leave that little one to slumber, quit the duty which is love,

Through the chiming of Ave Mary spread those bird wings white as snow,
Whether starwards, whether sunwards, be the way their angels go?

One more service yet, dear angel, find him there beyond the blue,
Tell him how I loved the message he interpreted so true!

Sir Rennell Rodd.

VERONA

From *Italy*

Verona is one of the most interesting towns of Venetia and its graceful gardens make it one of the most beloved. The beauty of the gardens is not due to artificial fantasies but to Nature who has so embellished the town that it brings delight to those who live there. Terraced hillsides, where "footsteps like our dreams rise ever higher" lead us through avenues of glorious cypresses. How many centuries have passed since wayfarers first began to seek the comfort of these venerable trees! From the vantage gained by higher climbing along the red brick stairs we may look out across the plain where Constantine defeated the army of Maxentius. Other historic events pass in review as we gaze out over this plain. Theodoric vanquished Odoacer out there on the horizon and from Verona Charlemagne once led his victorious armies south towards Rome.

"Is this the Mincius?
Are those the distant turrets of Verona?
And shall I sup where Juliet at the Masque
First saw and loved, and now by him who came
That night a stranger, sleeps from age to age?
Such questions hourly do I ask myself;
And not a stone, in a cross-way, inscribed
'To Mantua'—and 'To Ferrara'—but excites
Surprise, and doubt and self-congratulation.
Oh, Italy, how beautiful thou art!"

SAMUEL ROGERS.

ODE: THE MEDITERRANEAN

We may enter this Old Roman Lake through the Straits of Gibraltar where the Pillars of Hercules marked the western boundary of the Ancient World; we may make a short sail from Genoa to Naples; or we may take an excursion from one of the many famous ports to the historic islands lying on its broad expanse. Whichever way we go, we find historic legends and tales of war and peace; they rise on every hand, recalling the part this great waterway has played in history. Phoenician galleys, Roman triremes, Spanish corsairs, English and French men-of-war, and Italian liners have passed this way before us.

A mood of revery and romance fills our soul and we will do well to read and ponder the lines of Santayana's Ode.

Of thee the Northman by his beachèd galley
Dreamt, as he watched the never-setting Ursa
And longed for summer and thy light, O sacred
    Mediterranean.

Unseen he loved thee; for the heart within him
Knew earth had gardens where he might be blessed
Putting away long dreams and aimless, barbarous
    Hunger for battle.

The foretaste of thy languors thawed his bosom;
A great need drove him to thy caverned islands
From the gray, endless reaches of the outer
    Desert of ocean.

He saw thy pillars, saw thy sudden mountains
Wrinkled and stark, and in their crooked gorges,
'Neath peeping pine and cypress, guessed the torrent
    Smother in flowers.

Thine incense to the sun, thy gathered vapours,
He saw suspended on the flanks of Taurus,
Or veiling the snowed bosom of the virgin
    Sister of Atlas.

Ode: The Mediterranean

He saw the luminous top of wide Olympus,
Fit for the happy gods; he saw the pilgrim
River, with rains of Ethiopia flooding
    Pupulous Egypt.

And having seen, he loved thee. His racked spirit,
By the breath tempered and the light that clothes thee,
Forgot the monstrous gods, and made of Nature
    Mistress and mother.

The more should I, O fatal sea, before thee
Of alien words make echoes to thy music;
For I was born where first the rills of Tagus
    Turn to the westward.

And wandering long, alas! have need of drinking
Deep of the patience of thy perfect sadness,
O thou that constant through the change of ages,
    Beautiful ever.

Never wast wholly young and void of sorrows,
Nor ever canst be old, while yet the morning
Kindles thy ripples, or the golden evening
    Dyes thee in purple.

Thee, willing to be tamed but still untamable,
The Roman called his own until he perished,
As now the busy English hover o'er thee,
    Stalwart and noble.

But all is naught to thee, while no harsh winter
Congeals thy fountains, and the blown Sahara
Chokes not with dreadful sand thy deep and placid
    Rock-guarded havens.

Thou carest not what men may tread thy margin;
Nor I, while from some heather-scented headland
I may behold thy beauty, the eternal
    Solace of mortals.

                    GEORGE SANTAYANA.

A DIVINE BARRIER

In the "Passage of the Apennines" Shelley has expressed the deep emotion that filled his soul as he journeyed along the heights of Italy's "Divine Barrier." The traveler of today, as he rides in the smoky monster of the rails through this barrier of the Apennines, may find some reason for the dearth of present-day poems. It was the old-time traveler who walked or rode leisurely along the steep mountain paths and picturesque valley highways and lingered by the wayside shrines, who found inspiration for poems like those of Shelley and Savage-Armstrong.

If we admit that on a certain plain
The world was fashioned, that this great machine
Was by a god designed, the Apennines
Along the Latian watches he enwove,
A barrier scarce by mountain paths approached.
Nature feared envy and deemed it not enough
To oppose the Alps to the invading North.

G. F. SAVAGE-ARMSTRONG.

PASSAGE OF THE APENNINES

Surely Italy possesses a strange dynamic spell which has enabled her to hold the poetic souls of the past. This country "on the fair side of the Alps" has been of untold influence in their poetic and artistic development. Chaucer, Milton, Shelley, Goethe and Keats visited this land of song and sunshine to find their muse a constant companion.

On his way southward Shelley lingered for a while at Milan and hoped to find a retreat on the shores of Lake Como. Failing to find this ideal spot he started towards Pisa and Florence and it was on this journey, as he was crossing the great mountain ridge of Italy, that he wrote this lovely fragment.

Listen, Listen, Mary mine,
To the whisper of the Apennine,
It bursts on the roof like the thunder's roar,
Or like the sea on a northern shore,
Heard in its raging ebb and flow
By the captives pent in the cave below.
The Apennine in the light of day
Is a mighty mountain dim and gray,
Which between the earth and sky doth lay;
But when night comes, a chaos dread
On the dim starlight then is spread,
And the Apennine walks abroad with the storm.

Percy Bysshe Shelley.

ITALY
PART II
ITALIAN LAKES

SIRMIO: LAGO DI GARDA

Well to the east of Lake Como lies the beautiful Lake Garda which Virgil describes in the Georgics. Between the towns of Desenzano and Peschiera is the narrow promontory of Sirmio where Catullus had a villa. Although the site is marked by ruins, they are of a later period and are not historically associated with the great Roman.

The town not far away, has little that recalls the days when the pleasure-loving Romans made these lakes their favorite summer resort.

Sweet Sirmio! thou, the very eye
   Of all peninsulas and isles,
That in our lakes of silver lie,
   Or sleep, enwreathed by Neptune's smiles,—

How gladly back to thee I fly!
   Still doubting, asking,—can it be
That I have left Bithynia's sky,
   And gaze in safety upon thee?

O, what is happier than to find
   Our hearts at ease, our perils past;
When, anxious long, the lightened mind
   Lays down its load of care at last;

When, tired with toil o'er land and deep,
   Again we tread the welcome floor
Of our own home, and sink to sleep
   On the long-wished-for bed once more.

This, this it is, that pays alone
   The ills of all life's former track.
Shine out, my beautiful, my own
   Sweet Sirmio! greet thy master back.

And thou, fair lake, whose water quaffs
    The light of heaven like Lydia's sea,
Rejoice, rejoice,—let all that laughs
    Abroad, at home, laugh out for me.

CATULLUS
(Translated by Thomas Moore).

TO SAINT CHARLES BORROMEO
ON THE MASSACRE AT MILAN

Many travelers have stood on the shores of Lago Maggiore at Stresa or Baveno and looked out across the waters of Lago Maggiore towards the Borromean Islands, where resided the Counts Carlo and Guilio Borromeo.

Charles Borromeo was born in 1538 and, some thirty years later, was made Cardinal and Archbishop of Milan. We may look upon the body of the Cardinal dressed in his pontifical robes and jewels, as he lies under the high altar in the Cathedral of Milan; or, we may stand beside the colosal statue of the Saint on the heights above Arona. We shall find added interest if we but realize how unceasing were his efforts in establishing schools, colleges and asylums, and how untiring was his devotion to his people when Milan was plague-stricken in 1576.

I

Saint, beyond all in glory, who surround
    The throne above!
Thy placid brow no thorn blood-dropping crown'd,
    No grief came o'er thy love,

II

Save what they suffer'd whom the Plague's dull fire
    Wasted away,
Or those whom Heaven at last let worse Desire
    Sweep with soft swoop away.

III

If thou art standing high above the place
    Where Verban gleams,
Where Art and Nature give thee form and space
    As best beseems,

IV

Look down on thy fair country, and most fair
  The sister isles!
Where gratitude eternal mounts with prayer,
  Where spring eternal smiles;

V

Watch over that brave youth who bears thy name,
  and bears it well,
Unmindful never of the sacred flame
  With which his temples swell

VI

When praise from thousands breathes beneath thy
  shrine,
  And incense steeps
Thy calm brow bending over them, for thine
  Is bent on him who weeps;

VII

And, O most holy one! what tears are shed
  Thro' all thy town!
Thou wilt with pity on the brave and dead,
  God will with wrath, look down.

WALTER SAVAGE LANDOR.

CADENABBIA
[LAKE OF COMO]

Rose-clad Cadenabbia is far-famed for its beautiful sunsets. The shadow of Monte Crocione slowly creeps from the surface of Lake Como up the mountain slopes above Varema, and changes the green-clad mountains to deep purple. When at last the sun sinks below the horizon, the crest of Grigna still glows in a gorgeous rose-red against a sky slowly growing darker with the twilight hours.

No sound of wheels or hoof-beat breaks
   The silence of the summer day,
As by the loveliest of all lakes
   I while the idle hours away.

I pace the leafy colonnade
   Where level branches of the plane
Above me weave a roof of shade
   Impervious to the sun and rain.

At times a sudden rush of air
   Flutters the lazy leaves o'erhead,
And gleams of sunshine toss and flare
   Like torches down the path I tread.

By Somariva's garden gate
   I make the marble stairs my seat,
And hear the water, as I wait,
   Lapping the steps beneath my feet.

The undulation sinks and swells
   Along the stony parapets,
And far away the floating bells
   Tinkle upon the fisher's nets.

Silent and slow, by tower and town
　　The freighted barges come and go,
Their pendant shadows gliding down
　　By town and tower submerged below.

The hills sweep upward from the shore,
　　With villas scattered one by one
Upon their wooded spurs, and lower
　　Bellaggio blazing in the sun.

And dimly seen, a tangled mass
　　Of walls and woods, of light and shade,
Stands, beckoning up the Stelvio Pass
　　Varenna with its white cascade.

I ask myself, Is this a dream?
　　Will it all vanish into air?
Is there a land of such supreme
　　And perfect beauty anywhere?

Sweet vision! Do not fade away:
　　Linger until my heart shall take
Into itself the summer day,
　　And all the beauty of the lake.

Linger until upon my brain
　　Is stamped an image of the scene,
Then fade into the air again,
　　And be as if thou hadst not been.

　　　　　　　HENRY WADSWORTH LONGFELLOW.

THE LAKE OF COMO

There are many ways of approaching this most fascinating of all Italian lakes. From the roads that wind over the lofty plateau, rich in vineyards, meadows and wooded glades, a scene of romantic beauty unfolds itself below us.

Painters find it impossible to reproduce the delicate transparency of the atmosphere in these lake valleys. Many travelers come here to gratify the eye, forgetful of the history and traditions of the district. Here the élite of all Rome sought a retreat from the corruptions of the City of the Seven Hills and the Plinys found respite from their cares in the abounding country life.

To the student, Lake Como has its mediaeval and its classical zones. From Como to Colico the great center of interest in the art and history of the Middle Ages was around Menaggio; while the classical zone ended near the wooded heights around the Villa Serbelloni or the Pinito de Bellagio. Should the traveler stop to rest along these shores his sojourn will be all the more enjoyable if, as he looks upon these historic waters, he can be guided by the words of another who came this way before him.

Uprisen betimes, our journey we renewed,
Led by the stream, ere noon-day magnified
Into a lordly river, broad and deep,
Dimpling along in silent majesty,
With mountains for its neighbours, and in view
Of distant mountains and their snowy tops,
And thus proceeding to Locarno's Lake,
Fit resting place for such a visitant.
Locarno! spreading out in width like Heaven,
How dost thou cleave to the poetic heart,
Bask in the sunshine of the memory;
And Como! thou, a treasure whom the earth
Keeps to herself, confined as in a depth
Of Abyssinian privacy. I spake
Of thee, thy chestnut woods, and garden plots
Of Indian corn tended by dark-eyed maids;

Thy lofty steeps, and pathways roofed with vines,
Winding from house to house, from town to town,
Sole link that binds them to each other; walks
League after league, and cloistral avenues,
Where silence dwells if music be not there:
While yet a youth undisciplined in verse,
Through fond ambition of that hour I strove
To chat your praise; nor can approach you now
Ungreeted by a more melodious Song,
Where tones of Nature smoothed by learned Art
May flow in lasting current. Like a breeze
Or sunbeam over your domain I passed
In motion without pause; but ye have left
Your beauty with me, a serene accord
Of forms and colours, passive, yet endowed
In their submissiveness with power as sweet
And gracious, almost might I dare to say,
As virtue is, or goodness; sweet as love,
Or the remembrance of a generous deed,
Or mildest visitations of pure thought,
When God, the giver of all joy, is thanked
Religiously, in silent blessedness;
Sweet as this last herself, for such it is.

With those delightful pathways we advanced,
For two days' space, in presence of the Lake,
That, stretching far among the Alps, assumed
A character more stern. The second night,
From sleep awakened, and misled by sound
Of the church clock telling the hours with strokes
Whose import then we had not learned, we rose
By moonlight, doubting not that day was nigh,
And that meanwhile, by no uncertain path,
Along the winding margin to the lake,
Led, as before, we should behold the scene

The Lake of Como

Hushed in profound repose. We left the town
Of Gravedona with this hope; but soon
Were lost, bewildered among woods immense,
And on a rock sate down, to wait for day.
An open place it was, and overlooked,
From high, the sullen water far beneath,
On which a dull red image of the moon
Lay bedded, changing oftentimes its form
Like an uneasy snake. From hour to hour
We sate and sate, wondering as if the night
Had been ensnared by witchcraft. On the rock
At last we stretched our weary limbs for sleep,
But could not sleep, tormented by the stings
Of insects, which, with noise like that of noon,
Filled all the woods: the cry of unknown birds;
The mountains, more by blackness visible
And their own size, than any outward light;
The breathless wilderness of clouds; the clock
That told, with unintelligible voice,
The widely parted hours; the noise of streams,
And sometimes rustling motions nigh at hand,
That did not leave us free from personal fear;
And lastly, the withdrawing moon, that set
Before us, while she still was high in heaven—
These were our food; and such a summer's night
Followed that pair of golden days that shed
On Como's Lake, and all that round it lay,
Their fairest, softest, happiest influence.

      WILLIAM WORDSWORTH.

ITALY
PART III
MILAN

THE CATHEDRAL OF MILAN

"O Milan, O the enchanting quires,
The giant windows' blazon'd fires,
  The height, the space, the gloom, the glory!
A mount of marble, a hundred spires!

"I climb'd the roofs at break of day;
Sun-smitten Alps before me lay.
  I stood among the silent statues,
And statued pinnacles, mute as they."

TENNYSON, The Daisy.

Is there a cathedral south of the Alps more famous or more expressive of the spirit of Gothic architecture? Without the glory of her magnificent cathedral, Milan might still be a modern and prosperous city, but her most dazzling jewel would be sorely missed.

In the bright Italian sunshine or in the shadows of a summer evening this forest of marble pinnacles rises in inspiring grandeur. When compared with the northern cathedrals its decorations of a thousand statues and its spires of glittering white marble may seem trivial, but it will always remain a veritable miracle of craftsmanship. Perhaps these workmen of olden times sought to perpetuate in marble the form of Monte Rosa, lying off to the north among the conspicuous peaks around Zermatt. Like a magnificent design of frost work turned to marble it must, as long as it is spared the ravages of time, remain the glory of the chief city of the Lombard Plain.

With steps subdued, silence, and labour long
I reached the marble roofs. Awe vanquished dread.
White were they as the summit of Mont Blanc,
  When noontide parleys with that mountain's head.
The far-off Alps, by morning tinged with red,
Blushed through the spires that round in myriads sprung:

The Cathedral of Milan

A silver gleam the wind-stirred poplars flung
   O'er Lombardy's green sea below me spread,
Of these I little saw. In trance I stood;
   Ere death, methought, admitted to the skies;
Around me, like a heavenly multitude
   Crowning some specular mount of Paradise,
Thronged that angelic concourse robed in stone:
   The sun, ascending, in their faces shone!

AUBREY DE VERE.

LINES WRITTEN ON THE ROOF OF MILAN CATHEDRAL

'A mount of marble, a hundred spires.'

How many have climbed the winding stairs of the Cathedral at Milan to see its forest of graceful needles shimmering in the amber sunlight,—so grand, so solemn, so vast and yet so delicate—"an anthem in stone, a poem wrought in marble!" And yet how many have looked out across the thriving and prosperous city without understanding any of the story the city and plain unfold. Is he not to be pitied who cannot vision at least some of the historic panorama that rises before him here? Perhaps the following lines will awaken his imagination.

The long, long night of utter loneliness,
Of conflict, pain, defeat, and sore distress,
Hath vanished; and I stand as one whose life
Wages with death a scarcely winning strife,
Here on this mount of marble. Like a sea
Waveless and blue, the sky's transparency
Bathes spire and statue. Was it man or God
Who built these domes, whereon the feet have trod
Of eve and night and morn with rose and gold
And silver and strange symbols manifold
Of shadow? Fabric not of stone but mist
Or pearl or cloud beneath heaven's amethyst
Glitters the marvel: cloud congealed to shine
Through centuries with lustre crystalline;
Pearl spiked and fretted like an Orient shell;
Mist on the frozen fern-wreaths of a well.
Not God's but man's work this: God's yonder fane,
Reared on the distant limit of the plain,
From azure into azure, to blue sky
Shooting from vapours blue that folded lie
Round valley-basements, robed in royal snow,
Wherefrom life-giving waters leaping flow,

Lines Written on the Roof of Milan Cathedral

Aerial Monte Rosa!—God and man
Confront each other, with this narrow span
Of plain to part them, try what each can do
To make applauding Seraphs from the blue
Lean marvel-smitten, or alight with song
Upon the glittering peaks, or clustering throng
The spacious pathways. God on man's work here
Hath set his signature and symbol clear;
Man's soul that thinks and feels, to God's work there
Gives life, which else were cold and dumb and bare.
God is man's soul; man's soul a spark of God:
By God in man the dull terrestrial clod
Becomes a thing of beauty; thinking man
Through God made manifest, outrival can
His handiwork of nature. Do we dream
Mingling reality with things that seem?
Or is it true that God and man appear
One soul in sentient art self-conscious here,
One soul o'er senseless nature stair by stair
Raised to create by comprehending there!

JOHN ADDINGTON SYMONDS.

THE LAST SUPPER

(By Leonardo da Vinci, in the Refectory
of the Convent of Maria della Grazia, Milan)

The low, gloomy, Dominican church of Santa Maria della Grazia in Milan had been the favorite oratory of Beatrice d'Este, wife of Ludovico il Moro, the great patron of Leonardo da Vinci. With a sinister presentiment, the Duchess Beatrice had been ever reluctant to leave the oratory. Now that death had called her, Ludovico was affected by a paroxysm of religious feeling. A hundred times a day masses were said for her repose of soul. To her memory, Leonardo painted on the walls of the Church of the refectory, The Last Supper, now in pathetic and irreparable ruin. A door has been cut through it, but the traveler can still see one of the three or four world masterpieces. Painted in oil on plaster, it scarcely retained its perfection for fifty years. The great painting is blotched and disfigured indeed, terribly so, but somehow even to inexpert eyes, there is a power and majesty in the ruined forms and faces beside which the copies look cheap and ordinary. There is quite enough left to assist the imagination, and as you pore over it, and try to think yourself back into the mind of the painter, the outlines and colors come faintly back, the face of the Saviour is filled with its old dignity, its old pathos, its old divine humanity, and you look indeed at The Last Supper of our Lord.

Tho' searching damps and many an envious flaw
   Have marred this Work; the calm ethereal grace,
   The love deep-seated in the Saviour's face,
The mercy, goodness, have not failed to awe
The Elements; as they do melt and thaw
   The heart of the Beholder—and erase
   (At least for one rapt moment) every trace
Of disobedience to the primal law.
The annunciation of the dreadful truth
   Made to the Twelve, survives: lip, forehead, cheek,

And hand reposing on the board in ruth
  Of what it utters, while the unguilty seek
Unquestionable meanings—still bespeak
A labour worthy of eternal youth!

WILLIAM WORDSWORTH.

ITALY
PART IV
ASSISI

THE SERMON OF ST. FRANCIS

St. Francis looked upon the everyday world round about him and found it full of beauty. The birds of the air, the beasts of the fields, even the wind, the rain and the sun, were his little brothers. Truly he was the "little brother of the poor." He "anticipated all that is most liberal in the modern mood: the love of nature, the love of animals."

St. Francis may well be called the Father of the Renaissance, for in the thirteenth century the people of the little Umbrian towns and villages where he visited listened to him as to no one else. His idealism inspired the great artists of Umbria, who left on the frescoed walls of Italy's great churches the story of his life. Matthew Arnold does not hesitate to give the "poor little man of God" a place among the great geniuses of all time.

St. Francis' part in life was to bring religion to the people. His soul yearned for the poverty and suffering which were the common fate of the majority of mankind. "He listens," it was said of him, "to those to whom God himself will not listen."

Up soared the lark into the air,
A shaft of song, a winged prayer,
As if a soul, released from pain
Were flying back to heaven again.

St. Francis heard; it was to him
An emblem of the Seraphim;
The upward motion of the fire,
The light, the heat, the heart's desire.

Around Assisi's convent gate
The birds, God's poor who cannot wait,
From moor and mere and darksome wood
Came flocking for their dole of food.

"O brother birds," St. Francis said,
"Ye come to me and ask for bread,
But not with bread alone to-day
Shall ye be fed and sent away.

"Ye shall be fed, ye happy birds,
With manna of celestial words;
Not mine, though mine they seem to be,
Not mine, though they be spoken through me,

"O, doubly are ye bound to praise
The great Creator in your lays;
He giveth you your plumes of down,
Your crimson hoods, your cloaks of brown.

"He giveth you your wings to fly
And breathe a purer air on high,
And careth for you everywhere,
Who for yourselves so little care!"

With flutter of swift wings and songs
Together rose the feathered throngs,
And singing scattered far apart;
Deep peace was in St. Francis' heart.

He knew not if the brotherhood
His homily had understood;
He only knew that to one ear
The meaning of his words was clear.

    HENRY WADSWORTH LONGFELLOW.

ITALY
PART V
GENOA

GENOA

"Dost thou remember," wrote Petrarch, who saw the city as it was in the fourteenth century—"Dost thou remember when the Genoese were the happiest people on earth, and their country appeared a celestial residence even as the Elysian fields are painted? From the side of the sea, what an aspect it presented! Towers which seemed to threaten the firmament, hills covered with olives and oranges, marble palaces perched on the summit of the rocks, with delicious retreats beneath them where art conquered nature, and at the sight of which the very sailors checked the splashing of their oars, all intent to regard."

Like all the towns along the Riviera, Genoa has passed through stern and troubled times. She has been raided by Normans and Saracens and she has fought her greatest duel with Pisa. Glory came to her with the Crusades, for her galleys and skilled warriors were needed by kings and knights for the deliverance of the Holy Sepulchre.

"Many a gallant knight stepped on board the great ships in that lovely harbor and paid good red gold for transportation of himself and his men-at-arms to alien lands, where their bones were soon to whiten in the desert."

Ah! what avails it, Genoa, now to thee
That Doria, feared by monarchs, once was thine?
  Univied ruin! in thy sad decline
From virtuous greatness, what avails that he
Whose prow descended first the Hesperian sea,
  And gave our world her mate beyond the brine,
Was nurtured, whilst an infant, at thy knee?—
  All things must perish,—all but things divine.
Flowers, and the stars, and virtue,—these alone,
  The self-subsisting shapes, or self-renewing,
Survive. All else are sentenced. Wisest were
That builder who should plan with strictest care
(Ere yet the wood was felled or hewn the stone)
  The aspect only of his pile in ruin!

AUBREY DE VERE.

GENOA

"Oh, Genoese! ye men at variance
With every virtue, full of every vice,
Wherefore are ye not scattered from the world?"

DANTE, *Divina Comedia*.

Little did Dante realize that this city, standing at the northwestern point of Italy, would be the birthplace of the discoverer of a new world to which many of his countrymen would emigrate. One of the powerful cities of the Middle Ages, Genoa contested with Venice, Pisa and Florence for the supremacy of the Mediterranean. Dante's uncomplimentary reference shows the hatred in which she was held by her rivals.

When seen from the sea in those old days, a grand wall of terraced mountains rose like an amphitheatre about her, and marble palaces and churches overlooked her blue bay. To the east and west lies the well known Riviera region of France and Italy where "mountains kiss high heaven, and the waves clasp one another," and towns and villages are so charmingly situated that travelers long to tarry in this beautiful and picturesque region.

I am where mountains round me shine;
But in sweet vision truer than mine eyes
I see pale Genoa's marble crescent rise
Between the water and the Apennine.

On the sea-bank she couches like a deer,
A creature giving light with her soft sheen,
While the blue ocean and the mountain green
Pleased with the wonder always gaze on her.

And day and night the mild sea-murmur fills
The corridors of her cool palaces,
Taking the freshness from the orange trees,
A fragrant gift into the peaceful hills.

And from the balustrades into the street,
From time to time there are voluptuous showers,
Gentle descents, of shaken lemon flowers
Snapped by the echo of the passing feet.

And when the sun his noonday height hath gained,
How mute is all that slumbrous Apennine,
Upon whose base the streaks of green turf shine,
With the black olive-gardens interveined!

How fair it is when, in the purple bay,
Of the soft sea the clear edged moon is drinking,
Or the dark sky amid the shipmasts winking
With summer lightning over Corsica!

O Genoa! thou art a marvellous birth—
A clasp which joins the mountains and the sea:
And the two powers do homage unto thee
As to a matchless wonder of the earth.

Can life be common life in spots like these
Where they breathe breath from orange gardens
  wafted?
O joy and sorrow surely must be grafted
On stems apart for these bright Genoese.

The place is islanded amid her mirth,
The very girdle of her beauty thrown
About her in men's minds, a virgin zone,
Marks her a spot unmated on the earth.

I hear the deep coves of the Apennine,
Filled with a gentle trouble of sweet bells:
And the blue tongues of sea that pierce the dells,
As conscious of the Virgin's feast day shine.

For Genoa the Proud for many an age
Hath been pre-eminent as tributary
Unto the special service of St. Mary,
The sinless Virgin's chosen appanage.

I see the street with very stacks of flowers
Choked up, a wild and beautiful array,
And in my mind I thread my fragrant way
Once more amid the rich and cumbrous bowers.

And unforgotten beauty! by the Bay,
I see two boys and the little maiden
With crimson tulips for the Virgin laden,
Wending along the road from Spezzia.

F. W. FABER.

GENOA

Gently, as roses die, the day declines;
  On the charmed air there is a hush the while;
And delicate are the twilight-tints that smile
Upon the summits of the Apennines.
The moon is up; and o'er the warm wave shines
  A faery bridge of light, whose beams beguile
  The fancy to some far and fortunate isle,
Which love in solitude unlonely shrines.
The blue night of Italian summer glooms
  Around us: over the crystalline swell
I gaze on Genoa's spires and palace-domes:
  City of cities, the superb, farewell!
  The beautiful, in nature's bloom, is thine:
  And Art hath made it deathless and divine!

WILLIAM GIBSON.

ITALY
PART VI
VENICE

THE PIAZZA OF ST. MARK AT MIDNIGHT

It might be well for the traveler who stands alone in the great square of St. Mark's in Venice, to read this poem in the light of what Ruskin tells us of the Republic whose captains and navies have departed but whose glory is eternal.

"Not in the wantonness of wealth, not in vain ministry to the desire of the eyes or pride of life, were those marbles hewn into transparent strength, and those arches arrayed in the colors of the iris. There is a message written in the dyes of them that once was written in blood and a sound in the echoes of their vaults that one day shall fill the vault of heaven.

"He shall return to do judgment and justice. The strength of Venice was given her so long as she remembered this; her destruction found her when she had forgotten this; and it found her irrevocably because she forgot it without excuse."

Hushed is the music, hushed the hum of voices;
Gone is the crowd of dusky promenaders—
Slender-waisted, almond-eyed Venetians,
Princes and paupers. Not a single footfall
Sounds in the arches of the Procuratie.
One after one, like sparks of cindered paper,
Faded the lights out in the goldsmiths' windows.
Drenched with the moonlight lies the still Piazza.

Fair as the palace builded for Aladdin,
Yonder St. Mark uplifts its sculptured splendour—
Intricate fretwork, Byzantine mosaic,
Colour on colour, column upon column,
Barbaric, wonderful, a thing to kneel to!
Over the portal stand the four gilt horses,
Gilt hoof in air, and wide distended nostril,
Fiery, untamed, as in the days of Nero.

The Piazza of St. Mark at Midnight

Skyward, a cloud of domes and spires and crosses;
Earthward, black shadows flung from jutting stonework.
High over all the slender Campanile
Quivers, and seems a falling shaft of silver!

Hushed is the music, hushed the hum of voices,
From coigne and cornice and fantastic gargoyle,
At intervals the moan of dove or pigeon,
Fairly faint, floats off into the moonlight.
This, and the murmur of the Adriatic,
Lazily restless, lapping the mossed marble,
Staircase or buttress, scarcely breaks the stillness,
Deeper each moment seems to grow the silence,
Denser the moonlight in the still Piazza.
Hark! on the tower above the ancient gateway,
The twin bronze Vulcans, with their ponderous hammers,
Hammer the midnight on their brazen bell there!

THOMAS BAILEY ALDRICH.

ODE ON VENICE

To music, painting or poetry must remain the task of weaving into our vision of the present, a murmur of the life that belonged to ages past. In Venice there is such a "perpetual miracle of change" that the traveler seems confronted by a story writ in water. Ruskin once called Venice a "ghost upon the sands of the sea so bereft of all but her loveliness that we might well doubt, as we watched her faint reflections in the mirage of the lagoon, which was the city and which the shadow." Beloved by Turner, Shelley and Whistler we may well listen to the love of the Bride of the Adriatic that another famous traveler has expressed in verse.

I

Oh Venice! Venice! when thy marble walls
  Are level with the waters, there shall be
A cry of nations o'er thy sunken halls,
  A loud lament along the sweeping sea!
If I, a northern wanderer, weep for thee,
What should thy sons do?—anything but weep:
And yet they only murmur in their sleep,
In contrast with their fathers—as the slime,
The dull green ooze of the receding deep,
Is with the dashing of the spring-tide foam
That drives the sailor shipless to his home,
Are they to those that were; and thus they creep,
Crouching and crab-like, through their sapping streets.
Oh! agony—that centuries should reap
No mellower harvest! Thirteen hundred years
Of wealth and glory turn'd to dust and tears,
And every monument the stranger meets,
Church, palace, pillar, as a mourner greets;
And even the Lion all subdued appears,
And the harsh sound of the barbarian drum,
With dull and daily dissonance, repeats

The echo of thy tyrant's voice along
The soft waves, once all musical to song,
That heaved beneath the moonlight with the throng
Of gondolas—and to the busy hum
Of cheerful creatures, whose most sinful deeds
Were but the overbeating of the heart,
And flow of too much happiness, which needs
The aid of age to turn its course apart
From the luxuriant and voluptuous flood
Of sweet sensations, battling with the blood.
But these are better than the gloomy errors,
The weeds of nations in their last decay,
When Vice walks forth with her unsoften'd terrors,
And Mirth is madness, and but smiles to slay;
And Hope is nothing but a false delay,
The sick man's lightning half an hour ere death,
When Faintness, the last mortal birth of Pain,
And apathy of limb, the dull beginning
Of the cold staggering race which Death is winning,
Steals vein by vein and pulse by pulse away:
Yet so relieving the o'er-tortured clay,
To him appears renewal of his breath,
And freedom the mere numbness of his chain;
And then he talks of life, and how again
He feels his spirit soaring—albeit weak,
And of the fresher air, which he would seek:
And as he whispers knows not that he gasps,
That his thin finger feels not what it clasps,
And so the film comes o'er him, and the dizzy
Chamber swims round and round, and shadows busy,
At which he vainly clutches, flit and gleam,

Ode on Venice

Till the last rattle chokes the strangled scream,
And all is ice and blackness,—and the earth
That which it was the moment ere our birth.

II

There is no hope for nations!—Search the page
  Of many thousand years—the daily scene,
The flow and ebb of each recurring age;
  The everlasting to be which hath been,
  Hath taught us nought, or little: still we lean
On things that rot beneath our weight, and wear
Our strength away in wrestling with the air:
For 'tis our nature strikes us down: the beasts
Slaughter'd in hourly hecatombs for feasts
Are of as high an order—they must go
Even where their driver goads them, though to slaughter.
Ye men, who pour your blood for kings as water,
What have they given your children in return?
A heritage of servitude and woes,
A blindfold bondage, where your hire is blows.
What! do not yet the red-hot plough-shares burn,
O'er which you stumble in a false ordeal,
And deem this proof of loyalty the real:
Kissing the hand that guides you to your scars,
And glorying as you tread the glowing bars?
All that your sires have left you, all that Time
Bequeaths of free, and History of sublime,
Spring from a different theme! Ye see and read,
Admire and sigh, and then succumb and bleed!
Save the few spirits who, despite of all,
And worse than all, the sudden crimes engender'd
By the down-thundering of the prison-wall,
And thirst to swallow the sweet waters tender'd,
Gushing from Freedom's fountains, when the crowd,

Madden'd with centuries of drought, are loud,
And trample on each other to obtain
The cup which brings oblivion of a chain
Heavy and sore, in which long yoked they plough'd
The sand,—or if there sprung the yellow grain,
'Twas not for them, their necks were too much bow'd,
And their dead palates chew'd the cud of pain:
Yes! the few spirits,—who, despite of deeds
Which they abhor, confound not with the cause
Those momentary starts from Nature's laws,
Which, like the pestilence and earthquake, smite
But for a term, then pass, and leave the earth
With all her seasons to repair the blight
With a few summers, and again put forth
Cities and generations—fair when free—
For, Tyranny! there blooms no bud for thee!

III

Glory and Empire! once upon these towers
 With Freedom—godlike Triad! how ye sate!
The league of mightiest nations, in those hours
 When Venice was an envy, might abate
 But did not quench her spirit; in her fate
All were enwrapp'd: the feasted monarchs knew
 And loved their hostess, nor could learn to hate,
Although they humbled—with the kingly few
The many felt, for from all days and climes
She was the voyager's worship; even her crimes
Were of the softer order—born of Love.
She drank no blood, nor fatten'd on the dead,
But gladden'd where her harmless conquests spread,
For these restored the Cross, that from above

Ode on Venice

Hallow'd her sheltering banners, which incessant
Flew between earth and the unholy Crescent,
Which, if it waned and dwindled, Earth may
   thank
The city it has clothed in chains, which clank
Now, creaking in the ears of those who owe
The name of Freedom to her glorious struggles;
Yet she but shares with them a common woe,
And call'd the 'kingdom' of a conquering foe,
But knows what all—and, most of all, *we*
   know—
With what set gilded terms a tyrant juggles!

IV

The name of Commonwealth is past and gone
   O'er the three fractions of the groaning globe;
Venice is crush'd, and Holland deigns to own
   A sceptre, and endures the purple robe;
If the free Switzer yet bestrides alone
His chainless mountains, 'tis but for a time;
For tyranny of late is cunning grown,
And in its own good season tramples down
The sparkles of our ashes. One great clime,
Whose vigorous offspring by dividing ocean
Are kept apart and nursed in the devotion
Of Freedom, which their fathers fought for, and
Bequeath'd—a heritage of heart and hand,
And proud distinction from each other land,
Whose sons must bow them at a monarch's
   motion,
As if his senseless sceptre were a wand
Full of the magic of exploded science—
Still one great clime, in full and free defiance,
Yet rears her crest, unconquer'd and sublime,

Above the far Atlantic!—She has taught
Her Esau-brethren that the haughty flag,
The floating fence of Albion's feebler crag,
May strike to those whose red right hands have bought
Rights cheaply earn'd with blood. Still, still for ever,
Better, though each man's life-blood were a river,
That it should flow, and overflow, than creep
Through thousand lazy channels in our veins,
Damm'd like the dull canal with locks and chains,
And moving, as a sick man in his sleep,
Three paces, and then faltering: better be
Where the extinguish'd Spartans still are free,
In their proud charnel of Thermopylae,
Than stagnate in our marsh,—or o'er the deep
Fly, and one current to the ocean add,
One spirit to the souls our fathers had,
One freeman more, America! to thee!

LORD BYRON.

VENICE

A FRAGMENT

'Tis midnight—but it is not dark
Within thy spacious place, Saint Mark!
The Lights within, the Lamps without,
Shine above the revel rout.
The brazen Steeds are glittering o'er
The holy building's massy door,
Glittering with their collars of gold,
The goodly work of the days of old—
And the wingèd Lion stern and solemn
Frowns from the height of his hoary column,
Facing the palace in which doth lodge
The ocean-city's dreaded Doge.
The palace is proud—but near it lies,
Divided by the 'Bridge of Sighs,'
The dreary dwelling where the State
Enchains the captives of their hate:
These—they perish or they pine;
But which their doom may none divine:
Many have pass'd that Arch of pain,
But none retraced their steps again.

It is a princely colonnade!
And wrought around a princely place,
When that vast edifice display'd
Looks with its venerable face
Over the far and subject sea,
Which makes the fearless isles so free!
And 'tis a strange and noble pile,
Pillar'd into many an isle:
Every pillar fair to see,
Marble—jasper—and porphyry—
The church of Saint Mark—which stands hard by

With fretted pinnacles on high,
And Cupola and minaret;
More like the mosque of orient lands,
Than the fanes wherein we pray,
And Mary's blessèd likeness stands.—

       Lord Byron.

VENICE

On rosy Venice' breast
The gondola's at rest;
No fisher is in sight,
   Not a light.

Lone seated on the strand,
Uplifts the lion grand
His foot of bronze on high
   Against the sky.

As if with resting wing
Like herons in a ring,
Vessels and shallops keep,
   Their quiet sleep,

Upon the vapoury bay;
And when the light winds play,
Their pennons, lately whist,
   Cross in the mist.

The moon is now concealed,
And now but half revealed,
Veiling her face so pale
   With starry veil.

In convent of Sainte-Croix
Thus doth the abbess draw
Her ample-folded cape
   Round her fair shape.

The palace of the knight,
The staircases so white,
The solemn porticos
   Are in repose.

Each bridge and thoroughfare,
The gloomy statues there,
The gulf which trembles so
   When the winds blow,

All still, save guards who pace,
With halberds long, their space,
Watching the battled walls
   Of arsenals.

o o o o o o o o o o o o

ALFRED DE MUSSET
(Translated by C. F. BATES).

VENICE BY DAY

The splendour of the Orient, here of old
   Throned with the West, upon a waveless sea,
   Her various-vested, resonant jubilee
Maintains, though Venice hath been bought and sold.
In their high stalls of azure and of gold
   Yet stand, above the servile concourse free,
   Those brazen steeds,—the Car of Victory
Hither from far Byzantium's porch that rolled.
The winged Lions, Time's dejected thralls,
   Glare with furled plumes. The pictured shapes that glow
Like sunset clouds condensed upon the walls,
   Still boast old wars, or feasts of long ago;
     And still the sun his amplest glory pours
     On all those swelling domes and watery floors.

                        Aubrey De Vere.

VENICE IN THE EVENING

"The shadows were falling to the eastward. The hush of night was stealing on the world. The cares of life seemed disappearing down the radiant west together with the God of Day. Between us and the setting sun there seemed to fall a shower of powdered gold. The entire city was pervaded by a golden light which yet was perfectly transparent, like the purest ether.

"As we drew nearer to the Grand Canal the scene grew even more enchanting. In the refulgent light the city lay before us like a beautiful mirage, enthroned upon a golden bank between two seas—the ocean and the sky. Her streets seemed filled with liquid sunshine. The steps of her patrician palaces appeared entangled in the meshes of a golden net. The neighboring islands looked like jeweled wreckage floating from a barge of gold. The whole effect was that of a poem without words, illustrated by Titian, and having for a soft accompaniment the ripple of the radiant waves.

"I have seen many impressive sights in many climes; but for triumphant beauty, crystallized in stone and glorified by the setting sun, I can recall no scene more matchless in its loveliness than that which I enjoyed, when, on this richly tinted sea, I watched the Bride and Sovereign of the Adriatic pass to the curtained chamber of the night enveloped in a veil of gold."

J. L. STODDARD.

Alas! mid all this pomp of the ancient time,
    And flush of modern pleasure, dull Decay
O'er the bright pageant breathes her shadowy gray.
As on from bridge to bridge I roam and climb,
It seems as though some wonder-working chime
    (Whose spell the vision raised and still can sway)
To some far source were ebbing fast away;
As though, by man unheard, with voice sublime
It bade the sea-born Queen of Cities follow
    Her sire into his watery realm far down—
Beneath my feet the courts sound vast and hollow;

And more than evening's darkness seems to frown
On sable barks that, swift yet trackless, fleet
Like dreams o'er dim lagune and watery street.
       AUBREY DE VERE.

LIDO

During the days when hordes of barbarians swept in fierce bands across mountain barriers into the sunny plains of Lombardy, the deluge led by Attila, scourge of God, poured into Italy. Refugees, seeking escape, came to the shores of the Adriatic.

The forms of nature at work here are the mountains, the rivers and the sea. The rivers and mountains made the plain, and the rivers and the sea made those large sheets of tidal waters that are separated from the Adriatic by a thin line of sandy dunes, known as the "Lido." The lagoon of Venice, whose surface covers some one hundred and sixty square miles, was once the estuary of three large rivers. Now the sand bank or "Lido," that keeps out the stormy waves of the Adriatic, is famous for its magnificent hotels and bathing beaches.

    I went to greet the full May-moon
    On that long narrow shoal
    Which lies between the still Lagoon
    And the open ocean's roll.

    How pleasant was that grassy shore,
    When one for months had been
    Shut up in streets,—to feel once more
    One's foot fall on the green!

    There are thick trees too in that place;
    But straight from sea to sea,
    Over a rough uncultured space,
    The path goes drearily.

    I passed along, with many a bound,
    To hail the fresh free wave;
    But, pausing, wonderingly found
    I was treading on a grave.

Then, at one careless look, I saw
That, for some distance round,
Tombstones, without design or law,
Were scattered on the ground.

Of Pirates or of mariners
I deemed that these might be
The fitly chosen sepulchres,
Encircled by the sea.

But there were words inscribed on all,
I' the tongue of a far land,
And marks of things symbolical,
I could not understand.

They are the graves of that sad race
Who from their Syrian home,
For ages, without resting-place,
Are doomed in woe to roam;

Who, in the days of sternest faith,
Glutted the sword and flame,
As if a taint of moral death
Were in their very name:

And even under laws most mild,
All shame was deemed their due,
And the nurse told the Christian child
To shun the cursèd Jew.

Thus all their gold's insidious grace
Availed not here to gain
For their last sleep a seemlier place
Than this bleak-featured plain.

Apart, severely separate,
On the verge of the outer sea,
Their home of death is desolate
As their life's home could be.

The common sand-path had defaced
And pressed down many a stone;
Others can be but faintly traced
I' the rank grass o'er them grown.

I thought of Shylock,—the fierce heart
Whose wrongs and injuries old
Temper, in Shakespeare's world of art,
His lusts of blood and gold;

Perchance that form of broken pride
Here at my feet once lay,—
But lay alone,—for at his side
There was no Jessica!

Fondly I love each island-shore,
Embraced by Adrian's waves;
But none has Memory cherished more
Than Lido and its grave.

LORD HOUGHTON.

TO VENICE

Venice still remains unique among the cities of the Old World. Defying the centuries, she is still victorious over the waves of time and the forces of nature that would engulf her. You may bow down to the majesty and power of Rome, and long remember the stern palaces and arcades of Florence, but the Sea-queen, Venice, builder of jeweled St. Mark's, touches a heart-string that responds to no other places of human habitation. To the lover of the beautiful in Nature it brings the spell of an enchantress.

Dishonour'd hast thou been, but not debased,
   O Venice! he hastes onward who will bring
The girdle that enclosed thy virgin waist,
   And will restore to thee thy bridal ring.

Venice! on earth are reptiles who lift high
   The crested head, both venomous and strong
Are they; and many by their fangs shall die,
   But one calm watcher crushes them ere long.

So fare whoever twists in tortuous ways,
   Strown with smooth promises and broken vows,
Who values drunken shouts, not sober praise,
   And spurns the scanty pittance Truth allows.

                          WALTER SAVAGE LANDOR.

THE VENETIAN GONDOLIER

What would Venice be without the gondola, and the old *gauzer* at every *tragetta*, or landing place, who with boat hook pulls the gondola into place close to the steps and holds it there until the occupants are seated for a ride on the canals.

There is romance in every line of the Venetian Gondola. In form it is the result of centuries of slow evolution, but the word gondola is supposed to mean *quick*. Now painted black, the decorations must have been gay and gorgeous prior to 1094 when the Senate found it necessary to check the rivalry in color.

Looking at the peculiarly shaped prow one wonders what the significance of this design might be. The weight of the ferrule balances the weight of the gondolier in the stern, but in form it is unique and belongs solely to Venice. Shaped something like an old Viking ship, the ferrule has six cross pieces to represent the six sections of the city and one going inward to represent the Lido. The top reminds one of the Doge's cap.

In days gone by the gondolier had many interesting cries, but today, "A-eol-a," "watch out" is about the only one the modern wayfarer is apt to hear during his sojourn in Venice.

Of course, modernity is pouring into all the cities of the Old World. Changes are certain. The old in Venice is disappearing but will the gondolier vanish? The *vaporettas* or motor boats are increasing in number. It may be that the next generation will not see Venice in all her romance and beauty, but many believe that the romance of this city will ever defy modernity and live on for future generations to enjoy. Let us pray that this be so.

Here rest the weary oar!—soft airs
   Breathe out in the o'erarching sky;
And Night—sweet Night—serenely wears
   A smile of peace: her noon is nigh.

Where the tall fir in quiet stands,
   And waves, embracing the chaste shores,
Move over sea-shells and bright sands,
   Is heard the sound of dipping oars.

The Venetian Gondolier

Swift o'er the wave the light bark springs,
   Love's midnight hour draws lingering near;
And list!—his tuneful viol strings
   The young Venetian Gondolier.

Lo! on the silver-mirrored deep,
   On earth, and her embosomed lakes,
And where the silent rivers sweep,
   From the thin cloud fair moonlight breaks.

Soft music breathes around, and dies
   On the calm bosom of the sea;
Whilst in her cell the novice sighs
   Her vespers to her rosary.

At their dim altars bow fair forms,
   In tender charity for those,
That, helpless left to life's rude storms,
   Have never found this calm repose.

The bell swings to its midnight chime,
   Relieved against the deep blue sky.
Haste!—dip the oar again—'tis time
   To seek Genevra's balcony.

              HENRY WADSWORTH LONGFELLOW.

VENICE

White swan of cities, slumbering in thy nest
    So wonderfully built among the reeds
    Of the lagoon, that fences thee and feeds,
As sayeth thy old historian and thy guest!
White water-lily, cradled and carressed
    By ocean streams, and from the silt and weeds
    Lifting thy golden filaments and seeds,
Thy sun-illumined spires, thy crown and crest!
White phantom city, whose untrodden streets
    Are rivers, and whose pavements are the shifting
    Shadows of palaces and strips of sky;
I wait to see thee vanish like the fleets
    Seen in mirage, or towers of cloud uplifting
    In air their unsubstantial masonry.

                    HENRY WADSWORTH LONGFELLOW.

MOURN NOT FOR VENICE

Mourn not for Venice—let her rest
  In ruin, 'mong those States unblest,
Beneath whose gilded hoofs of pride,
Where'er they trampled, Freedom died.
No—let us keep our tears for them,
  Where'er they pine, whose fall hath been
Not from a blood-stain'd diadem,
  Like that which deck'd this ocean-queen,
But from high daring in the cause
  Of human Rights—the only good
And blessed strife, in which man draws
  His mighty sword on land or flood.

Mourn not for Venice; though her fall
  Be awful, as if Ocean's wave
Swept o'er her, she deserves it all,
  And Justice triumphs o'er her grave.
Thus perish ev'ry King and State,
  That run the guilty race she ran,
Strong but in ill, and only great
  By outrage against God and man.

True, her high spirit is at rest
  And all those days of glory gone,
When the world's waters, east and west,
  Beneath her white-wing'd commerce shone;
When, with her countless barks she went
To meet the Orient Empire's might,
And her Giustinianis sent
  Their hundred heroes to that fight.

Vanish'd are all her pomps, 'tis true,
  But mourn them not—for vanish'd too,
(Thanks to that Pow'r, who, soon or late,

Hurls to the dust the guilty Great,)
Are all the outrage, falsehood, fraud,
  The chains, the rapine, and the blood,
That fill'd each spot, at home, abroad,
  Where the Republic's standard stood.
Desolate Venice! when I track
Thy haughty course through cent'ries back;
Thy ruthless pow'r, obey'd but curst—
  The stern machinery of thy State,
Which hatred would, like steam, have burst
  Had stronger fear not chill'd ev'n hate;—
Thy perfidy, still worse than aught
Thy own unblushing Sarpi taught;—
Thy friendship, which, o'er all beneath
Its shadow, rain'd down dews of death;—
Thy Oligarchy's Book of Gold,
  Closed against humble Virtue's name,
But open'd wide for slaves who sold
  Their native land to thee and shame;—
Thy all-pervading host of spies,
  Watching o'er ev'ry glance and breath,
Till men look'd in each other's eyes,
  To read their chance of life or death;—
Thy laws, that made a mart of blood,
  And legalized the assassin's knife;—
Thy sunless cells beneath the flood,
  And racks, and Leads, that burnt out life;—
When I review all this, and see
The doom that now hath fall'n on thee;
Thy nobles, tow'ring once so proud,
Themselves, beneath the yoke now bow'd,—
A yoke, by no one grace redeem'd,
Such as, of old, around thee beam'd,
But mean and base as e'er yet gall'd,
Earth's tyrants, when, themselves, enthrall'd,—

I feel the moral vengeance sweet,
And smiling o'er the wreck, repeat:
'Thus perish ev'ry King and State,
   That tread the steps which Venice trod,
Strong but in ill, and only great
   By outrage against man and God!'

THOMAS MOORE.

VENICE

"The rising moon shines upon pale palaces, dim and splendid, and breaks in silver arrows and broad white gleams upon the ripples of the canal, still,—yet alive with a hundred reflections, and a soft pulsation and twinkle of life. The lights glitter above and below—every star, every lamp doubled. Then comes the measured sweep of the oars, and you are away on the silent, splendid road, all darkling, yet alive. Not a sound less harmonious and musical than the soft splash of the water against the marble steps and grey walls, the waves' plash against your boat, the wild cry of the boatmen as they round each sharp corner, or the singing of some wandering boatful of musicians on the Grand Canal, disturbs the quiet. Across the flat Lido, from the Adriatic, comes a little breath of fresh wind; and when, out of a maze of narrow water-lanes, you shoot out into the breadth and glorious moonlight of the Grand Canal, and see the lagoon go widening out, a plane of dazzling silver, into the distance, and great churches and palaces standing up pale against the light, what words can describe the novel, beautiful scene! 'The poet alone can come nearest to the power to give expression to the emotions the traveller feels.'"

J. L. STODDARD.

I

Night on the Adriatic, night!
   And like a mirage of the plain,
With all her marvellous domes of light,
   Pale Venice looms along the main.

No sound from the receding shore,
   No sound from all the broad lagoon,
Save where the light and springing oar
   Brightens our track beneath the moon;

Or save where yon high campanile
   Gives to the listening sea its chime;
Or where those dusky giants wheel
   And smite the ringing helm of Time.

'Tis past,—and Venice droops to rest;
    Alas! hers is a sad repose,
While in her brain and on her breast
    Tramples the vision of her foes.

Erewhile from her sad dream of pain
    She rose upon her native flood,
And struggled with the Tyrant's chain,
    Till every link was stained with blood.

The Austrian pirate, wounded, spurned,
    Fled howling to the sheltering shore,
But, gathering all his crew, returned
    And bound the Ocean Queen once more.

'Tis past,—and Venice prostrate lies,—
    And, snarling round her couch of woes,
The watch-dogs, with the jealous eyes,
    Scowl where the stranger comes and goes.

II

Lo! here awhile suspend the oar;
    Rest in the Mocenigo's shade,
For Genius hath within this door
    His charmed, though transient, dwelling made.

Somewhat of "Harold's" spirit yet,
    Methinks, still lights these crumbling walls;
For where the flame of song is set
    It burns, though all the temple falls.

Oh, tell me not those days were given
    To Passion and her pampered brood;
Or that the eagle stoops from heaven
    To dye his talons deep in blood.

I hear alone his deathless strain
   From sacred inspiration won,
As I would only watch again
   The eagle when he nears the sun.

III

O, would some friend were near me now,
   Some friend well tried and cherished long,
To share the scene; but chiefly thou,
   Sole source and object of my song.

By Olivola's dome and tower,
   What joy to clasp thy hand in mine,
While through my heart this sacred hour
   Thy voice should melt like mellow wine.

What time or place so fit as this
   To bid the gondolier withhold,
And dream through one soft age of bliss
   The olden story, never old?

The domes suspended in the sky
   Swim all above me broad and fair;
And in the wave their shadows lie,—
   Twin phantoms of the sea and air.

O'er all the scene a halo plays,
   Slow fading, but how lovely yet;
For here the brightness of past days
   Still lingers, though the sun is set.

Oft in my bright and boyish hours
   I lived in dreams what now I live,
And saw these palaces and towers
   In all the light romance can give.

They rose along my native stream,
   They charmed the lakelet in the glen;
But in this hour the waking dream
   More frail and dreamlike seems than then.

A matchless scene, a matchless night,
   A tide below, a moon above;
An hour for music and delight,
   For gliding gondolas and love!

But here, alas! you hark in vain,—
   When Venice fell her music died;
And voiceless as a funeral train,
   The blackened barges swim the tide.

The harp which Tasso loved to wake,
   Hangs on the willow where it sleeps,
And while the light strings sigh or break
   Pale Venice by the water weeps.

IV

'Tis past, and weary droops the wing
   That thus hath borne me idly on;
The thoughts I have essayed to sing
   Are but as bubbles touched and gone.

But, Venice, cold his soul must be,
   Who, looking on thy beauty, hears
The story of thy wrongs, if he
   Is moved to neither song nor tears.

To glide by temples fair and proud,
   Between deserted marble walls,
Or see the hireling foeman crowd
   Rough-shod her noblest palace halls;

To know her left to vandal foes
   Until her nest be robbed and gone;
To see her bleeding breast, which shows
   How dies the Adriatic swan;

To know that all her wings are shorn,
   That Fate has written her decree,
That soon the nations here shall mourn
   The lone Palmyra of the sea,

Where waved her vassal flags of yore
   By valour in the Orient won;
To see the Austrian vulture soar,
   A blot against the morning sun;

To hear a rough and foreign speech
   Commanding the old ocean mart,—
Are mournful sights and sounds that reach,
   And wake to pity, all the heart.

THOMAS BUCHANAN READ.

FOR ONE OF GIAN BELLINI'S LITTLE ANGELS

Of the famous Venetian school of painting Giovanni Bellini is counted among its greatest masters. Ruskin claimed that "Giovanni Bellini is the only artist who appears to me to have united in equal and magnificent measures, justness of drawing, nobleness of coloring, and perfect manliness of treatment, with the purest religious feeling. He did, as far as it is possible to do it, instinctively and uneffectively, what the Caracci only pretended to do. Titian colors better but has not his piety. Leonardo draws better, but has not his color. Angelico is more heavenly, but has not his manliness, far less his powers of art." With such a painter it is no wonder that his angels should be happy and cheerful boys in the full, exuberant bloom of youth. Where he discovered that wonderful music of color which is found in no other school, we need not here attempt to answer. We do feel however, that in his "little angels" on the steps of the throne of the Madonna, with their singing, their lutes and violins, he has given us outward symbols of his deep musical feeling.

My task it is to stand beneath the throne,
   To stand and wait, while those grave presences,
Prophet and priest and saint and seraph, zone
   Our Lady with the Child upon her knees:
   They from mild lips receive the messages
Of peace and love, from whence to men below
They shower soft-falling like pure flakes of snow.

I meanwhile wait; and very mute must be
   My music, lest I break the golden trance
Of bliss celestial, or with childish glee
   Trouble the fount of divine utterance.
   Yet when those lips are tired of speech, perchance
It may be that the royal Babe will lie
And slumber to my whispered lullaby:

For One of Gian Bellini's Little Angels

Then all those mighty brows will rest, and peace
   Descend like dew on that high company.
Therefore I stand and wait, but do not cease
   To clasp my lute, that silver melody,
   When our dear Lady bends her smile on me,
Forth from my throat and from these thrilling strings
Dove-like may soar and spread ethereal wings.

JOHN ADDINGTON SYMONDS.

THE INVITATION TO THE GONDOLA

Come forth; for Night is falling,
   The moon hangs round and red
On the verge of the violet waters,
   Fronting the daylight dead.

Come forth; the liquid spaces
   Of sea and of sky are as one,
Where outspread angel flame-wings
   Brood o'er the buried sun.

Bells call to bells from the islands,
   And far-off mountains rear
Their shadowy crests in the crystal
   Of cloudless atmosphere.

A breeze from the sea is wafted;
   Lamp-litten Venice gleams
With her towers and domes uplifted
   Like a city seen in dreams.

Her water-ways are atremble
   With melody far and wide,
Borne from the phantom galleys
   That o'er the darkness glide.

There are stars in heaven, and starry
   Are the wandering lights below:
Come forth! for the Night is calling,
   Sea, city, and sky are aglow!

                JOHN ADDINGTON SYMONDS.

VENICE

Venice, thou Siren of sea-cities, wrought
   By mirage, built on water, stair o'er stair,
   Of sunbeams and cloud-shadows, phantom-fair,
With naught of earth to mar thy sea-born thought!
Thou floating film upon the wonder-fraught
   Ocean of dreams! Thou hast no dream so rare
   As are thy sons and daughters, they who wear
Foam-flakes of charm from thine enchantment caught!

O dark brown eyes! O tangles of dark hair!
   O heaven-blue eyes, blond tresses where the breeze
   Plays over sun-burned cheeks in sea-blown air!
Firm limbs of moulded bronze! frank debonair
   Smiles of deep-bosomed women! Loves that seize
Man's soul, and waft her on storm-melodies!

                              JOHN ADDINGTON SYMONDS.

IN A GONDOLA

Suggested by Mendelssohn's Andante in G Minor
Book 1, Lied 6, of the "Lieder ohne Worte"

I

In Venice! This night so delicious—its air
   Full of moonlight, and passionate snatches of song,
   And quick cries, and perfume of romances, which throng
To my brain, as I steal down this marble sea-stair,
        And my gondola comes:

   And I hear the slow, rhythmical weep of the oar
   Drawing near and more near—and the noise of the prow,
   And the sharp, sudden splash of her stoppage—and now
I step in; we are off o'er the street's heaving floor,
        As my gondola glides—
Away past these palaces silent and dark,
   Looming ghostly and grim o'er their bases, where clings
   Rank sea-weed which gleams, flecked with light, as it swings
To the plash of the waves, where they reach the tide-mark
On the porphyry blocks—with a song full of dole,
        A forlorn barcarole,
           As my gondola glides.

II

And the wind seems to sigh through that lattice
  rust-gnawn,
  A low dirge for the past: the sweet past when it
    played
  In the pearl-braided hair of some beauty, who
    stayed
But one shrinking half-minute—her mantle close-
  drawn
O'er the swell of her bosom and cheeks passion-
  pale,
  Ere her lover came by, and they kissed. 'They
    are clay,
  Those fire-hearted men with the regal pulse-play.'
'They are dust!' sighs the wind with its whisper of
  wail;
  'Those women snow-fair, flower-sweet, passion-
    pale!'
And the waves make reply with their song full of
  dole,
      Their forlorn barcarole,
      As my gondola glides.

III

Dust—those lovers! But love ever lives, ever new,
  Still the same: so we shoot into bustle and light,
  And lamps from the festal casinos stream bright
On the ripples; and here's the Rialto in view;
And black gondolas, spirit-like, cross or slide past,
  And the gondoliers cry to each other: a song
  Far away, from sweet voices in tune, dies along
The waters moon-silvered. So on to the vast

In a Gondola

Shadowy span of an arch where the oar-echoes leap
   Through chill gloom from the marble; then moonlight once more,
And laughter and strum of guitars from the shore,
And sonorous bass-music of bells booming deep
   From Saint Mark's. Still those waves with their song full of dole,
        Their forlorn barcarole,
        As my gondola glides.

IV

Here the night is voluptuous with odorous sighs
   From verandas o'erstarred with dim jessamine flowers,
   Their still scent deep-stirred by the tremulous showers
Of a nightingale's notes as his song swells and dies—
        While my gondola glides.

V

Dust—those lovers!—who floated and dreamed long ago,
   Gazed, and languished, and loved, on these waters—where I
Float and dream and gaze up in the still summer sky,
Whence the great stars look down—as they did long ago:
Where the moon seems to dream with my dreaming—disc-hid
   In a gossamer veil of white cirrus—then breaks
   The dream-spell with a pensive half-smile, as she wakes

To new splendour. But lo! while I mused we have slid
From the open, the stir, down a lonely lane-way,
  Into hush and dark shadow! fresh smells of the sea
  Come cool from beyond; a faint lamp mistily
Hints fair shafts and quaint arches, in crumbling decay;
  And the waves still break in with their song full of dole,
      Their forlorn barcarole,
      As my gondola glides.

VI

Then the silent lagune stretched away through the night,
  And the stars, and the fairy-like city behind,
  Domes and spires rising spectral and dim: till the mind
Becomes tranced in a vague, subtle maze of delight;
And I float in a dream, lose the present—or seem
  To have lived it before. Then a sense of deep bliss,
  Just to breathe—to exist—in a night such as this;
Just to feel what I feel, drowns all else. But the gleam
Of the lights, as we turn to the city once more,
  And the music, and clangor of bells booming slow,
  And this consummate vision—Saint Mark's! the star-glow
For a background—crowns all. Then I step out on shore.
  The Piazzetta! my life-dream accomplished at last,
      (As my gondola goes)

In a Gondola

I am here: here alone with the ghost of the past!
But the waves still break in with their song full of dole,
   Their forlorn barcarole,
    As my gondola goes;
And the pulse of the oar swept through silvery spray
Dies away in the gloom, dies away, dies away,—
   Dies away—dies away—!

JOHN TODHUNTER.

ON THE EXTINCTION OF THE VENETIAN REPUBLIC

"Let us lie back in our gondola to take one last look at Venice. We are going to leave the City of the Lagoons, perhaps never to return. As the waves rise and fall in the sunset glow, they seem to be of molten gold and the foam, lace of precious metal. As the sun sank lower and lower, as it had done day after day and century after century, it cast its halo as it were over a city whose captains and navies had departed but whose memory and influence are eternal. Over and above all that is selfish and cruel in the whole wonderful story there sinks into you now as the day wanes the marvel of the jewelled city, built on marshy islets, lifted from these muddy lagoons, raised in strength and beauty by iron hands and patient hearts to be one of the famous spots of the whole earth. Few cities have brought forth for our encouragement so many generations of stout-hearted citizens. Few cities have done their part in the world's work as manfully. Only two at most have left the world so brilliant a flowering of beauty. So for the good work and for beauty, for palaces and fishers' huts, for St. Mark and for the painters, for sun color and swift gondola, for all that is Venice, let the world give thanks."

LAVELL, *Italian Cities*

Once did She hold the gorgeous east in fee;
And was the safeguard of the west: the worth
Of Venice did not fall below her birth,
Venice, the eldest Child of Liberty.

She was a maiden City, bright and free;
No guile seduced, no force could violate;
And, when she took unto herself a Mate,
She must espouse the everlasting Sea.

And what if she had seen those glories fade,
Those titles vanish, and that strength decay;
Yet shall some tribute of regret be paid

On the Extinction of the Venetian Republic

When her long life hath reached its final day:
Men are we, and must grieve when even the Shade
Of that which once was great, is passed away.
                              WILLIAM WORDSWORTH.

ITALY
PART VII
PISA

PISA

Strange indeed has been the destiny of this city, once Genoa's Tuscan rival. "Pitiless Pisa" was her name while trade and maritime greatness gave her power; but now, humbled and humiliated, she must look to her past for consolation, and to that once famous square where the Duomo, the Leaning Tower, the Baptistry and Campo Santo recall her place in vitalizing Italian art.

Pisa will always be known as the teacher of Florence, that sister city far up the Valley of the Arno; the place of Florence in the world of art is due, to a great extent, to Niccola and to his son, Giovanni. These two artists lived and worked in Pisa while she was approaching her fateful defeat at Meloria.

For her contributions to humanity, Pisa would be forgotten; but Pisa, silent and grass-grown though her streets may be, will always be remembered as the one that passed on to Florence the torch of her artistic strength and inspiration.

On the Lung' Arno, in each stately street,
   The silence is a hunger and craves food
   Like Ugolino cowering o'er his brood.
Sad Pisa! in thy garments obsolete
Still grand, the sceptre fallen at thy feet,
   An impuissant queen of solitude,
   Thine inconsolable gaze speaks widowhood
Fixed on the river, voiceless and deplete.
A trance more lovely—lo! not many rods
   From the shrunk Arno, a more slumbrous air,
   A dream of heaven in marble rich and rare!
Oppressed with sleep the Campanile nods;
   But in the Campo Santo's hush of breath,
   Orcagna's pathos paints, not Sleep but Death!

                                WILLIAM GIBSON.

EVENING: PONTE A MARE, PISA

Pisa, once the rival of Florence and Genoa, is today so quiet and sleepy that it seems almost moribund. Few travelers have time for more than a passing visit to the old open square with its four famous buildings. These now seem to cluster into a corner of her ancient walls, as if seeking protection from the slow decay of time and from the dangers that her people have so often experienced from foes beyond the Alps.

For Shelley, Pisa became "a little nest of singing birds." In his great yellow house on the Lung' Arno Galileo, he abandoned himself to his poetic mood when the news of Keats' death in Rome brought sadness to his little group of friends. Byron lived across the Arno, that famous stream on which both Pisa and Florence stand.

For the traveler of today an evening walk about the dreamy city, and a pleasant hour of lingering on the old bridge across the river, may seem a loss of time. A casual hurried glimpse at the Cathedral, Baptistry, Campo Santo, and leaning Tower enables the modern traveler to check these off the list of "places I have seen" and that suffices. But if you would get the true spell of the city, stay and dream awhile of the past. Listen to the great bells of the Campanile ring out a benediction over a city whose history has been written, and watch the Tower as it inclines its fairy form as though weary of the burden of a glory long departed.

I

The sun is set; the swallows are asleep;
    The bats are flitting fast in the gray air;
The slow soft toads out of damp corners creep,
    And evening's breath, wandering here and there
Over the quivering surface of the stream,
Wakes not one ripple from its summer dream.

II

There is no dew on the dry grass to-night,
    Nor damp within the shadow of the trees;
The wind is intermitting, dry, and light;
    And in the inconstant motion of the breeze
The dust and straws are driven up and down,
And whirled about the pavement of the town.

III

Within the surface of the fleeting river
   The wrinkled image of the city lay,
Immovably unquiet, and for ever
   It trembles, but it never fades away;
Go to the . . .
You, being changed, will find it then as now.

IV

The chasm in which the sun has sunk is shut
   By darkest barriers of cinereous cloud,
Like mountain over mountain huddled—but
   Growing and moving upwards in a crowd,
And over it a space of watery blue,
Which the keen evening star is shining thro'.

                           PERCY BYSSHE SHELLEY.

ITALY
PART VIII
FLORENCE

ANDREA DEL SARTO
(Called "The Faultless Painter")

The traveler visiting the Pitti Palace in Florence, with its incomparable art treasures, may well allow the following poem by Robert Browning to serve as a "translation into song" of the picture called "Andrea del Sarto and his Wife." The poet has given us a re-creation of the Andrea described by Vasari.

His wonderful craftsmanship had won for the artist the name of Andrea *senza errori*, (the faultless painter). He might have competed with Raphael or Michael Angelo, had he not been ruined as an artist and as a man by his beautiful, but soulless wife, Lucrezia del Fede. Led and lured on by this beautiful woman, he outraged his conscience, lowered his ideals, and, losing heart and hope, fell into a melancholy repetition of a single type—his wife's.

Michael Angelo once said to Raphael: "There is a little man in Florence who, were he ever employed on such great works as these, would bring out the sweat upon your brow."

Before the traveler leaves the Palace it would be worth his while to walk out on the balcony that overlooks the Arno and the house where the Brownings once lived, and read this poem. Could one find a truer picture of the great painter's failure in life and the woman who brought about his downfall?

Julia Cartwright tells us that one day in the winter of 1570, when the artist Jacopo da Empoli was copying Andrea del Sarto's "Birth of the Virgin" in the Court of the Annunciata, an old woman of eighty stopped to speak to him on her way to mass, and, pointing to the figure of the handsome young matron in the picture, told him that this was her portrait and that she herself was Lucrezia del Fede, the widow of the artist who painted the fresco. She had vexed him in his lifetime, and abandoned him on his death-bed, but it was still her greatest pride to remember that she had been the wife of the famous master—"Andrea senza errori."

But do not let us quarrel any more,
No, my Lucrezia; bear with me for once:
Sit down and all shall happen as you wish.
You turn your face, but does it bring your heart?

I'll work then for your friend's friend, never fear,
Treat his own subject after his own way,
Fix his own time, accept too his own price,
And shut the money into this small hand
When next it takes mine. Will it? tenderly?
Oh, I'll content him,—but to-morrow, Love!
I often am much wearier than you think,
This evening more than usual, and it seems
As if—forgive now—should you let me sit
Here by the window with your hand in mine
And look a half-hour forth on Fiesole,
Both of one mind, as married people use
Quietly, quietly the evening through,
I might get up to-morrow to my work
Cheerful and fresh as ever. Let us try.
To-morrow how you shall be glad for this!
Your soft hand is a woman of itself,
And mine the man's bared breast she curls inside.
Don't count the time lost, neither; you must serve
For each of the five pictures we require:
It saves a model. So! keep looking so—
My serpentining beauty, rounds on rounds!
—How could you ever prick those perfect ears,
Even to put the pearl there! oh, so sweet—
My face, my moon, my everybody's moon,
Which everybody looks on and calls his,
And, I suppose, is looked on by in turn,
While she looks—no one's: very dear, no less.
You smile? why, there's my picture ready made,
There's what we painters call our harmony!
A common grayness silvers everything,—
All in a twilight, you and I alike
—You, at the point of your first pride in me
(That's gone, you know),—but I, at every point;

My youth, my hope, my art, being all toned down
To yonder sober pleasant Fiesole.
There's the bell clinking from the chapel-top;
That length of convent-wall across the way
Holds the trees safer, huddled more inside;
The last monk leaves the garden; days decrease,
And autumn grows, autumn in everything.
Eh? the whole seems to fall into a shape
As if I saw alike my work and self
And all that I was born to be and do,
A twilight-piece. Love, we are in God's hand.
How strange now looks the life he makes us lead;
So free we seem, so fettered fast we are!
I feel he laid the fetter: let it lie!
This chamber for example—turn your head—
All that's behind us! You don't understand
Nor care to understand about my art,
But you can hear at least when people speak:
And that cartoon, the second from the door
—It is the thing, Love! so such thing should be,—
Behold Madonna!—I am bold to say.
I can do with my pencil what I know,
What I see, what at bottom of my heart
I wish for, if I ever wish so deep—
Do easily, too—when I say, perfectly,
I do not boast, perhaps: yourself are judge,
Who listened to the Legate's talk last week,
And just as much they used to say in France
At any rate 'tis easy, all of it!
No sketches first, no studies, that's long past:
I do what many dream of all their lives,
—Dream? strive to do, and agonize to do,
And fail in doing. I could count twenty such

On twice your fingers, and not leave this town,
Who strive—you don't know how the others
   strive
To paint a little thing like that you smeared
Carelessly passing with your robes afloat,—
Yet do much less, so much less, Someone says,
(I know his name, no matter)—so much less!
Well, less is more, Lucrezia: I am judged.
There burns a truer light of God in them,
In their vexed beating stuffed and stopped-up
   brain,
Heart, or whate'er else, than goes on to prompt
This low-pulsed forthright craftsman's hand of
   mine.
Their works drop groundward, but themselves,
   I know,
Reach many a time a heaven that's shut to me,
Enter and take their place there sure enough,
Though they come back and cannot tell the
   world.
My works are nearer heaven, but I sit here.
The sudden blood of these men! at a word—
Praise them, it boils, or blame them, it boils too.
I, painting from myself and to myself,
Know what I do, am unmoved by men's blame
Or their praise either. Somebody remarks
Morello's outline there is wrongly traced,
His hue mistaken; what of that? or else,
Rightly traced, and well ordered; what of that?
Speak as they please, what does the mountain
   care?
Ah, but a man's reach should exceed his grasp,
Or what's a heaven for? All is silver-gray
Placid and perfect with my art: the worse!
I know both what I want and what might gain,

Andrea del Sarto

And yet how profitless to know, to sigh
"Had I been two, another and myself,
Our head would have o'erlooked the world!"
No doubt.
Yonder's a work now, of that famous youth
The Urbinate who died five years ago.
('Tis copied, George Vasari sent it me.)
Well, I can fancy how he did it all,
Pouring his soul, with kings and popes to see,
Reaching, that heaven might so replenish him,
Above and through his art—for it gives away;
That arm is wrongly put—and there again—
A fault to pardon in the drawing's lines,
Its body, so to speak: its soul is right,
He means right—that, a child may understand.
Still, what an arm! and I could alter it:
But all the play, the insight and the stretch—
Out of me, out of me! And wherefore out?
Had you enjoined them on me, given me soul,
We might have risen to Rafael, I and you!
Nay, Love, you did give all I asked, I think—
More than I merit, yes, by many times.
But had you—oh, with the same perfect brow,
And perfect eyes, and more than perfect mouth,
And the low voice my soul hears, as a bird
The fowler's pipe, and follows to the snare—
Had you, with these the same, but brought a mind!
Some women do so. Had the mouth there urged
"God and the glory! never care for gain.
The present by the future, what is that?
Live for fame, side by side with Agnolo!
Rafael is waiting: up to God, all three!"
I might have done it for you. So it seems:
Perhaps not. All is as God over-rules.

Andrea del Sarto

Beside, incentives come from the soul's self;
The rest avail not. Why do I need you?
What wife had Rafael, or has Agnolo?
In this world who can do a thing, will not;
And who would do it, cannot, I perceive:
Yet the will's somewhat—somewhat, too, the
    power—
And thus we half-men struggle. At the end,
God, I conclude, compensates, punishes.
'Tis safer for me, if the award be strict,
That I am something underrated here,
Poor this long while, despised, to speak the truth.
I dared not, do you know, leave home all day,
For fear of chancing on the Paris lords.
The best is when they pass and look aside;
But they speak sometimes; I must bear it all.
Well may they speak! That Francis, that first
    time,
And that long festal year at Fontainebleau!
I surely then could sometimes leave the gound,
Put on the glory, Rafael's daily wear,
In that humane great monarch's golden look,—
One finger in his beard or twisted curl
Over his mouth's good mark that made the
    smile,
One arm about my shoulder, round my neck,
The jingle of his gold chain in my ear,
I painting proudly with his breath on me,
All his court round him, seeing with his eyes,
Such frank French eyes, and such a fire of souls
Profuse, my hand kept plying by those hearts,—
And, best of all, this, this, this face beyond,
This in the background, waiting on my work,
To crown the issue with a last reward!
A good time, was it not, my kingly days?

Andrea del Sarto

And had you not grown restless . . . but I
  know—
'Tis done and past; 'twas right, my instinct said;
Too live the life grew, golden and not gray,
And I'm the weak-eyed bat no sun should tempt
Out of the grange whose four walls make his
  world.
How could it end in any other way?
You called me, and I came home to your heart.
The triumph was—to reach and stay there; since
I reached it ere the triumph, what is lost?
Let my hands frame your face in your hair's gold,
You beautiful Lucrezia that are mine!
"Rafael did this, Andrea painted that;
The Roman's is the better when you pray,
But still the other's Virgin was his wife."
Men will excuse me. I am glad to judge
Both pictures in your presence; clearer grows
My better fortune, I resolve to think.
For, do you know, Lucrezia, as God lives,
Said one day Angolo, his very self,
To Rafael . . . I have known it all these
  years . . .
(When the young man was flaming out his
  thoughts
Upon a palace-wall for Rome to see,
Too lifted up in heart because of it)
"Friend, there's a certain sorry little scrub
Goes up and down our Florence, none cares how,
Who, were he set to plan and execute
As you are, pricked on by your popes and kings,
Would bring the sweat into that brow of yours!"
To Rafael's!—and indeed the arm is wrong.
I hardly dare . . . yet, only you to see,

Give the chalk here—quick, thus the line should go!
Ay, but the soul! he's Rafael! rub it out!
Still, all I care for, if he spoke the truth,
(What he? why, who but Michel Agnolo?
Do you forget already words like those?)
If really there was such a chance, so lost,—
Is, whether you're—not grateful—but more pleased.
Well, let me think so. And you smile indeed!
This hour has been an hour! Another smile?
If you would sit thus by me every night
I should work better, do you comprehend?
I mean that I should earn more, give you more.
See, it is settled dusk now; there's a star;
Morello's gone, the watch-lights show the wall,
The cue-owls speak the name we call them by.
Come from the window, Love,—come in, at last,
Inside the melancholy little house
We built to be so gay with. God is just.
King Francis may forgive me: oft at nights
When I look up from painting, eyes tired out,
The walls become illumined, brick from brick
Distinct, instead of mortar, fierce bright gold,
That gold of his I did cement them with!
Let us but love each other. Must you go?
That Cousin here again? he waits outside?
Must see you—you, and not with me? Those loans?
More gaming debts to pay? you smiled for that?
Well, let smiles buy me! have you more to spend?
While hand and eye and something of heart
Are left me, work's my ware, and what's it worth?

Andrea del Sarto

I'll pay my fancy. Only let me sit
The gray remainder of the evening out,
Idle, you call it, and muse perfectly
How I could paint, were I but back in France,
One picture, just one more—the Virgin's face,
Not yours this time! I want you at my side
To hear them—that is, Michel Agnolo—
Judge all I do, and tell you of its worth.
Will you? To-morrow, satisfy your friend.
I take the subjects for his corridor,
Finish the portrait out of hand—there, there,
And throw him in another thing or two
If he demurs; the whole should prove enough
To pay for this same Cousin's freak. Beside,
What's better and what's all I care about,
Get you the thirteen scudi for the ruff!
Love, does that please you? Ah, but what does he,
The Cousin! what does he to please you more?

I am grown peaceful as old age to-night.
I regret little, I would change still less.
Since there my past life lies, why alter it?
The very wrong to Francis!—it is true
I took his coin, was tempted and complied,
And built this house and sinned, and all is said.
My father and my mother died of want.
Well, had I riches of my own? you see
How one gets rich! Let each one bear his lot.
They were born poor, lived poor, and poor they
    died;
And I have laboured somewhat in my time
And not been paid profusely. Some good son
Paint my two hundred pictures—let him try!
No doubt, there's something strikes a balance.
    Yes,

You loved me quite enough, it seems to-night.
This must suffice me here. What would one have?
In heaven, perhaps, new chances, one more chance—
Four great walls in the New Jerusalem,
Meted on each side by the angel's reed,
For Leonard, Rafael, Agnolo and me
To cover—the three first without a wife,
While I have mine! So—still they overcome
Because there's still Lucrezia,—as I choose.

    Again the Cousin's whistle! Go, my Love.

ROBERT BROWNING.

APPROACH TO FLORENCE

From *Childe Harold's Pilgrimage*

Only by walking around the hills about Florence do we get a true idea of the infinite variety of the hill-lands to be found in Tuscany. Covered with olive trees and vines, with here and there a patch of wheat, these hills are cultivated like gardens. To the visitor, the city has a setting like the landscapes in a Leonardo or a Raphael—the horizon is so often bounded by a line of dark trees relieved against a sky of blue.

No matter from what direction you may gaze upon this "City of the Miracle," it is always impressive. The great dome of Brunelleschi, the Palazzo Vecchio, Santa Croce, the Badia, Santa Maria Novella, the cupola of Michael Angelo's tombs for the Medici and Giotto's heaven-ascending campanile, rise in triumphant acclaim above the lesser buildings of the old city.

But Arno wins us to the fair white walls,
Where the Etrurian Athens claims and keeps
A softer feeling for her fairy halls.
Girt by her theatre of hills, she reaps
Her corn and wine and oil, and Plenty leaps
To laughing life, with her redundant horn.
Along the banks where smiling Arno sweeps
Was modern luxury of commerce born,
And buried learning rose, redeemed to a new morn.

LORD BYRON.

SANTA CROCE

From *Childe Harold's Pilgrimage*

Towards the end of "The Thirteenth, Greatest of Centuries," a small shrine stood where now we see the Westminster Abbey of Italy, the great Franciscan Church of Santa Croce. The first stone of the new church was laid on Holy Cross Day and so, the proud citizens called the church Santa Croce. Some of the glory that once hung about it still lingers, for here Michael Angelo, Machiavelli, Leonardo, Mazzini, and Galileo are buried and Dante's empty tomb might well have held the ashes of Florence's greatest son had not death in exile been his lot. His marble statue, in the famous square before the Church, gazes towards Ravenna that welcomed him when exiled from his native city.

> "From Heaven his spirit came, and robed in clay
> The realms of justice and of mercy trod:
> Then rose a living man to gaze on God,
> That he might make the truth as clear as day
> For that pure star, that brightened with its ray
> The undeserving nest where I was born,
> The whole wide world would be a prize to scorn;
> None but his Maker can due guerdon pay.
> I speak of Dante, whose high work remains
> Unknown, unhonored by that thankless brood,
> Who only to just men deny their wage.
> Were I but he! Born for like lingering pains,
> Against his exile coupled with his good
> I'd gladly change the world's best heritage."

In Santa Croce's holy precincts lie
Ashes which make it holier, dust which is
Even in itself an immortality,
Though there were nothing save the past, and this
The particle of those sublimities
Which have relapsed to chaos;—here repose
Angelo's, Alfieri's bones, and his,

The starry Galileo's, with his woes;
Here Machiavelli's earth returned to whence it rose.

These are four minds, which, like the elements,
Might furnish forth creation;—Italy!
Time, which hath wronged thee with a thousand rents
Of thine imperial garment, shall deny
And hath denied, to every other sky,
Spirits which soar from ruin: thy decay
Is still impregnate with divinity,
Which gilds it with revivifying ray;
Such as the great of yore, Canova is to-day.

But where repose the all-Etruscan three,—
Dante, and Petrarch, and, scarce less than they,
The Bard of Prose, creative spirit! he
Of the Hundred Tales of love,—where did they lay
Their bones, distinguished from our common clay
In death as life? Are they resolved to dust,
And have their country's marbles naught to say?
Could not her quarries furnish forth one bust?
Did they not to her breast their filial earth intrust?

Ungrateful Florence! Dante sleeps afar,
Like Scipio, buried by the upbraiding shore;
Thy factions, in their worse than civil war,
Proscribed the bard whose name forevermore
Their children's children would in vain adore
With the remorse of ages; and the crown
Which Petrarch's laureate brow supremely wore,
Upon a far and foreign soil had grown,
His life, his fame, his grave, though rifled,—not thine own.

Boccaccio to his parent earth bequeathed
His dust,—and lies it not her Great among,
With many a sweet and solemn requiem breathed
O'er him who formed the Tuscan's siren
    tongue,—
That music in itself, whose sounds are song,
The poetry of speech? No; even his tomb
Uptorn, must bear the hyena bigots wrong,
No more amongst the meaner dead find room,
Nor claim a passing sigh, because it told for whom.

And Santa Croce wants their mighty dust;
Yet for this want more noted, as of yore
The Caesar's pageant, shorn of Brutus' bust,
Did but of Rome's best son remind her more.
Happier Ravenna! on thy holy shore,
Fortress of falling empire, honoured sleeps
The immortal exile;—Arqua, too, her store
Of tuneful relics proudly keeps,
While Florence vainly begs her banished dead, and
    weeps.

                                          LORD BYRON.

SANTA MARIA DEL FIORE

Let us stand for a moment and gaze in admiration at one of the world's great buildings, the Duomo of Florence. Built from the designs of Arnolfo with Brunelleschi's dome, grandest of all earthly architectural creations, it stands on the site of the old church of S. Salvatore and S. Reparata. Perhaps it does not have the strange appeal of an English cathedral, or the romantic interest and mysticism of Notre Dame, but it is, nevertheless, more human than the great Gothic churches of the North. Unlike Santa Croce, few frescoes or works of art grace its interior, but it is a church where man may find religious inspiration and feel the presence of God in its shadowy spaces.

Summits and vales, slim cypresses and pines—
Arno and April and the Apennines!

And Giotto's captive dream (what dream has ending?)
Lifting his Florence up to God for friending.

Her dream enfolded his. She willed and waited,
Conceived her popes and princes, and created.

Mother and Muse was she of mighty singers;
Grave Dante drank her breast; the beauty-bringers

In cell and cloister felt her mood and fashioned
Mystic Madonnas palely unimpassioned,

With cherubean Babes and saints immortal,
High men and humble kneeling at the portal.

She was the pale Madonna, hers the story
Of pilgrim lords at pause before her glory.

And for the Babe she showed them Beauty solely
The while they worshipped: "Holy, O Thou holy!"

Fear was her fault, too cold a doubt of duty,
Of brows that burned, of hearts that beat, for Beauty.

So Florence fell. Yet strangely sweet and vernal
Beauty is born again in her eternal!

Summits and vales, slim cypresses and pines—
Arno and April and the Apennines!

GEORGE HERBERT CLARKE.

GIOTTO'S CAMPANILE

    Like the lily in an Annunciation by Fra Lippi stands Giotto's Campanile beside the cathedral of Santa Maria del Fiore in Florence. Its four stories, rising from the pavement of the piazza in their jeweled beauty, marked the close of the great artist's life and the achievements of his genius which combined "skill of hand and tenderness of heart." Of all living Christian works there is none so perfect as this Shepherd's Tower. Under the gleam and shadow of its marbles, the morning light is haunted by the ghost of Giotto who died too soon to see the realization of his fairest dream. Dante sat on a nearby stone to watch the workmen carve its precious reliefs. Andrea Pisano, Donatello, Taddeo Gaddi and Francesco Talenti here planned and carved for future generations to wonder and admire. Charles V., entering the city after besieging it, declared that the Campanile "ought to have a case made for it, so that it might be shown as one would a jewel."

Enchased with precious marbles, pure and rare,
    How graciously it soars, and seems the while
    From every polished stage to laugh and smile,
Playing with sportive gleams of lucid air!
Fit resting-place methinks its summit were
    For a descended angel! happy isle,
    Mid life's rough sea of sorrow, force, and guile,
For saint of royal race, or vestal fair,
In this seclusion,—call it not a prison,—
    Cloistering a bosom innocent and lonely.
      O Tuscan Priestess! gladly would I watch
      All night one note of thy loud hymn to catch
Sent forth to greet the sun, when first, new-risen,
    He shines on that aerial station only!

                              Aubrey De Vere.

IN FLORENCE

O Tuscan days, my true, gold-hearted days,
With thy deep skies and fleecy clouds afloat,
Like the dropped petals of some moon-pale flower;

With thy still sunset, zephyr-stirrèd hour,
Thy evening bird with thrilled melodious throat . . .
Gone, gone from me, my golden Tuscan day.

Once wert thou with me in fair Florence, crown
Of all that perfect, flower-filled Italy.
Thy name, O Florence, like a song doth fill

With memories the gray unblossoming still
That girts me round and holds me fast from thee—
From thee, O peaceful, perfect Tuscan town.

Thy lang'rous hush at even-tide just stirred
By some faint convent chime from very far,
Thy murmurous Arno speeding on its way,

And in the East a shadow wan and gray,
Kindled to brightness by a single star,
And somewhere in the West a singing bird.

All mem'ries. And the window whence my eyes
Saw Ponte Vecchio with its old-time mien,
Like some rich gem set deep in thy gold heart;

And faint Fiesole, where pale clouds start,
Dusted with leafy olive-trees, gray-green,
That fade off in the shadow-girted skies.

O Florence, my fair Florence, I would stray
Once more to-day, as in that dear dead time,
Along thy streets at golden mid-noon's hour,

In Florence

Till thy old Duomo and thy slender tower
Rose up before me with its mid-noon chime,
And haply step therein. All twilight gray,

With a faint trail of incense on the air,
And the low murmured hidden monotone
Of priests at holy mass. So, entered in,

How still it seemed after the city's din,
How solemn sweet the organ's vibrant tone.
I did not pray. The silence was a prayer.

Then out again into the rain of gold
Flooding the broad gay piazza everywhere . . .
A flutter of white wings, a flock of birds

Let loose, like some sweet tumult of love words,
Floating and sweeping through the sun-cleft air,
To peck the golden grain some hands would hold.

In those Spring days (Spring comes with tend'rer
    look,
And far more lavish hands to that sweet place,
My little Tuscan town, than to this clime,

Cold England and its fogs) I used to climb
Thy Colli, Florence—climbing, reach the place
Where thy sweet face lies stretched out like a book;

Lies stretched out like a soft smile, caught and
    kept
From the Past's fast-sealed lips, or like a flower
Yielding its petals up to the blue sky.

And when I strayed back to the city,
Found all things flooded with the sunset hour
Save Ponte Vecchio, where the shadows crept.

Elsewhere at night—the amorous Tuscan night,
When the white moon had climbed the silver stair
The fair stars make for their most lowly Queen—

How sweet from out the casement far to lean,
And feel the fragrance of the dewy air,
And see the whole world bathed in silver light!

Warm Tuscan sun! in that last dreaming lull
'Twixt night and day, along the Western ways
Thy tender light hath set from me fore'er:

Set, with my first lost love, lost dream, lost prayer . . . .
O Tuscan days! my true, gold-hearted days,
Thy lips are dumb, and mine are sorrowful.

Thy earth beneath my feet is cold and brown,
The skies are netted in a blank, gray shroud,
The mournful rain is dripping from the eaves. . . .

Lost—like a flower too deep-sunk in the leaves;
Lost—like a white star hidden by a cloud,
I see thee now, O little Tuscan town!

CORA FABBRI.

GIOTTO'S TOWER

How many lives, made beautiful and sweet
   By self-devotion and by self-restraint,
   Whose pleasure is to run without complaint
   On unknown errands of the Paraclete,
Wanting the reverence of unshodden feet,
   Fail of the nimbus which the artists paint
   Around the shining forehead of the saint,
   And are in their completeness incomplete!
In the old Tuscan town stands Giotto's tower,
   The lily of Florence blossoming in stone,—
   A vision, a delight, and a desire,—
The builder's perfect and centennial flower,
   That in the night of ages bloomed alone,
   But wanting still the glory of the spire.
              HENRY WADSWORTH LONGFELLOW.

IL PONTE VECCHIO DI FIRENZE

Gaddi mi fece; il Ponte Vecchio sono;
   Cinquecent' anni già sull' Arno pianto
   Il piede, come il suo Michele Santo
   Piantò sul draco. Mentre ch' io ragiono
Lo vedo torcere con flebil suono
   Le rilucenti scaglie. Ha questi affranto
   Due volte i miei maggior. Me solo intanto
   Neppure muove, ed io non l' abbandono.
Io mi rammento quando fur cacciati
   I Medici; pur quando Ghibellino
   E Guelfo fecer pace mi rammento.
Fiorenza i suoi giojelli m' ha prestati;
   E quando penso ch' Agnolo il divino
   Su me posava insuperbir mi sento.
                            HENRY WADSWORTH LONGFELLOW.

THE OLD BRIDGE AT FLORENCE

Who does not know the old bridge at Florence! Tourists on their way to the jewelry stores on the south side of the Arno stop to look into the quaint shops that line its roadway. A few linger for a moment at the open central span where the bronze bust of Benvenuto Cellini has watched so many amble by.

Along the second story of this old bridge runs a covered passageway connecting the Pitti Palace with the Palazzo Vecchio. Vasari, that garrulous historian of painters, built it for Cosimo I so that he might pass without interruption from the Palace to the Palazzo. Today, along this corridor which now connects the Uffizi and the Pitti, one sees hundreds of portraits of famous Florentines. This long passageway could tell many a story of the trysts of the Cardinal, the son of Cosimo I and Violante Martelli. At one time the historic gallery was threatened with destruction, but Victor Emmanuel's emphatic veto saved the romantic old bridge.

Who does not recall George Eliot's *Romola* and the description of Tito's last efforts to escape the destiny awaiting him, as he was dragged along the Ponte Vecchio by the mob?

"Yes,—they were at the arches. In that moment Tito, with bloodless face and eyes dilated, had one of the self-preserving inspirations that come in extremity. With a sudden desperate effort he mastered the clasp of his belt, and flung belt and scarsella forward towards a yard of clear space against the parapet, crying in a ringing voice, 'There are the diamonds! there is gold!'

"In the instant the hold on him was relaxed and there was a rush towards the scarsella. He threw himself on the parapet with a desperate leap, and the next moment plunged, —plunged with a great splash into the dark river far below."

Taddeo Gaddi built me. I am old,
   Five centuries old. I plant my foot of stone
   Upon the Arno, as St Michael's own
Was planted on the dragon. Fold by fold

Beneath me as it struggles, I behold
 Its glistening scales. Twice hath it overthrown
 My kindred and companions. Me alone
It moveth not, but is by me controlled.

I can remember when the Medici
 Were driven from Florence; longer still ago
 The final wars of Ghibelline and Guelf.
Florence adorns me with her jewelry;
 And when I think that Michel Angelo
 Hath leaned on me, I glory in myself.

HENRY WADSWORTH LONGFELLOW.

MASACCIO
IN THE BRANCACCI CHAPEL

Across the Arno from where the usual Florentine visitor finds his hotel, is the Church and Monastery of Sta. Maria della Carmine, built for the Carmelite friars in 1475. Some three hundred years later the building was destroyed by fire. Disastrous as this conflagration was, the celebrated Brancacci Chapel in the southern transept was only partially injured. Here the paintings by Masaccio and Filippino Lippi inaugurated a new period in art. Raphael came here and copied these pictures seven times. On the pilasters the story of Adam and Eve, under the Tree of Knowledge and the Expulsion from Paradise, offer a fitting introduction to the scenes depicted in the twelve compartments into which the frescoes of the chapel are divided.

St. Peter heals Tabitha, and cures a cripple at the Temple's Gate. In the scene of his preaching and baptism, the youth, who has thrown off his garment and stands shivering with cold, forms an epoch in art. "As a revelation of feeling it is supremely expressive."

Masaccio, the youthful painter who had such a profound influence upon the painters of his time, stands midway between Giotto and Michael Angelo. "In considering these works, their superiority over all that painting had till then achieved or attempted as such there seems a kind of break in the progression of Art, as if Masaccio had overleapt suddenly the limits which his predecessors had found impassable."

What might not art have become in the hands of this marvellous youth if he had lived to round out a long life of honor and distinction like Michael Angelo or Titian, instead of meeting death in an unknown tavern somewhere on the way from Florence to Rome.

> He came to Florence long ago,
> And painted here these walls, that shone
> For Raphael and for Angelo,
> With secrets deeper than his own,
> Then shrank into the dark again,
> And died, we know not how or when.

The shadows deepened, and I turned
Half-sadly from the fresco grand;
'And is this,' mused I, 'all ye earned,
High-vaulted brain and cunning hand,
That ye to greater men could teach
The skill yourselves could never reach?'

'And who were they,' I mused, 'that wrought
Through pathless wilds, with labour long,
The highways of our daily thought?
Who reared those towers of earliest song
That lift us from the throng to peace
Remote in sunny silences?'

Out clanged the Ave Mary bells,
And to my heart this message came:
'Each clamorous throat among them tells
What strong-souled martyrs died in flame
To make it possible that thou
Should'st here with brother-sinners bow.

'Thoughts that great hearts once broke for, we
Breathe cheaply in the common air;
The dust we trample heedlessly
Throbbed once in saints and heroes rare,
Who perished, opening for their race
New pathways to the commonplace.

'Henceforth, when rings the health to those
Who live in story and in song;
O nameless Dead! who now repose,
Safe in Oblivion's chambers strong;
One cup of recognition true
Shall silently be drained to you!'

JAMES RUSSELL LOWELL.

SPRING

A PICTURE IN THE ACCADEMIA OF FLORENCE, BY SANDRO BOTTICELLI

The riddle of this famous painting may be left unsolved in Rossetti's sonnet, but it brings an added charm to the allegory if we believe that it was painted to perpetuate the memory of Simonetta Cattaneo Vespucci, a fair lady of the court of Lorenzo de Medici. We see her again in the "Birth of Venus" and "Mars and Venus." Simonetta lived but a short time longer. Lorenzo later spoke of her to a friend one evening, as, turning to a star of unusual brilliancy, he observed: "There is no need for wonder, since the soul of that most gentle lady has either been transformed into yon star or has joined herself to it."

What masque of what old wind-withered New-Year
  Honours this Lady? Flora wanton-eyed
  For birth, and with all flowrets prankt and pied:
Aurora, Zephyrus, with mutual cheer
Of clasp and kiss: the Graces circling near,
  'Neath bower-linked arch of white arms glorified:
  And with those feathered feet which hovering glide
O'er Spring's brief bloom, Hermes the harbinger.

Birth-bare, not death-bare yet, the young stems stand,
  This Lady's temple-columns: o'er her head
  Love wings his shaft. What mystery here is read
Of homage or of hope? But how command
  Dead Springs to answer? And how question here
  These mummers of that wind-withered New-Year?

Dante Gabriel Rossetti.

ODE TO THE WEST WIND

Just outside the old walls of Florence, we find the Cascine Gardens extending along the Arno. Many tourists during the summer months drive along its dusty paths overhung with brown dust-laden branches and perhaps they too, have heard the rustling of the winds through the trees as Shelley once heard the West Wind.

I

O wild West Wind, thou breath of Autumn's being,
Thou, from whose unseen presence the leaves dead
Are driven, like ghosts from an enchanter fleeing,

Yellow, and black, and pale, and hectic red,
Pestilence-stricken multitudes: O thou,
Who chariotest to their dark wintry bed

The wingèd seeds, where they lie cold and low,
Each like a corpse within its grave, until
Thine azure sister of the spring shall blow

Her clarion o'er the dreaming earth, and fill
(Driving sweet buds like flocks to feed in air)
With living hues and odours plain and hill;

Wild Spirit, which art moving everywhere;
Destroyer and preserver; Hear, Oh hear!

II

Thou on whose stream, 'mid the steep sky's commotion,
Loose clouds like earth's decaying leaves are shed,
Shook from the tangled boughs of Heaven and Ocean,

Angels of rain and lighting: there are spread
On the blue surface of thine airy surge,
Like the bright hair uplifted from the head

Of some fierce Mænad, even from the dim verge
Of the horizon to the zenith's height
The locks of the approaching storm. Thou dirge

Of the dying year, to which this closing night
Will be the dome of a vast sepulchre,
Vaulted with all thy congregated might

Of vapours, from whose solid atmosphere
Black rain, and fire, and hail will burst: Oh hear!

III

Thou who didst waken from his summer dreams
The blue Mediterranean, where he lay,
Lulled by the coil of his crystàlline streams,

Beside a pumice isle in Baiæ's bay,
And saw in sleep old palaces and towers
Quivering within the wave's intenser day,

All overgrown with azure moss and flowers
So sweet, the sense faints picturing them! Thou
For whose path the Atlantic's level powers

Cleave themselves into chasms, while far below
The sea-blooms and the oozy woods which wear
The sapless foliage of the ocean, know

Thy voice, and suddenly grow gray with fear,
And tremble and despoil themselves: Oh hear!

IV

If I were a dead leaf thou mightest bear;
If I were a swift cloud to fly with thee;
A wave to pant beneath thy power, and share

The impulse of thy strength, only less free
Than thou, O uncontrollable! If even
I were as in my boyhood, and could be

The comrade of thy wanderings over heaven,
As then, when to outstrip thy skiey speed
Scarce seemed a vision; I would ne'er have striven

As thus with thee in prayer in my sore need.
Oh lift me as a wave, a leaf, a cloud!
I fall upon the thorns of life! I bleed!

A heavy weight of hours has chained and bowed
One too like thee: tameless, and swift, and proud.

V

Make me thy lyre, even as the forest is:
What if my leaves are falling like its own!
The tumult of thy mighty harmonies

Will take from both a deep, autumnal tone,
Sweet though in sadness. Be thou, spirit fierce,
My spirit! be thou me, impetuous one!

Drive my dead thoughts over the universe
Like withered leaves, to quicken a new birth!
And, by the incantation of this verse,

Scatter, as from an unextinguisht hearth
Ashes and sparks, my words among mankind!
Be through my lips to unawakened earth

The trumpet of a prophecy! O, wind,
If Winter comes, can Spring be far behind?

       PERCY BYSSHE SHELLEY.

ON THE MEDUSA OF LEONARDO DA VINCI IN THE FLORENTINE GALLERY

No better introduction could be found to this poem than the words of Walter Pater in his chapter on Leonardo da Vinci.

"All these swarming fancies unite in the Medusa of the Uffizi. Vasari's story of an earlier Medusa, painted on a wooden shield, is perhaps an invention; and yet, properly told, has more of the air of truth about it than anything else in the whole legend. For its real subject is not the serious work of a man, but the experiment of a child. The lizards and glow-worms and other strange small creatures which haunt an Italian vineyard bring before one the whole picture of a child's life in a Tuscan dwelling—half castle, half farm—and are as true to nature as the pretended astonishment of the father for whom the boy has prepared a surprise. It was not in play that he painted that other Medusa, the one great picture which he left behind him in Florence. The subject has been treated in various ways; Leonardo alone cuts to its centre; he alone realises it as the head of a corpse, exercising its powers through all the circumstances of death. What may be called the fascination of corruption penetrates in every touch its exquisitely finished beauty. About the dainty lines of the cheek the bat flits unheeded. The delicate snakes seem literally strangling each other in terrified struggle to escape from the Medusa brain. The hue which violent death always brings with it is on the features; features singularly massive and grand, as we catch them inverted, in a dexterous foreshortening, crown foremost, like a great calm stone against which the wave of serpents breaks."

I

It lieth, gazing on the midnight sky,
    Upon the cloudy mountain peak supine;
Below, far lands are seen tremblingly;
    Its horror and its beauty I divine.
Upon its lips and eyelids seems to lie
    Loveliness like a shadow, from which shine,

On the Medusa of Leonardo da Vinci

Fiery and lurid, struggling underneath,
The agonies of anguish and of death.

II

Yet it is less the horror than the grace
    Which turns the gazer's spirit into stone;
Whereon the lineaments of that dead face
    Are graven, till the characters be grown
Into itself, and thought no more can trace;
    'Tis the melodious hue of beauty thrown
Athwart the darkness and the glare of pain,
Which humanize and harmonize the strain.

III

And from its head as from one body grow,
    As grass out of a watery rock,
Hairs which are vipers, and they curl and flow
    And their long tangles in each other lock,
And with unending involutions show
    Their mailèd radiance, as it were to mock
The torture and the death within, and saw
The solid air with many a ragged jaw.

IV

And from a stone beside, a poisonous eft
    Peeps idly into those Gorgonian eyes;
Whilst in the air a ghastly bat, bereft
    Of sense, has flitted with a mad surprise
Out of the cave this hideous light had cleft,
    And he comes hastening like a moth that hies
After a taper; and the midnight sky
Flares, a light more dread than obscurity.

V

'Tis the tempestuous loveliness of terror;
   For from the serpents gleams a brazen glare
Kindled by that inextricable error,
   Which makes a thrilling vapour of the air
Become a (   ) and ever-shifting mirror
   Of all the beauty and the terror there—
A woman's countenance, with serpent locks,
Gazing in death on heaven from those wet rocks.

                PERCY BYSSHE SHELLEY.

ON THE PERSEUS AND MEDUSA Of BENVENUTO CELLINI, AT FLORENCE

The Piazza della Signoria is as much the heart of Florence as the Piazza San Marco is the heart of Venice. On festival days the crowds from the Duomo came along the Via Calzaioli to this square so full of memories and art. Here republican orators have thundered, and dependencies of the state have paid their tribute and homage. The old square has witnessed the Ordeal by Fire, the Bonfire of Vanities and the tragedy of Savonarola's death at the stake. You can still see the spot, for it is marked by a large bronze disk.

The Loggia de Lanzi forms the south angle of the Piazza. Constructed as a public meeting hall of the Priors, it is now an open air art gallery. Its beauty so appealed to Michael Angelo that he is said to have pronounced it incapable of improvement.

Of all the sculptured groups gathered together here the Perseus and Medusa, by Benvenuto Cellini, is the masterpiece. "It soars into a region of authentic, if not pure and sublime, inspiration." The story of its casting is delightfully told in his autobiography.

In what fierce spasms upgathered, on the plain
Medusa's headless corpse has quivering sunk,
While all the limbs of that undying trunk
To their extremest joint with torture strain;
But the calm visage has resumed again
Its beauty,—the orbed eyelids are let down,
As though a living sleep might once more crown
Their placid circlets, guiltless of all pain.
And thou—is thine the spirit's swift recoil,
Which follows every deed of acted wrath,
That holding in thine hand this lovely spoil,
Thou dost not triumph, feeling that the breath
Of life is sacred, whether it inform,
Loathly or beauteous, man or beast or worm?

Richard Chenevix Trench.

BY THE ARNO

From any one of the six bridges that span the broad channel of the Arno one gets an animated and glorious view of the city. Lofty mountains stand guard on the north and east, and pleasant valleys branch out in all directions, surrounding the city with a lovely setting well in keeping with her own charm and beauty. From the southeast to the northwest the Arno, like a liquid diagonal, cuts the city in two. At times it is not a very prepossessing river but it has played a tremendous rôle in the many vicissitudes of the city's history. The walls that once encircled the City of Flowers are gone, but the old Arno flows on as she did when Savonarola thundered his threats at Pope and Medici beneath Brunelleschi's Dome and when Michael Angelo fortified the heights of San Miniato.

> The oleander on the wall
> Grows crimson in the dawning light,
> Though the grey shadows of the night
> Lie yet on Florence like a pall.
>
> The dew is bright upon the hill,
> And bright the blossoms overhead,
> But ah! the grasshoppers have fled,
> The little Attic song is still.
>
> Only the leaves are gently stirred
> By the soft breathing of the gale,
> And in the almond-scented vale
> The lonely nightingale is heard.
>
> The day will make thee silent soon,
> O nightingale sing on for love!
> While yet upon the shadowy grove
> Splinter the arrows of the moon.

By the Arno

Before across the silent lawn
In sea-green mist the morning steals,
And to love's frightened eyes reveals
The long white fingers of the dawn

Fast climbing up the eastern sky
To grasp and slay the shuddering night,
All careless of my heart's delight,
Or if the nightingale should die.

OSCAR WILDE.

AT FLORENCE

"How little dreams
The traveller of today who sees thee glass
Thy sunny charms within the Arno's breast
How oft they've reddened with thy children's blood."

Florence is an old city and has always been noted for its beauty. In fact, few cities can vie with it for situation. Lying in the Valley of the Arno and surrounded by cultivated hills where the olive and the vine grow in such profusion, it was well called Florentia by the Romans when they made it the northern terminus of the Via Cassia. Ruined by the invasion of northern tribes, it later arose to be a feudal city and a free commune—Guelphs and Ghibellines, Bianci and Neri, quarreled for mastery. In our wanderings through the streets of Florence we find memories of Dante, Savonarola, Michael Angelo, Donatello and the Medici. Church, palace, and old bridge all speak of the past.

Under the shadow of a stately Pile,
   The dome of Florence, pensive and alone,
   Nor giving heed to aught that passed the while,
I stood, and gazed upon a marble stone,
The laurelled Dante's favourite seat. A throne,
   In just esteem, it rivals; though no style
   Be there of decoration to beguile
The mind, depressed by thought of greatness flown.

As a true man, who long had served the lyre,
   I gazed with earnestness, and dared no more.
   But in his breast the mighty Poet bore
A Patriot's heart, warm with undying fire.
Bold with the thought, in reverence I sate down,
And, for a moment, filled that empty Throne.

                        WILLIAM WORDSWORTH.

ITALY
PART IX
ROME

THE CATACOMBS

It was perhaps due to Roman opposition that so many of the earliest churches built over the tombs of martyrs, were founded outside the walls of the Eternal City. When Honorius, in the fifth century, deprived the old faith of all its temples, Christian places of worship increased rapidly. Among the most famous of these places, which date back to those years of the great change from Pagan to Christian Rome, are the Catacombs. In the plains that stretch away from Rome to the Alban and Sabine Hills these subterranean passages were excavated in the soft *tufa* from twenty-five to seventy-five feet below the surface of the earth. If placed in a continuous line they would extend about five hundred and fifty miles.

Among the most famous are the Catacombs of St. Calixtus, St. Agnes and St. Domitilla.

Departed Brothers, generous, brave,
   Who for the faith have died,
   Nor its pure Source denied,
Your bodies from devouring flames to save;
   Honour on earth, and bliss in heaven,
   Be to your saintly valour given.

And we, who, left behind, pursue
   The pilgrim's weary way
   To realms of glorious day,
Shall raise our fainting souls with thoughts of you.
   Honour on earth, and bliss in heaven,
   Be to your saintly valour given!

Your ashes, mingled with the dust,
   Shall yet be forms more fair
   Than here breathed vital air,
When earth again gives up her precious trust.
   Honour on earth, and bliss in heaven,
   Be to your saintly valour given!

The trump of angels shall proclaim,
  With tones far-sent and sweet,
  Which countless hosts repeat,
The generous Martyr's never-fading name.
  Honour on earth, and bliss in heaven,
  Be to your saintly valour given!

JOANNA BAILLIE.

ROME

From *Childe Harold's Pilgrimage*

O Rome, my country! city of the soul!
The orphans of the heart must turn to thee,
Lone mother of dead empires, and control
In their shut breasts their petty misery.
What are our woes and sufferance? Come and see
The cypress, hear the owl, and plod your way
O'er steps of broken thrones and temples, Ye!
Whose agonies are evils of a day—
A world is at our feet as fragile as our clay.

The Niobe of nations! there she stands,
Childless and crownless, in her voiceless woe;
An empty urn within her wither'd hands,
Whose holy dust was scattered long ago:
The Scipios' tomb contains no ashes now;
The very sepulchres lie tenantless
Of their heroic dwellers;—dost thou flow,
O Tiber, through a marble wilderness?
Rise, with thy yellow waves, and mantle her distress!

. . . .

Alas, the lofty city! and alas,
The trebly hundred triumphs! and the day
When Brutus made the dagger's edge surpass
The conqueror's sword in bearing fame away!
Alas, for Tully's voice, and Virgil's lay,
And Livy's pictured page!—But these shall be
Her resurrection; all beside—decay.
Alas, for Earth, for never shall we see
The brightness in her eye she bore when Rome was free!

Lord Byron.

ST. PETER'S BY MOONLIGHT

When twilight falls upon the Eternal City we leave our hotel and wander across the Tiber to the Borgo, the Vatican quarter of the city, where emperors and kings once had their gardens, and Nero, his circus. The moonlight night lends enchantment to the shadowy church and greatest of palaces. In the square in front stands the obelisk like a stately sentinel between the sweeping curves of Bernini's colonnade. On the balustrade above the church, the figures of Christ and the Apostles seem more stonily silent. Only a lighted window here and there, like lonely stars, break the gloomy curtain of the palace walls. The moonbeams fall aslant the sparkling fountains and add a touch of jeweled splendor to the shadowy glory of the scene.

Could it be that St. Peter was crucified near this spot and that yonder in the church, under the baldachin of pagan bronze, the Prince of the Apostles still lies?

No longer the shouts of a boisterous populace echo from the walls of the circus which once had been lighted by the burning forms of martyred Christians, but some of the old walls still support this greatest of churches, built to commemorate the teaching of the Christ for whom they suffered.

Low hung the moon when first I stood in Rome;
   Midway she seemed attracted from her sphere,
   On those twin fountains shining broad and clear
Whose floods, not mindless of their mountain home,
Rise there in clouds of rainbow mist and foam.
   That hour fulfilled the dream of many a year:
   Through that thin mist, with joy akin to fear,
The steps I saw, the pillars, last, the dome.
A spiritual empire there embodied stood;
   The Roman church there met me face to face:
   Ages, sealed up, of evil and of good
Slept in that circling colonnade's embrace.
   Alone I stood, a stranger and alone,
   Changed by that stony miracle to stone.

AUBREY DE VERE.

THE RUINS OF ROME

The curtain in the great drama of the story of Rome has fallen on Senate and Forum, only to rise again on a new and united Italy. Of ancient Rome we can see today only ruins, but she has contributed in large measure to our language, religion and laws. One who walks amidst her ruined palaces, amphitheatres and temples should always bear in mind that, although the Romans could not build for all ages, they did bequeath four lasting monuments that have a strange power to resist the ravages of time: "an example of a highly centralized government, a consummate system of law, a body of literature which luminously sets forth the deeds and ideals of classical times, and Latin Christianity." Of these the ruins of the Imperial City are everywhere eloquent.

I

Thou stranger, which for Rome in Rome here seekest,
And nought of Rome in Rome perceivst at all,
These same olde walls, olde arches, which thou seest,
Olde palaces, is that which Rome men call.
Beholde what wreake, what ruine, and what wast,
And how that she, which with her mightie powre
Tam'd all the world, hath tam'd herself at last;
The pray of Time, which all things doth devowre!
Rome now of Rome is th' onely funerall,
And onely Rome of Rome hath victorie;
Ne ought save Tyber hastning to his fall
Remaines of all: O worlds inconstancie!
   That which is firme doth flit and fall away,
   And that is flitting doth abide and stay.

II

These heapes of stones, these old walls, which ye see,
Were first enclosures but of salvage soyle;
And these brave pallaces, which maystred bee
Of Time, were shepheards cottages somewhile.

Then tooke the shepheards kingly ornaments,
And the stout hynde armed his right hand with
    steele:
Eftsoones their rule of yearely Presidents
Grew great, and sixe months greater a great deele;
Which, made perpetuall, rose to so great height,
That thence th' Imperiall Eagle rooting tooke,
Till th' heaven it selfe, opposing gainst her might,
Her powers to Peters successor betooke;
   Who, shepheardlike, (as Fates the same fore-
    seeing),
   Doth shew that all things turne to their first
    being.

III

O that I had the Thracian Poets harpe,
For to awake out of th' infernall shade
Those antique Caesars, sleeping long in darke,
The which this aunciant City whilome made!
Or that I had Amphions instrument,
To quicken, with his vitall notes accord,
The stonie ioynts of these old walls now rent,
By which th' Ausonian light might be restor'd!
Or that at least I could, with pencill fine,
Fashion the pourtraicts of these palacis,
By paterne of great Virgils spirit divine!
I would assay with that which in me is,
   To builde, with levell of my loftie style,
   That which no hands can evermore compyle.

                        JOACHIM DU BELLAY.
      (Translated by EDMUND SPENSER.)

AFTER A LECTURE ON SHELLEY

After the body of Shelley was burned on the shore at Viareggio, in accordance with the Greek custom, his ashes were buried in Rome. Here, too, were brought the ashes of Edward Trelawney, for whose tomb in the Protestant Cemetery Shelley had written these lines:

"These are two friends whose lives were undivided;
So let their memory be, now they have glided
Under the grave; let not their bones be parted
For their two hearts in life were single hearted."

It is interesting to know that the old seaman in Millais' picture, "The North West Passage," in the Tate Gallery, is a portrait of this adventurous and romantic soul.

In 1819 Shelley lost his eldest child, the idol of his heart. No parent can see the tomb of the great poet without recalling the lines with which the bereaved father uttered his lament:

"Here its ashes find a tomb
But beneath this pyramid
Thou art not,—if a thing divine
Like thee can die,—thy funeral shrine
Is thy mother's grief and mine."

One broad, white sail in Spezzia's treacherous bay;
  On comes the blast; too daring bark, beware!
The cloud has clasped her; lo! it melts away;
  The wide, waste waters, but no sail is there.

Morning: a woman looking on the sea;
  Midnight: with lamps the long veranda burns;
Come, wandering sail, they watch, they burn for thee!
  Suns come and go, alas! no bark returns.

And feet are thronging on the pebbly sands,
  And torches flaring in the weedy caves,
Where'er the waters lay with icy hands
  The shapes uplifted from their coral graves.

Vainly they seek; the idle quest is o'er;
    The coarse, dark women, with their hanging locks,
And lean, wild children gather from the shore
    To the black hovels bedded in the rocks.

But Love still prayed, with agonizing wail,
    "One, one last look, ye heaving waters, yield!"
Till Ocean, clashing in his jointed mail,
    Raised the pale burden on his level shield.

Slow from the shore the sullen waves retire;
    His form a nobler element shall claim;
Nature baptized him in ethereal fire,
    And death shall crown him with a wreath of flame.

Fade, mortal semblance, never to return;
    Swift is the change within thy crimson shroud;
Seal the white ashes in the peaceful urn;
    All else has risen in yon silvery cloud.

Sleep where thy gentle Adonais lies,
    Whose open page lay on thy dying heart,
Both in the smile of those blue-vaulted skies,
    Earth's fairest dome of all divinest art.

Breathe for his wandering soul one passing sigh,
    O happier Christian, while thine eye grows dim,
In all the mansions of the house on high,
    Say not that Mercy has not one for him!

                        OLIVER WENDELL HOLMES.

THE NAME WRIT IN WATER
(Piazza di Spagna, Rome)

The Spirit of the Fountain speaks:

Yonder's the window my poet would sit in
   While my song murmured of happier days;
Mine is the water his name has been writ in,
   Sure and immortal my share in his praise.

Gone are the pilgrims whose green wreaths here
     hung for him,—
   Gone from their fellows like bubbles of foam;
Long shall outlive them the songs have been sung
     for him;
   Mine is eternal—or Rome were not Rome.

Far on the mountain my fountain was fed for him,
   Bringing soft sounds that his nature loved best:
Sighing of pines that had fain made a bed for him;
   Seafaring rills, on their musical quest.

Bells of the fairies at eve, that I rang for him;
   Nightingale's glee, he so well understood;
Chant of the dryads at dawn, that I sang for him;
   Swish of the snake at the edge of the wood.

Little he knew 'twixt his dreaming and sleeping,
   The while his sick fancy despaired of his fame,
What glory I held in my loverly keeping:
   Listen! my waters will whisper his name.

                        ROBERT UNDERWOOD JOHNSON.

TO SHELLEY

Shelley! whose song so sweet was sweetest here,
We knew each other little; now I walk
Along the same green path, along the shore
Of Lerici, along the sandy plain
Trending from Lucca to the Pisan pines
Under whose shadow scattered camels lie,
The old and young, and rarer deer uplift
Their knotty branches o'er high-feathered fern.
Regions of happiness! I greet ye well;
Your solitudes, and not your cities, stayed
My steps among you; for with you alone
Converst I, and with those ye bore of old.
He who beholds the skies of Italy
Sees ancient Rome reflected, sees beyond,
Into more glorious Hellas, nurse of Gods
And godlike men: dwarfs people other lands.
Frown not, maternal England! thy weak child
Kneels at thy feet and owns in shame a lie.

WALTER SAVAGE LANDOR.

TWO GRAVES

Thou hast not lost all glory, Rome!
  With thee have found their quiet home
Two, whom we followers most admire
  Of those that swell our sacred quire;
And many a lowered voice repeats:
  'Hush! here lies Shelley! here lies Keats!'
                WALTER SAVAGE LANDOR.

BELISARIUS

"Ignorance, tradition, imagination, romance,—call it what you will,—has chosen the long-closed Pincian Gate for the last station of the blind Belisarius." The legend tells how this leader of armies, this destroyer and maker of popes, this one-time favorite of Theodora, led by a small child begged alms at the gate of the city he had once entered as a conqueror.

It is perhaps a truer story that he drove Pope Silverius into exile and later repenting of his deed, built the small church of Santa Maria de' Crociferi behind the Trevi fountain. For fourteen hundred years there has been a tablet on the east wall of the church toward the Via de' Poli telling of the repentance of the soldier of Justinian, who conquered Africa, reduced Ravenna, delivered Rome from the Goths and at last rescued Constantinople. He did not die in exile and disgrace but was honored for his daring deeds and loyal service to his Emperor.

    I am poor and old and blind;
    The sun burns me, and the wind
        Blows through the city gate,
    And covers me with dust
    From the wheels of the august
        Justinian the Great.

    It was for him I chased
    The Persians o'er wild and waste,
        As General of the East;
    Night after night I lay
    In their camps of yesterday;
        Their forage was my feast.

    For him, with sails of red,
    And torches at masthead,
        Piloting the great fleet,
    I swept the Afric coasts
    And scattered the Vandal hosts,
        Like dust in a windy street.

For him I won again
The Ausonian realm and reign,
   Rome and Parthenope;
And all the land was mine
From the summits of Apennine
   To the shores of either sea.

For him, in my feeble age,
I dared the battle's rage,
   To save Byzantium's state,
When the tents of Zabergan
Like snow-drifts overran
   The road to the Golden Gage.

And for this, for this, behold!
Infirm and blind and old,
   With gray, uncovered head,
Beneath the very arch
Of my triumphal march,
   I stand and beg my bread!

Methinks I still can hear,
Sounding distinct and near,
   The Vandal monarch's cry,
As, captive and disgraced,
With majestic step he paced,—
   "All, all is Vanity!"

Ah! vainest of all things
Is the gratitude of kings;
   The plaudits of the crowd
Are but the clatter of feet
At midnight in the street,
   Hollow and restless and loud.

But the bitterest disgrace
Is to see forever the face
  Of the Monk of Ephesus!
The unconquerable will
This, too, can bear;—I still
  Am Belisarius!
      Henry Wadsworth Longfellow.

JUGURTHA

Almost in the shadows of the Arch of Septimius Severus, in the northern corner of the Roman Forum, is the little church of San Guiseppe dei Falegnanie, built above the Mamertine prison, the state prison of Ancient Rome. The Tullianum, as the lower cell is called, is no doubt one of the oldest buildings in Rome. Here criminals and captives awaited execution. There is a tradition that St. Peter and St. Paul were confined in this part of the prison and that the spring now trickling through the cell began to flow at the bidding of Saint Peter so that he might baptise the jailors who afterwards suffered martyrdom.

In the days of Jugurtha, no stairs led down to the lower cell and the prisoners were lowered through a hole in the stone floor. Imprisonment as a punishment was unknown in Rome but victims were detained in the upper prison, pending trial.

When Jugurtha, King of Numidia, was lowered into the Tullianum, he remarked to his executioners: "My, what a cold bath you Romans give."

Even today, as we enter into its chilly atmosphere, we think of how Cicero brought Lentulus across the Forum to this same prison and how Sejanus, the favorite of Tiberius, was strangled in its depths.

To avoid the ill-omen of mentioning death, Cicero, after the Catilinarian conspirators had been executed, and their bodies dragged to the nearby Scalae Gemoniae, or Stairs of Mourning, proclaimed in cold triumph, "vixerunt"—they have lived.

How cold are thy baths, Apollo!
   Cried the African monarch, the splendid,
As down to his death in the hollow
   Dark dungeons of Rome he descended,
   Uncrowned, unthroned, unattended;
How cold are thy baths, Apollo!

How cold are thy baths, Apollo!
   Cried the Poet, unknown, unbefriended,

As the vision, that lured him to follow,
   With the mist and the darkness blended,
   And the dream of his life was ended;
How cold are thy baths, Apollo!

            HENRY WADSWORTH LONGFELLOW.

THE CONSPIRACY OF RIENZI

So many places in Rome recall the story of Cola di Rienzi, the Last of the Tribunes. We think of that night of vigil in one of the chapels of St. John Lateran, where his life was threatened, and of the bath in that famous porphyry sarcophagus in which Constantine was baptized.

Near that marble ascent which rises as a grand monumental entrance to the Palace of the Senators and designed by the poet, painter, sculptor, architect, Michael Angelo—the great Rienzi fell—just at the foot of one of the Egyptian lionesses on the balustrade at the bottom of the steps. Not far away has been placed a bronze statue of Cola di Rienzi, who, seeking to restore the sovereignty of the ancient city rather than the liberty of mankind, rose to the highest civic honors but forgot the people who had helped him rise. At last they joined his enemies, the Colonnas, and when he tried to escape in disguise they dragged him here and left him to die.

Above, in the center of the magnificent court, is the famous equestrian statue of Marcus Aurelius, the one equestrian statue that takes us back to the days of Imperial Rome. In the stormy days of Rienzi we hear of this statue figuring in a festival given in honor of the Tribune. On that day wine was made to flow from the nostrils of the horse. "Those good old days!" many an American is heard to say as he hears this story for the first time.

'Twas a proud moment—ev'n to hear the words
  Of Truth and Freedom 'mid these temples breath'd,
And see, once more, the Forum shine with swords,
  In the Republic's sacred name unsheath'd—
That glimpse, that vision of a brighter day,
  For his dear Rome, must to a Roman be,
Short as it was, worth ages pass'd away
  In the dull lapse of hopeless slavery.

'Twas on a night of May, beneath that moon,
Which had, through many an age, seen Time untune

The strings of this Great Empire, till it fell
From his rude hands, a broken, silent shell—
The sound of the church clock, near Adrian's
    Tomb,
Summon'd the warriors, who had risen for
    Rome,
To meet unarm'd—with none to watch them
    there,
But God's own eye,—and pass the night in
    pray'r.
Holy beginning of a holy cause,
When heroes, girt for Freedom's combat, pause
Before high Heav'n and, humble in their might,
Call down its blessing on the coming fight.
At dawn, in arms, went forth the patriot band;
And as the breeze, fresh from the Tiber, fann'd
Their gilded gonfalons, all eyes could see
    The palm-tree there, the sword, the keys of
        Heav'n—
Types of the justice, peace, and liberty,
    That were to bless them, when their chains were
        riv'n.
On to the Capitol the pageant moved
    While many a Shade of other times, that still
Around that grave of grandeur sighing roved,
    Hung o'er their footsteps up the Sacred Hill,
And heard its mournful echoes, as the last
High-minded heirs of the Republic pass'd.

'Twas then that thou, their Tribune (Name,
    which brought
Dreams of lost glory to each patriot's thought),
Didst, with a spirit Rome in vain shall seek
To wake up in her sons again, thus speak:—

'Romans! look around you!—on this sacred place
  There once stood shrines, and gods, and god-
    like men.
What see you now? what solitary trace
  Is left of all, that made Rome's glory then?
The shrines are sunk, the Sacred Mount bereft
  Ev'n of its name—and nothing now remains
But the deep mem'ry of that glory, left
  To whet out pangs, and aggravate our chains!
But shall this be?—our sun and sky the same,—
  Treading the very soil our fathers trode,—
What with'ring curse hath fall'n on soul and
    frame,
  What visitation hath there come from God,
To blast our strength, and rot us into slaves,
Here, on our great forefathers' glorious graves?
It cannot be—rise up ye Mighty Dead,—
  If we, the living, are too weak to crush
These tyrant priests, that o'er your empire tread,
  Till all but Romans at Rome's tameness blush.
'Happy Palmyra! in thy desert domes,
  Where only date-trees sigh and serpents hiss;
And thou, whose pillars are but silent homes
  For the stork's brood, superb Persepolis!
Thrice happy both, that your extinguish'd race
Have left no embers—no half-living trace—
No slaves, to crawl around the once proud spot,
Till past renown in present shame's forgot,
While Rome, the Queen of all, whose very
    wrecks,
  If lone and lifeless through a desert hurl'd,
Would wear more true magnificence than decks
  Th' assembled thrones of all th' existing
    world—

Rome, Rome alone, is haunted, stain'd, and curst,
　Through ev'ry spot her princely Tiber laves,
By living human things—the deadliest, worst,
　This earth engenders—tyrants and their slaves!
And we—oh shame!—we who have ponder'd o'er
　The patriot's lesson and the poet's lay;
Have mounted up the streams of ancient lore,
　Tracking our country's glories all the way—
Ev'n we have tamely, basely, kiss'd the ground
　Before that Papal Power—that Ghost of Her,
The World's Imperial mistress—sitting, crown'd,
　And ghastly, on her mould'ring sepulchre!
But this is past:—too long have lordly priests
　And priestly lords, led us, with all our pride
With'ring about us—like devoted beasts,
　Dragg'd to the shrine, with faded garlands tied.
'Tis o'er—the dawn of our deliv'rance breaks!
Up from the sleep of centuries awakes
The Genius of the Old Republic, free
As first he stood, in chainless majesty,
And sends his voice through ages yet to come,
Proclaiming: Rome! Rome! Rome! Eternal Rome!'

THOMAS MOORE.

THE COLISEUM

"A mighty monument to heathen brutality and Christian courage" and so vast that Juvenal says:

"Which in its public shows, unpeopled Rome,
And held, uncrowded, nations in its womb."

For centuries this mountainous ruin has been the quarry from which palaces and churches have been built. After the destruction of Jerusalem, Titus forced twelve thousand captive Jews to finish the titanic structure begun by his father Vespasian in A.D. 72.

"A ruin,—yet what ruin! from its mass
Walls, palaces, half-cities, have been reared;
Yet oft the enormous skeleton ye pass,
And marvel where the spoil could have appeared.
Hath it indeed been plundered, or but cleared?
Alas! developed, opens the decay,
When the colossal fabric's form is neared:
It will not bear the brightness of the day,
Which streams too much on all years, man, have reft away.

"But when the rising moon begins to climb
Its topmost arch, and gently pauses there;
When the stars twinkle through the loops of time,
And the low night-breeze waves along the air,
The garland-forest, which the gray walls wear,
Like laurels on the bald first Caesar's head;
When the light shines serene, but doth not glare,
Then in this magic circle raise the dead;
Heroes have trod this spot, 'tis on their dust ye tread."

BYRON, *Childe Harold's Pilgrimage.*

Type of the antique Rome! Rich reliquary
Of lofty contemplation left to Time
By buried centuries of pomp and power!
At length, at length, after so many days
Of weary pilgrimage and burning thirst
(Thirst for the springs of lore that in thee lie),

I kneel, an altered and a humble man,
Amid thy shadows, and so drink within
My very soul thy grandeur, gloom, and glory!

Vastness, and age, and memories of old!
Silence, and desolation, and dim night!
I feel ye now,—I feel ye in your strength,—
O spells more sure than e'er Judæan king
Taught in the gardens of Gethsemane!
O charms more potent than the rapt Chaldee
Ever drew down from out the quiet stars!

Here, where a hero fell, a column falls!
Here, where the mimic eagle glared in gold,
A midnight vigil holds the swarthy bat!
Here, where the dames of Rome their gilded
    hair
Waved to the wind, now wave the reed and
    thistle!
Here, where on golden throne the monarch lolled,
Glides, spectre-like, unto his marble home,
Lit by the wan light of the hornèd moon,
The swift and silent lizard of the stones!

But stay! these walls, these ivy-clad arcades,
These mouldering plinths, these sad and blackened
    shafts,
These vague entablatures, this crumbling frieze,
These shattered cornices, this wreck, this ruin,
These stones,—alas! these gray stones,—are they
    all,
All of the famed and the colossal left
By the corrosive hours to fate and me?
"Not all," the echoes answer me,—"not all!
Prophetic sounds and loud arise forever
From us and from all ruin unto the wise,

As melody from Memnon to the sun.
We rule the hearts of mightiest men, we rule
With a despotic sway all giant minds.
We are not impotent,—we pallid stones.
Not all our power is gone, not all our fame,
Not all the magic of our high renown,
Not all the wonder that encircles us,
Not all the mysteries that in us lie,
Not all the memories that hang upon
And cling around about us as a garment,
Clothing us in a robe of more than glory."
EDGAR ALLAN POE.

I AM IN ROME

No visitor to Rome will get the message of pathos and disaster which the storms of centuries have left amid the ruined temples and palaces, unless he tries to see the grandeur, the glory and the power that once was Rome's.

It is no easy task for the imagination to reconstruct ancient Rome from crumbling walls and isolated columns, which here and there stand like skeletons of masonry. They are mere suggestions of the life, beauty and heart-beat of the Eternal City, whose legions once tramped along the highways of the Empire from the Firth of Forth to the Euphrates. The mists of too many centuries cloud the vision of the past of this great city. Ancient, mediaeval and modern Rome lie in inextricable confusion for him who looks but cannot see.

"Who could believe," laments Jerome, "that Rome built upon the conquest of the whole world, would fall to the ground? that the mother herself would become the tomb of her people? that all the regions of the East, of Africa, and Egypt, once ruled by the queenly city, would be filled with troops of slaves and handmaidens?"

I am in Rome! Oft as the morning-ray
Visits these eyes, waking at once I cry,
Whence this excess of joy? What has befallen me?
And from within a thrilling voice replies,
Thou art in Rome! A thousand busy thoughts
Rush on my mind, a thousand images;
And I spring up as girt to run a race!

Thou art in Rome! the City, where the Gauls,
Entering at sun-rise through her open gates,
And, through her streets silent and desolate,
Marching to slay, thought they saw Gods, not men:
The City that, by temperance, fortitude,
And love of glory, tower'd above the clouds,
Then fell—but, falling, kept the highest seat,

I am in Rome

And in her loneliness, her pomp of woe,
Where now she dwells, withdrawn into the wild,
Still o'er the mind maintains, from age to age,
Her empire undiminish'd.

                    There, as though
Grandeur attracted Grandeur, are beheld
All things that strike, ennoble—from the depths
Of Egypt, from the classic fields of Greece,
Her groves, her temples—all things that inspire
Wonder, delight!
    And I am there!

SAMUEL ROGERS.

FRAGMENT ON KEATS

WHO DESIRED THAT ON HIS TOMB SHOULD BE INSCRIBED—

'Here lieth One whose name was writ on water.'
    But, ere the breath that could erase it blew,
Death, in remorse for that fell slaughter,
    Death, the immortalizing winter, flew
    Athwart the stream,—and time's printless torrent grew
A scroll of crystal, blazoning the name
    Of Adonais.—

Percy Bysshe Shelley.

KEATS
From *Adonais*

XXIX
Peace, peace! he is not dead, he doth not sleep—
He hath awakened from the dream of life—
'Tis we, who lost in stormy visions, keep
With phantoms an unprofitable strife,
And in mad trance strike with our spirit's knife
Invulnerable nothings.—*We* decay
Like corpses in a charnel; fear and grief
Convulse us and consume us day by day,
And cold hopes swarm like worms within our living clay.

XL
He has outsoared the shadow of our night;
Envy and calumny and hate and pain,
And that unrest which men miscall delight,
Can touch him not and torture not again;
From the contagion of the world's slow stain
He is secure, and now can never mourn
A heart grown cold, a head grown gray in vain;
Nor, when the spirit's self has ceased to burn,
With sparkless ashes load an unlamented urn.

XLI
He lives, he wakes—'tis Death is dead, not he;
Mourn not for Adonais.—Thou young Dawn
Turn all thy dew to splendor, for from thee
The spirit thou lamentest is not gone;
Ye caverns and ye forests, cease to moan!
Cease ye faint flowers and fountains, and thou Air
Which like a mourning veil thy scarf hadst thrown

O'er the abandoned Earth, now leave it bare
Even to the joyous stars which smile on its despair!

XLII

He is made one with Nature: there is heard
His voice in all her music, from the moan
Of thunder to the song of night's sweet bird;
He is a presence to be felt and known
In darkness and in light, from herb and stone,
Spreading itself where'er that Power may move
Which has withdrawn his being to its own;
Which wields the world with never-wearied
    love,
Sustains it from beneath, and kindles it above.

                              PERCY BYSSHE SHELLEY.

VILLA BORGHESE

Not far from where Belisarius withstood one of the memorable sieges of the Goths, we enter one of the beautiful parks of Rome. "A scene that must have required generations and ages, during which growth, decay and man's intelligence wrought kindly together to render it so gently wild as we behold it now." Paul V. a Borghese pope, created this Elysium of delight and for three centuries it remained the royal residence of this family.

Today, known as the Villa Umberta, it is a treasure-house of art and sculpture. The present collection of statues and works of art was made possible by discoveries and excavations after the first great collection had been sold to Napoleon I. The present masterpieces of Bernini, Canova, Titian and others are fine enough to make us forget the loss of the first collection which now enriches the corridors and galleries of the Louvre.

A grace of winter breathing like the spring;
Solitude, silence, the thin whispering
Of water in the fountains, that all day
Talk with the leaves; the winds, gentle as they,
Rustle the silken garments of their speech
Rarely, for they keep silence, each by each,
The dim green silence of the dreaming trees,
Cypress and pine and the cloaked ilexes,
That winter never chills; and all these keep
A sweet and grave and unawakening sleep,
Reticent of its dreams, but hearing all
The babble of the fountains as they fall,
Chattering bright and irresponsible words
As in a baby-speech of liquid birds.

ARTHUR SYMONS.

ROME UNVISITED

"A man who has not been in Italy is always conscious of an inferiority for his not having seen what it is expected a man should see. It ought to be the business of every man's life to see Rome."—Dr. Samuel Johnson.

> "Then from the very soil of silent Rome,
> You shall grow wise, and walking, live again
> The lives of buried peoples, and become
> A child by right of that eternal home,
> Cradle and grave of empires on whose walls
> The sun himself subdued to reverence falls."

How many times we try to bring back the varied scenes and acts in that tremendous drama of Rome in the making. He who allows the spirit of Rome to gain hold of his heart will find that the very "stone will speak to him and even the dust under his footsteps will seem to bear with it something of human grandeur."

I

The corn has turned from grey to red,
   Since first my spirit wandered forth
   From the drear cities of the north,
And to Italia's mountains fled.

And here I set my face towards home,
   For all my pilgrimage is done,
   Although, methinks, yon blood-red sun
Marshals the way to Holy Rome.

O blessed Lady, who dost hold
   Upon the seven hills thy reign!
   O Mother without blot or stain,
Crowned with bright crowns of triple gold!

O Roma, Roma, at thy feet
   I lay this barren gift of song!
   For, ah! the way is steep and long
That leads unto thy sacred street.

II

And yet what joy it were for me
  To turn my feet unto the south,
  And journeying towards the Tiber mouth
To kneel again at Fiesole!

And wandering through the tangled pines
  That break the gold of Arno's stream,
  To see the purple mist and gleam
Of morning on the Apennines.

By many a vineyard-hidden home,
  Orchard, and olive-garden grey,
  Till from the drear Campagna's way
The seven hills bear up the dome!

. . . .

OSCAR WILDE.

THE GRAVE OF KEATS

"Under the pyramid which is the tomb of Cestius, and the massy walls and towers, now mouldering and desolate, which formed the circuit of ancient Rome, is the Protestant Cemetery. The cemetery is an open space among the ruins, covered in winter with violets and daisies. It might make one in love with death, to think that one should be buried in so sweet a place."

In the old part is the grave of Keats with the inscription:

> This Grave
> contains all that was mortal
> of a
> YOUNG ENGLISH POET
> who
> on his Death Bed
> in the Bitterness of his Heart
> at the Malicious Power of his Enemies
> Desired
> these Words to be engraved on his Tombstone
> *'Here lies One*
> *Whose Name Was Writ in Water.'*
> Feb. 24th, 1821.

Rid of the world's injustice, and his pain,
   He rests at last beneath God's veil of blue:
   Taken from life when life and love were new
The youngest of the martyrs here is lain,
Fair as Sebastian, and as early slain.
   No cypress shades his grave, no funeral yew,
   But gentle violets weeping with the dew
Weave on his bones an ever-blossoming chain.

O proudest heart that broke for misery!
   O sweetest lips since those of Mitylene!
   O poet-painter of our English land!
Thy name was writ in water—it shall stand:
   And tears like mine shall keep thy memory green,
   As Isabella did her Basil-tree.

OSCAR WILDE.

SHELLEY'S HOUSE

Shelley's life at Rome opened to him scenes of ancient grandeur that far surpassed his expectations. As he wandered among those "stories in stone," his soul imbibed forms of loveliness which became a part of himself. He gave us his Roman experiences in his great tragedy of *The Cenci* and in his sublime drama of *Prometheus Unbound*, chiefly written upon the mountainous ruins of the Baths of Caracala. Between April 26 and May 1, 1822, the Shelleys and two friends, Edward and Jane Williams, moved into the house, Casa Magni, on the Gulf of Spezzia, near Lerici. From Leghorn (near Spezzia) Shelley sailed his little boat, the *Ariel*,—on a journey from which he was never to return. The bodies of Shelley and his friend Williams were washed ashore. Byron, Hunt and Edward John Trelawny stood by as the bodies of the two were cremated on the sandy shore, Trelawny, in despair, snatching Shelley's unconsumed heart from the flames. The poet's ashes were later deposited in the English Cemetery at Rome beneath a marble slab inscribed:

PERCY BYSSHE SHELLEY
Cor Cordium
Natus IV. Aug. MDCCXCII
Obiit VII. Jul. MDCCCXXII
"Nothing of him doth fade
But doth suffer a sea change
Into something rich and strange."

Thou last, O Lerici, receive my song:
   Ilex and olive on the gleaming steep
Gray-green, descend to kiss the brilliant deep
Beautiful with clear winds; the golden leap
Of the far-snowing blue, with horned sweep,
Pours to yon purple sea-valley asleep,
Between fair mountains locked; and noon's high blaze
Turns to one melting sapphire all light's rays,
Wherein the wild wind blows, the wild wave strays,
While ocean from his azure censer sprays

Each scarlet poppy that the shore embays
Mid thickets of the rose; and all day long
The nightingales are waking, loud and strong,
Warbling unseen their unremitting song
Round Shelley's house, lest here I suffer wrong,
This day that gave me birth, pierced by the prong
Of absence, misery, loss; and, lest I weep,
Colour and light and music round me keep
Life's crystal, and this day of all my days
To be a temple of the soul upraise,
Where I may breathe and throb and muse, and long
Brood on the loves that to my bosom throng;
And from these splendours of earth, sea, and air,
Like Uriel issuing from the glorious sphere
That hides him with great beauty, everywhere
I feel the might of song that once dwelt here,
A shadow of loveliness approaching near,
A fragrance in the unseen atmosphere,
An intimate presence in the darkness dear;
I see, and see not! O, the sweet, the fair
Melodious death my sea-borne soul should bear
With yon blue waters whelmed, to meet him there,
My poet!—yet rather life to me belong!—
Sing, nightingales, flood the blind world with song!

GEORGE EDWARD WOODBERRY.

AT ROME

Is this, ye Gods, the Capitolian Hill?
Yon petty steep in truth the fearful Rock,
Tarpeian named of yore, and keeping still
That name, a local Phantom proud to mock
The Traveller's expectation?—Could our Will
Destroy the ideal power within, 'twere done
Thro' what men see and touch,—slaves wandering on,
Impelled by thirst of all but Heaven-taught skill.
Full oft, our wish obtained, deeply we sigh;
Yet not unrecompensed are they who learn,
From that depression raised, to mount on high
With stronger wing, more clearly to discern
Eternal things; and, if need be, defy
Change, with a brow not insolent, though stern.

WILLIAM WORDSWORTH.

NEAR ROME, IN SIGHT OF ST. PETER'S

Long has the dew been dried on tree and lawn:
   O'er man and beast a not unwelcome boon
   Is shed, the languor of approaching moon;
To shady rest withdrawing or withdrawn
Mute are all creatures, as this couchant fawn,
   Save insect-swarms that hum in air afloat,
   Save that the cock is crowing, a shrill note,
Startling and shrill as that which roused the dawn.
—Heard in that hour, or when, as now, the nerve
   Shrinks from the note as from a mistimed thing,
Oft for a holy warning it may serve,
   Charged with remembrance of *his* sudden sting,
His bitter tears, whose name the Papal Chair
And yon resplendent Church are proud to bear.

                  WILLIAM WORDSWORTH.

THE PILLAR OF TRAJAN

This grand and enduring monument of the Dacian wars now stands amid the ruins of the Forum of Trajan. The space where today you see broken columns and an army of stray cats was one of the striking sights of the ancient city. Two libraries, a basilica of splendid dimensions, a temple, a great equestrian statue of Trajan and a triumphal arch amazed the travelers who came here from all the provinces of the Roman world.

Domitian had accepted an ignominious peace, but Trajan, his successor, would not endure such conditions. After a bitter struggle, the Dacian leader, Decebalus, put an end to his own life and his army was destroyed. Trajan entrusted to Apollodonis of Damascus the design of a Forum which would immortalize the memory of his victory. It was to surpass in extent and splendor any similar work previously attempted.

The Pillar of Trajan in the Forum has stood as a memorial of the Dacian wars for eighteen centuries. At its base the ashes of the emperor once rested in a golden urn. Trajan was the only emperor whose remains were permitted to remain within the city walls. Peculiarly graceful, the column is formed of nineteen massive marble drums encircled by spiral bands picturing in relief the arms, arts, and costumes of Romans and Barbarians. No column of ancient Rome is better known and few have a more interesting history.

Where towers are crushed, and unforbidden weeds
O'er mutilated arches shed their seeds;
And temples, doomed to milder change, unfold
A new magnificence that vies with old;
Firm in its pristine majesty hath stood
A votive Column, spared by fire and flood:—
And, though the passions of man's fretful race
Have never ceased to eddy round its base,
Not injured more by touch of meddling hands
Than a lone obelisk, 'mid Nubian sands,
Or aught in Syrian deserts left to save
From death the memory of the good and brave.

The Pillar of Trajan

Historic figures round the shaft embost
Ascend, with lineaments in air not lost:
Still as he turns, the charmed spectator sees
Group winding after group with dream-like ease;
Triumphs in sunbright gratitude displayed,
Or softly stealing into modest shade.
—So, pleased with purple clusters to entwine
Some lofty elm-tree, mounts the daring vine;
The woodbine so, with spiral grace, and breathes
Wide-spreading odours from her flowery wreaths.

Borne by the Muse from rills in shepherds' ears
Murmuring but one smooth story for all years,
I gladly commune with the mind and heart
Of him who thus survives by classic art,
His actions witness, venerate his mien,
And study Trajan as by Pliny seen;
Behold how fought the Chief whose conquering sword
Stretched far as earth might own a single lord;
In the delight of moral prudence schooled,
How feelingly at home the Sovereign ruled;
Best of the good—in pagan faith allied
To more than Man, by virtue deified.

Memorial Pillar! 'mid the wrecks of Time
Preserve thy charge with confidence sublime—
The exultations, pomps, and cares of Rome,
Whence half the breathing world received its doom;
Things that recoil from language; that, if shown
By apter pencil, from the light had flown.
A Pontiff, Trajan *here* the Gods implores,
There greets an embassy from Indian shores;
Lo! he harangues his cohorts—*there* the storm
Of battle meets him in authentic form!

The Pillar of Trajan

Unharnessed, naked, troops of Moorish horse
Sweep to the charge; more high, the Dacian force,
To hoof and finger mailed;—yet, high or low,
None bleed, and none lie prostrate but the foe;
In every Roman, through all turns of fate,
Is Roman dignity inviolate;
Spirit in him pre-eminent, who guides,
Supports, adorns, and over all presides;
Distinguished only by inherent state
From honoured Instruments that round him wait;
Rise as he may, his grandeur scorns the test
Of outward symbol, nor will deign to rest
On aught by which another is deprest.
—Alas! that One thus disciplined could toil
To enslave whole nations on their native soil;
So emulous of Macedonian fame,
That, when his age was measured with his aim,
He drooped, 'mid else unclouded victories,
And turned his eagles back with deep-drawn sighs:
O weakness of the Great! O folly of the Wise!

Where now the haughty Empire that was spread
With such fond hope? her very speech is dead;
Yet glorious Art the power of Time defies,
And Trajan still, through various enterprise,
Mounts, in this fine illusion, toward the skies:
Still are we present with the imperial Chief,
Nor cease to gaze upon the bold Relief
Till Rome, to silent marble unconfined,
Becomes with all her years a vision of the Mind.

WILLIAM WORDSWORTH.

ITALY
PART X
NAPLES

STREET OF GOOD FORTUNE—POMPEII

A strange name, this, for a city street that met such a disastrous end. And yet the traveler who treads the pavements of this once buried city finds evidence on every hand that the inhabitants were a carefree, happy people, who little realized that "they danced over a volcano."

Bulwer Lytton's *The Last Days of Pompeii* tells the story, but when the traveler has seen with his own eyes the temples of Apollo and Jupiter, the Forum, the stepping stones, the gladiatorial barracks, the great theatre and the homes of many a wealthy citizen, he gets a deeper conception of the greatness, the wealth and power of that mighty people that measured its empire from the golden milestone of the Roman Forum.

For future generations it was a Street of Good Fortune, for here, in 1784, Charles III, the first Bourbon king of Naples, began the excavations which, in the years to follow, were to uncover the entire city and disclose the singular splendors of bronze, precious marbles and exquisite paintings that filled the doomed city.

The day was gray—a film of misty rain
Blew on a gentle wind through unroofed home,
Temple and marble bath. The stony lane
That once had been a street and looked toward
    Rome,
Was ghostly-still and broken and bereft;
The weeds had grown, a lizard crawled in fright
Across a rut by some swift chariot left,
Hastening in panic through that flame-shot night.
    The cool rain fell—we spoke of molten rock
Half-carelessly—of sudden death and fear,
We who were still so blithe and quick to mock,
Who baked our loaves, thinking to-morrow near;
While down Good Fortune Street, before our eyes,
A green hill hissed white spirals to the skies.

                             HORTENSE FLEXNER.

AMALFI

We who have driven by carriage or motor along the Amalfi Drive, will remember the delightful luncheon hours at the Capucini Monastery high above the Salernian Bay.

As we looked out from the vine-clad pergola over Amalfi, once a republic vying with Venice, Florence, Pisa and Genoa, but now sleepy and almost forgotten, we experienced emotions closely akin to those of the poet Longfellow as he penned these lines.

> Sweet the memory is to me
> Of a land beyond the sea,
> Where the waves and mountains meet;
> Where, amid her mulberry-trees
> Sits Amalfi in the heat,
> Bathing ever her white feet
> In the tideless summer seas.
>
> In the middle of the town,
> From its fountains in the hills,
> Tumbling through the narrow gorge,
> The Canneto rushes down,
> Turns the great wheels of the mills,
> Lifts the hammers of the forge.
>
> 'Tis a stairway, not a street,
> That ascends the deep ravine,
> Where the torrent leaps between
> Rocky walls that almost meet.
> Toiling up from stair to stair
> Peasant girls their burdens bear:
> Sunburnt daughters of the soil,
> Stately figures tall and straight,
> What inexorable fate
> Dooms them to this life of toil?
>
> Lord of vineyards and of lands,
> Far above the convent stands.

Amalfi

On its terraced walk aloof
Leans a monk with folded hands.
Placid, satisfied, serene,
Looking down upon the scene
Over wall and red-tiled roof;
Wondering unto what good end
All this toil and traffic tend,
And why all men cannot be
Free from care and free from pain
And the sordid love of gain,
And as indolent as he.

Where are now the freighted barks
From the marts of east and west?
Where the knights in iron sarks
Journeying to the Holy Land,
Glove of steel upon the hand,
Cross of crimson on the breast?
Where the pomp of camp and court?
Where the pilgrims with their prayers?
Where the merchants with their wares,
And their gallant brigantines
Sailing safely into port
Chased by corsair Algerines?
Vanished like a fleet of cloud,
Like a passing trumpet-blast,
Are those splendours of the past,
And the commerce and the crowd!
Fathoms deep beneath the seas
Lie the ancient wharves and quays,
Swallowed by the engulfing waves,
Silent streets, and vacant halls,
Ruined roofs and towers and walls;
Hidden from all mortal eyes
Deep the sunken city lies:
Even cities have their graves!

Amalfi

This is an enchanted land!
Round the headlands far away
Sweeps the blue Salernian bay
With its sickle of white sand:
Further still and furthermost
On the dim discovered coast
Paestum with its ruins lies,
And its roses all in bloom
Seem to tinge the fatal skies
Of that lonely land of doom.

On his terrace, high in air,
Nothing doth the good monk care
For such wordly themes as these.
From the garden just below
Little puffs of perfume blow,
And a sound is in his ears
Of the murmur of the bees
In the shining chest-nut trees;
Nothing else he heeds or hears.
All the landscape seems to swoon
In the happy afternoon;
Slowly o'er his senses creep
The encroaching waves of sleep,
And he sinks as sank the town,
Unresisting, fathoms down,
Into caverns cool and deep!

Walled about with drifts of snow,
Hearing the fierce north-wind blow,
Seeing all the landscape white,
And the river cased in ice,
Comes this memory of delight,
Comes this vision unto me
Of a long-lost Paradise
In the land beyond the sea.

   HENRY WADSWORTH LONGFELLOW.

MONTE CASSINO
TERRA DI LAVORO

In journeying between Rome and Naples the traveler obtains a view of the huge pile of the abbey of Monte Cassino. This famous monastery, founded by St. Benedict in the sixth century, was a center of mediaeval learning. It was built by the followers of St. Benedict who kept the torch of learning lighted during the Dark Ages.

If you climb the monumental staircase of the church, you will enter a portico of antique columns that came from a temple of Apollo. The bronze doors of the church will recall to you the beautiful craftsmanship of those workmen in far off Constantinople, who cast these portals when the city on the Bosphorus was still a Christian city.

Beautiful valley! through whose verdant meads
   Unheard the Garigliano glides along;—
The Liris, nurse of rushes and of reeds
   The river taciturn of classic song.

The Land of Labor and the Land of Rest,
   Where mediaeval towns are white on all
The hillsides, and where every mountain's crest
   Is an Etrurian or a Roman wall.

There is Alagna, where Pope Boniface
   Was dragged with contumely from his throne;
Sciarra Colonna, was that day's disgrace
   The Pontiff's only, or in part thine own?

There is Ceprano, where a renegade
   Was each Apulian, as great Dante saith,
When Manfred by his men-at-arms betrayed
   Spurred on to Benevento and to death.

There is Aquinum, the old Volscian town,
  Where Juvenal was born, whose lurid light
Still hovers o'er his birthplace like the crown
  Of splendor seen o'er cities in the night.

Doubled the splendor is, that in its streets
  The Angelic Doctor as a school-boy played,
And dreamed perhaps the dreams, that he repeats
  In ponderous folios for scholastics made.

And there, uplifted, like a passing cloud
  That pauses on a mountain summit high,
Monte Cassino's convent rears its proud
  And venerable walls against the sky.

Well I remember how on foot I climbed
  The stony pathway leading to its gate;
Above, the convent bells for vespers chimed,
  Below, the darkening town grew desolate.

Well I remember the low arch and dark,
  The courtyard with its well, the terrace wide,
From which, far down, the valley like a park,
  Veiled in the evening mists, was dim descried.

The day was dying, and with feeble hands
  Carressed the mountain-tops; the vales between
Darkened; the river in the meadow-lands
  Sheathed itself as a sword, and was not seen.

The silence of the place was like a sleep,
  So full of rest it seemed; each passing tread
Was a reverberation from the deep
  Recesses of the ages that are dead.

For, more than thirteen centuries ago,
   Benedict fleeing from the gates of Rome,
A youth disgusted with its vice and woe,
   Sought in these mountain solitudes a home.

He founded here his Convent and his Rule
   Of prayer and work, and counted work as prayer;
The pen became a clarion, and his school
   Flamed like a beacon in the midnight air.

What though Boccaccio, in his reckless way,
   Mocking the lazy brotherhood, deplores
The illuminated manuscripts, that lay
   Torn and neglected on the dusty floors?

Boccaccio was a novelist, a child
   Of fancy and of fiction at the best!
This the urbane librarian said, and smiled
   Incredulous, as at some idle jest.

Upon such themes as these, with one young friar
   I sat conversing late into the night,
Till in its cavernous chimney the wood-fire
   Had burnt its heart out like an anchorite.

And then translated, in my convent cell,
   Myself yet not myself, in dreams as I lay,
And, as a monk who hears the matin bell,
   Started from sleep;—already it was day.

From the high window I beheld the scene
   On which Saint Benedict so oft had gazed,—
The mountains and the valley in the sheen
   Of the bright sun,—and stood as one amazed.

Gray mists were rolling, rising, vanishing;
    The woodlands glistened with their jewelled crowns;
Far off the mellow bells began to ring
    For matins in the half-awakened towns.

The conflict of the Present and the Past,
    The ideal and the actual in our life,
As on a field of battle held me fast,
    Where this world and the next world were at strife.

For, as the valley from its sleep awoke,
    I saw the iron horses of the steam
Toss to the morning air their plumes of smoke,
    And woke, as one awaketh from a dream.

                    HENRY WADSWORTH LONGFELLOW.

AT AMALFI

Here might I rest for ever; here,
Till death, inviolate of fear,
  Descended cloud-like on calm eyes,
Enjoy the whisper of the waves
Stealing around those azure caves,
  The gloom and glory of the skies!

Great mother, Nature, on thy breast
Let me, unsoiled by sorrow, rest,
  By sin unstirred, by love made free:
Full-tried am I by years that bring
The blossoms of the tardy spring
  Of wisdom, thine adept to be.

In vain I pray: the wish expires
Upon my lip, as fade the fires
  Of youth in withered veins and weak;
Not mine to dwell, the neophyte
Of Nature, in her shrine of light,
  But still to strive and still to seek.

I have outgrown the primal mirth
That throbs in air and sea and earth;
  The world of worn humanity
Reclaims my care; at ease to range
Those hills, and watch their interchange
  Of light and gloom is not for me.

Dread Pan, to thee I turn: thy soul
That through the living world doth roll,
  Stirs in our heart an aching sense
Of beauty, too divinely wrought
To be the food of mortal thought,
  For earth-born hunger too intense.

At Amalfi

Breathless we sink before thy shrine;
We pour our spirits forth like wine;
   With trembling hands we strive to lift
The veil of airy amethyst,
That shrouds thy godhood like a mist;
   Then, dying, forth to darkness drift.

Thy life around us laughs, and we
Are merged in its immensity;
   Thy chanted melodies we hear,
The marrying clouds that meet and kiss
Between two silences; but miss
   The meaning, though it seems so clear.

From suns that sink o'er silent seas,
From myrtles 'neath the mountain breeze
   Shedding their drift of scented snow,
From fleeting hues, from sounds that swoon
On pathless hills, from night and noon,
   The inarticulate passions flow

They are thy minions, mighty Pan!
No priest hast thou; no muse or man
   Hath ever told, shall ever tell,
But each within his heart alone,
Awe-struck and dumb, hath learned to own
   The burden of thine oracle.

JOHN ADDINGTON SYMONDS.

AT CASTELLAMARE

Along the southern shores of the Bay of Naples are Sorrento, Castellamare and Capri, with their vineyards and cliffs and magnificent views of the sea. We may approach them by steamer from Naples, or drive along the far-famed road above the bay. Such a drive seems ideally beautiful until we reach the Salernian Bay farther southward and find our journey to Castellamare has been but a fitting introduction to the matchless drive to Amalfi. When the air is clear, the road, winding amid olive and lemon orchards, offers ever-recurring glimpses of the sea in all its gorgeous hues of blue.

Awake, my Myrto, with the birth of day,
    Forth to the meadow fare this first of May.

Not yet the sun with his o'ermastering might
    Hath dried the pearlets on the bud and bloom;
Still in pale skies trembles the star of night,
    Morn's herald star, and all the glorious gloom
    Is waiting for the dawn ro reillume
Her eyes of fire above the burning bay.

Awake, my Myrto, with the birth of day,
Forth to the meadow fare this first of May.

See in thick pleachèd garden-alleys green
    How rose by rose deep-sunken drinks the dew:
Sheathed in soft sleep they hide their silken sheen,
    Nor know the passion of fierce light that through
    Their crimson spheres will shoot when morn is new:
So sleep not we when love invites to play.

Awake, my Myrto, with the birth of day,
Forth to the meadow fare this first of May.

Ah, foolish rose! She hath one little hour
   To cast her sweetness on the amorous prime;
The kiss of noon her girlhood will deflower,
   The wanton bee about her lap will climb,
   And birds will sing their clear love-laden rhyme,
Till night descends that taketh all away.

Awake, my Myrto, with the birth of day,
Forth to the meadow fare this first of May.
JOHN ADDINGTON SYMONDS.

SORRENTO

A Fragment

On the southern side of the Bay of Naples, where the coast line curves westward towards Capri, we may well rest for at least an evening. Here is enchanting Sorrento, where the poet Tasso was born, and the novelist Marion Crawford lived.

The old Romans frequented these shores and lofty rocks to enjoy the beauty of scenery and climate.

> Fair fountains of man's art were there,
> Streams trickling down from stair to stair,
> And as, with lapse just audible,
> From font to font the waters fell,
> Around the lighted bubbles flew,
> Starring the leaves with points like dew:
> For tender myrtles near were set,
> And in this happy clime had met
> Unhoused the winter's deadliest air;
> And the pale lemon-flower was there,
> And the dark glittering leaves behind
> The fruit with its discoloured rind:
> While the long groves of orange made
> A screen sun-proof, an ample shade,
> With spacious avenues below,
> Where one might wander to and fro,
> Watching the little runnels creep
> Round every root, and duly steep
> With freshness all the thirsty soil;
> Or lift an hand for easiest spoil,
> And of the golden fruitage share,
> Cool-hanging in the morning air.
>
> RICHARD CHENEVIX TRENCH.

EPILOGUE

EPILOGUE

The days of travel are over and this may be our last return to the home-fire after many wanderings in foreign lands. Whether it is the last journey or is to be followed by other Old World quests, the memories of our trip are its richest blessings. We may return penniless, but if we have seen other peoples and other lands with the spirit of the poet we shall be wealthy in memories.

Let us like the Greek of old long "to see the cities of many men and to know their minds."

THE ENCHANTED TRAVELLER

We travelled empty-handed
With hearts all fear above,
For we ate the bread of friendship,
We drank the wine of love.

Through many a wondrous autumn,
Through many a magic spring,
We hailed the scarlet banners,
We heard the bluebird sing.

We looked on life and nature
With eager eyes of youth,
And all we asked or cared for
Was beauty, joy, and truth.

We found no other wisdom,
We learned no other way,
Than the gladness of the morning,
The glory of the day.

So all our earthly treasure
Shall go with us, my dears,
Aboard the Shadow Liner,
Across the sea of years.

BLISS CARMAN.

ON TRAVELING

And who would be a traveler
   And see the world afar,
What joys at Rome could equal home
   Where my two children are?
And what has Paris fair to show
   That I should sail away,
When I can sit at home and know
   Their pranks from day to day?

They say Japan is bright with charm
   And Orient customs lure,
But that they'd be delights for me
   I'm not so very sure;
For all the joys which are Japan's
   Would find me cold as stone
And glum of face, in such a place,
   If I were there alone.

I'd like to go to Oxford town,
   I'd like to sail the sea,
But bless your heart, I'll never start
   Until they can go with me.
For little joy I'd get from all
   The splendors I should find,
I should only grieve if I had to leave
   My loved ones all behind.

                    EDGAR A. GUEST.

TRAVELLER'S JOY

What went you, Pilgrim, for to see?
A sign or wonder-thing maybe?
Some marvel or a holy sight
As clerks in chronicles do write?
For you have gone and come again
Now tell us plain?

I saw the sky from rim to rim
Full-filled with light up to the brim
As though it were a mighty cup
To God's lip holden up.
I saw a river and a down,
A harbor and a little town,
A marshland blue with irises,
I saw all these.

Saw, too, a sedgy pond where lay
Lilies like anchored stars that Day
Had ravished from the summer night
And kept them there a-light.
I saw a hill-side gold with furze,
And wildrose banks and junipers
Distilling fragrance pungent-sweet:
I saw a path that called my feet
To go with it as any friend,
To heart's desire at the end.

Sooth, all of these! but mid them all
Did nothing wonderful befall?
No miracle?
Yea, but I have no word to tell
Of that great thing that happened me—
I saw the sea!

Traveller's Joy

O wide, and blue and infinite!
League upon league of space and light!
I think that down this sapphire floor
One might walk straight to heaven's door

And lift its golden latchet-bar,
Nor find it far
Or very strange, as one would guess,
After such earthly loveliness.
Poor pilgrim, is this all your store
Of tales to tell? Is there no more
Then this that any man might show?
Yea, all is told. How should you know
That I have looked on Beauty's face,
And being far from men a space
Have found at springs of Quietness
The hands that heal, the hands that bless—
Have known the sun and wind and trod
The holy earth and talked with God!

ARTHUR KETCHUM.

TRAVELS BY THE FIRESIDE

The ceaseless rain is falling fast,
    And yonder gilded vane,
Immovable for three days past,
    Points to the misty main.

It drives me in upon myself
    And to the fireside gleams,
To pleasant books that crowd my shelf,
    And still more pleasant dreams.

I read whatever bards have sung
    Of lands beyond the sea,
And the bright days when I was young
    Come thronging back to me.

In fancy I can hear again
    And Alpine torrent's roar,
The mule-bells on the hills of Spain
    The sea at Elsinore.

I see the convent's gleaming wall
    Rise from its groves of pine,
And towers of old cathedrals tall,
    And castles by the Rhine.

I journey on by park and spire,
    Beneath centennial trees,
Through fields with poppies all on fire,
    And gleams of distant seas.

I fear no more the dust and heat,
    No more I feel fatigue,
While journeying with another's feet
    O'er many a lengthening league

Travels by the Fireside

Let others traverse sea and land,
    And toil through various climes,
I turn the world round with my hand
    Reading these poets' rhymes.

From them I learn whatever lies
    Beneath each changing zone,
And see, when looking with their eyes,
    Better than with mine own.

HENRY WADSWORTH LONGFELLOW.

THE TRAVELLER'S RETURN

Sweet to the morning traveller
   The song amid the sky,
Where twinkling in the dewy light
   The skylark soars on high.

And cheering to the traveller
   The gales that round him play,
When faint and heavily he drags
   Along his noon-tide way.

And when beneath the unclouded sun
   Full wearily toils he,
The flowing water makes to him
   A soothing melody.

And when the evening light decays,
   And all is calm around,
There is sweet music to his ear
   In the distant sheep-bell's sound.

But oh! of all delightful sounds
   Of evening or of morn,
The sweetest is the voice of Love,
   That welcomes his return.

                                  ROBERT SOUTHEY.

AMERICA FOR ME

Perhaps some who come back will find in the bottoms of their hearts a deep longing for the Old World, and will not want to sing with Van Dyke his *"America for Me."*

For those who have lost their heart to the Old World we give below our version of the last stanza:

Oh, it's Rome again, and Rome again, Rome again for me!
I want a ship that's eastward bound to plough the rolling sea,
To the blessèd Land of Room Enough beyond the ocean bars,
Where the air is full of sunlight and the sky is full of stars.

T. W. H.

'Tis fine to see the Old World, and travel up and down
Among the famous palaces and cities of renown,
To admire the crumbly castles and the statues of the kings,—
But now I think I've had enough of antiquated things.

So it's home again, and home again, America for me!
My heart is turning home again, and there I long to be,
In the land of youth and freedom beyond the ocean bars,
Where the air is full of sunlight and the flag is full of stars.

Oh, London is a man's town, there's power in the air;
And Paris is a woman's town, with flowers in her hair;

And it's sweet to dream in Venice, and it's great to
    study Rome;
But when it comes to living there is no place like
    home.

I like the German fir-woods, in green battalions
    drilled;
I like the gardens of Versailles with flashing foun-
    tains filled;
But, oh, to take your hand, my dear, and ramble for
    a day
In friendly western woodland where Nature has her
    way!

I know that Europe's wonderful, yet something
    seems to lack:
The Past is too much with her, and the people
    looking back.
But the glory of the Present is to make the Future
    free,—
We love our land for what she is and what she is to
    be.

> *Oh, it's home again, and home again, America
>   for me.*
> *I want a ship that's westward bound to plough
>   the rolling sea,*
> *To the blessèd Land of Room Enough beyond
>   the ocean bars,*
> *Where the air is full of sunlight and the flag
>   is full of stars.*

INDEX

A

		PAGE
A Divine Barrier	G. F. Savage-Armstrong	206
A Passer-by	Robert Bridges	3
After a Lecture on Shelley	Oliver Wendell Holmes	339
Aladdin	James Russell Lowell	167
Albert Dürer's Studio	Josiah Gilbert Holland	121
Amalfi	Henry Wadsworth Longfellow	376
America for Me	Henry Van Dyke	399
An Alpine Picture	Thomas Bailey Aldrich	141
An Old Castle	Thomas Bailey Aldrich	85
Andrea del Sarto	Robert Browning	293
Approach to Florence	Lord Byron	303
At Amalfi	John Addington Symonds	383
At Castellamare	John Addington Symonds	385
At Fano	Sir Rennell Rodd	200
At Florence	William Wordsworth	329
At Rome	William Wordsworth	367

B

Bagpipe Player: Nuremberg Fountain	Leonora Speyer	137
Belisarius	Henry Wadsworth Longfellow	344
Browning at Asolo	Robert Underwood Johnson	187
By the Arno	Oscar Wilde	327

C

Cadenabbia	Henry Wadsworth Longfellow	215
Carcassonne	Gustave Nadaud	108
Castilian	Elinor Wylie	172
Castles in Spain	Henry Wadsworth Longfellow	163
Charlemagne	Mary Sinton Leitch	104

D

Dawn in Arqua	Lloyd Mifflin	198
Dawn on Mid-Ocean	John Hall Wheelock	11
Drachenfels	Lord Byron	117

E

Edinburgh	Alfred Noyes	56
Elegy Written in a Country Churchyard	Thomas Gray	20

	PAGE
England................Walter de la Mare	19
England................William Shakespeare	35
Evening: Ponte a Mare, Pisa....Percy Bysshe Shelley	288
Evening: Spain................W. J. Turner	170

F

For One of Gian Bellini's Little Angels	
John Addington Symonds	273
Fragment on Keats............Percy Bysshe Shelley	358

G

Gargoyle: Strasbourg Cathedral	
Gertrude Huntington McGiffert	107
Genoa......................Aubrey De Vere	235
Genoa............................F. W. Faber	236
Genoa......................William Gibson	239
Giotto's Campanile............Aubrey De Vere	309
Giotto's Tower.......Henry Wadsworth Longfellow	313

H

He Never Took a Vacation....John Warren Harper	9
Heather................Marguerite Wilkinson	68
Highland Mary................Robert Burns	47
Home Thoughts from Abroad......Robert Browning	16

I

I am in Rome................Samuel Rogers	356
I Wandered Lonely as a Cloud..William Wordsworth	40
Il Ponte Vecchio di Firenze	
Henry Wadsworth Longfellow	314
Implora Pace............Charles Lotin Hildreth	186
In a Gondola................John Todhunter	277
In Flanders Fields...............John McCrae	80
In Florence......................Cora Fabbri	310
In Old Rouen......Antoinette De Coursey Patterson	110
In the Galleries of the Louvre Charles Lewis Slattery	111
Inside of King's College Chapel, Cambridge	
William Wordsworth	42
Italian Scenery........Henry Wadsworth Longfellow	191
Italy............................A. W. Hare	182

J

Jugurtha............Henry Wadsworth Longfellow	347

Index 403

K

		PAGE
Keats	Percy Bysshe Shelley	359

L

La Marseillaise	Rouget de Lisle	98
Lake Leman	Lord Byron	142
Lido	Lord Houghton	258
Lines Written on the Roof of Milan Cathedral	John Addington Symonds	225
London Town	John Masefield	33

M

Masaccio	James Russell Lowell	317
Melrose Abbey	Sir Walter Scott	58
Milton in Italy	Walter Savage Landor	189
Monte Cassino	Henry Wadsworth Longfellow	379
Monument at Lucerne	John Kenyon	158
Mourn Not for Venice	Thomas Moore	265
My Heart's in the Highlands	Robert Burns	49

N

Near Amsterdam	S. Weir Mitchell	81
Near Rome, in Sight of St. Peter's	William Wordsworth	368
Night at Sea	Amelia Josephine Burr	4
Nightfall in Dordrecht	Eugene Field	74
Notre Dame	Théophile Gautier	100
Nuremberg	Henry Wadsworth Longfellow	123

O

Ode on a Distant Prospect of Eton College	Thomas Gray	26
Ode on Venice	Lord Byron	245
Ode: The Mediterranean	George Santayana	204
Ode to the West Wind	Percy Bysshe Shelley	320
On the Extinction of the Venetian Republic	William Wordsworth	282
On the Medusa of Leonardo da Vinci in the Florentine Gallery	Percy Bysshe Shelley	323
On the Perseus and Medusa of Benvenuto Cellini, at Florence	Richard Chenevix Trench	326
On the Tombs in Westminster Abbey	Francis Beaumont	15
On Traveling	Edgar A. Guest	393

Index

PAGE

P

Passage of the Apennines	Percy Bysshe Shelley	207
Petrarch's Tomb	Lord Byron	177
Pictures of the Rhine	George Meredith	133
Pisa	William Gibson	287
Prison of Tasso	Lord Byron	178

R

Robert Burns	Henry Wadsworth Longfellow	53
Rome	Lord Byron	335
Rome Unvisited	Oscar Wilde	362
Rule, Britannia	James Thomson	36

S

St. Peter's by Moonlight	Aubrey De Vere	336
San Terenzo	Andrew Lang	190
Santa Croce	Lord Byron	304
Santa Maria del Fiore	George Herbert Clarke	307
Sea-Fever	John Masefield	10
Shelley's House	George Edward Woodberry	365
Sirmio: Lago di Garda	Catullus	211
Skies Italian	Ruth Shepard Phelps	199
Sorrento: A Fragment	Richard Chenevix Trench	387
Spring	Dante Gabriel Rossetti	319
Stanzas to the Po	Lord Byron	180
Street of Good Fortune—Pompeii	Hortense Flexner	375

T

The Angelus	Florence Earle Coates	97
The Avon and the Thames	Arthur Upson	38
The Belfry of Bruges	Henry Wadsworth Longfellow	76
The Book-Stalls on the Seine	Charles Lewis Slattery	112
The Catacombs	Joanna Baillie	333
The Cathedral of Milan	Aubrey De Vere	223
The Chain of Princes Street	Elizabeth S. Fleming	51
The Coliseum	Edgar Allan Poe	353
The Conspiracy of Rienzi	Thomas Moore	349
The Enchanted Traveller	Bliss Carman	392
The Grave of Keats	Oscar Wilde	364
The Invitation to the Gondola	John Addington Symonds	275
The Lake of Como	William Wordsworth	217
The Last Supper	William Wordsworth	227
The Little Bells of Sevilla	Dora Sigerson Shorter	168

Index 405

	PAGE
The Lorelei..............*Thomas Bailey Aldrich*	115
The Name Writ in Water.*Robert Underwood Johnson*	341
The Old Bridge at Florence	
Henry Wadsworth Longfellow	315
The Piazza of St. Mark at Midnight	
Thomas Bailey Aldrich	243
The Pillar of Trajan..........*William Wordsworth*	369
The Prisoner of Chillon..............*Lord Byron*	145
The Rolling English Road.........*G. K. Chesterton*	17
The Ruins of Rome............*Joachim du Bellay*	337
The Sermon of St. Francis	
Henry Wadsworth Longfellow	231
The Simplon Pass............*William Wordsworth*	160
The Spires of Oxford................*W. M. Letts*	30
The Three Kings......*Henry Wadsworth Longfellow*	127
The Traveller's Return.............*Robert Southey*	398
The Trossachs....................*Sir Walter Scott*	61
The Venetian Gondolier	
Henry Wadsworth Longfellow	262
The Venus of Milo..........*Wilfrid Scawen Blunt*	88
The Wingèd Victory................*Bliss Carman*	94
To King Victor Emmanuel.......*Henry Lushington*	195
To Saint Charles Borromeo...*Walter Savage Landor*	213
To Shelley..................*Walter Savage Landor*	342
To the Avon.........*Henry Wadsworth Longfellow*	32
To the Ocean......................*Lord Byron*	5
To the Rhine......................*Lord Byron*	119
To the River Rhone...*Henry Wadsworth Longfellow*	106
To Venice...................*Walter Savage Landor*	261
Traveller's Joy................*Arthur Ketchum*	394
Travels by the Fireside.*Henry Wadsworth Longfellow*	396
Trees............................*Joyce Kilmer*	103
Two Graves...............*Walter Savage Landor*	343

U

Umbria........................*Laurence Binyon*	175
Upon Westminster Bridge September 3, 1802	
William Wordsworth	43

V

Venice........................*Alfred de Musset*	253
Venice.............*Henry Wadsworth Longfellow*	264
Venice..................*Thomas Buchanan Read*	268
Venice..................*John Addington Symonds*	276
Venice: A Fragment...................*Lord Byron*	251
Venice by Day..................*Aubrey De Vere*	255

		PAGE
Venice in the Evening	*Aubrey De Vere*	256
Verona	*Samuel Rogers*	203
Versailles	*Godfrey Fox Bradby*	90
Villa Borghese	*Arthur Symons*	361

W

Walter von der Vogelweid		
	Henry Wadsworth Longfellow	130
Wanderlust	*Gerald Gould*	8
Waterloo	*Lord Byron*	71

Y

| Ye Banks and Braes | *Robert Burns* | 50 |